YOU
and Your
Money

Florence M. Dennis ?

money

FINANCIAL TIMES

In an increasingly competitive world, it is quality
of thinking that gives an edge—an idea that opens new
doors, a technique that solves a problem, or an insight
that simply helps make sense of it all.

We work with leading authors in the various arenas
of business and finance to bring cutting-edge thinking
and best-learning practices to a global market.

It is our goal to create world-class print publications
and electronic products that give readers
knowledge and understanding that can then be
applied, whether studying or at work.

To find out more about our business
products, you can visit us at www.ftpress.com.

YOU
and Your
Money

A No-Stress Guide to
Becoming Financially Fit

Lois A. Vitt
Karen L. Murrell

Vice President, Editor-in-Chief: Tim Moore
Executive Editor: Jim Boyd
Editorial Assistant: Pamela Boland
Development Editor: Russ Hall
Associate Editor-in-Chief and Director of Marketing: Amy Neidlinger
Publicist: Amy Fandrei
Marketing Coordinator: Megan Colvin
Cover Designer: Chuti Prasertsith
Managing Editor: Gina Kanouse
Senior Project Editor: Kristy Hart
Copy Editor: Language Logistics LLC
Indexer: Susan Loper
Compositor: Moore Media, Inc.
Manufacturing Buyer: Dan Uhrig

© 2007 by Pearson Education, Inc.
Publishing as FT Press
Upper Saddle River, New Jersey 07458

FT Press offers excellent discounts on this book when ordered in quantity for bulk purchases or special sales. For more information, please contact U.S. Corporate and Government Sales, 1-800-382-3419, corpsales@pearsontechgroup.com. For sales outside the U.S., please contact International Sales at international@pearsoned.com.

Company and product names mentioned herein are the trademarks or registered trademarks of their respective owners.

Printed in the United States of America

First Printing, March 2007

ISBN 0-13-100310-0

Pearson Education LTD.
Pearson Education Australia PTY, Limited.
Pearson Education Singapore, Pte. Ltd.
Pearson Education North Asia, Ltd.
Pearson Education Canada, Ltd.
Pearson Educatión de Mexico, S.A. de C.V.
Pearson Education—Japan
Pearson Education Malaysia, Pte. Ltd.

Library of Congress Cataloging-in-Publication Data

Vitt, Lois A.
  It's about you and your money : a no stress guide to becoming financially fit / Lois A. Vitt, Karen Murrell. — 1st ed.
    p. cm.
  Includes bibliographical references and index.
  ISBN 0-13-100310-1 (pbk. : alk. paper) 1. Finance, Personal. I. Murrell, Karen. II. Title.
  HG179.V58 2007
  332.024—dc22
                              2006035936

To our children: mine, theirs, and yours.

LAV

To my parents—my first money management teachers.

KLM

CONTENTS

PART I
MAINTAINING A POSITIVE OUTLOOK   1

1
THE RIGHT STUFF   3

2
THE "NEW" AMERICAN DREAM   13

8

BECOMING A SAVVY CONSUMER 89

9

GETTING AND KEEPING GOOD CREDIT 103

Appendix
PERSONAL FINANCE EDUCATION
INTERNET SITES 277

Endnotes 293

Index 299

FOREWORD

My parents are now aged 93 and 90. They were 19 and 16 in 1929 as the nation moved into the Great Depression. As a result, my father had to transfer from a high-cost private college to the low-cost public university. He hitchhiked 30 miles to and from classes each day, spending three to five hours just getting to and from school. During the early years of their marriage, my folks ate graham crackers for dinner three nights a week. They never lived beyond their current income, never had credit cards, bought a home in their mid 30s, and paid off the mortgage in their 50s.

We went without many things that the "Joneses" had as I grew up, and the words "You should never try to keep up with the Joneses" still ring in my ears. My folks considered wants versus needs and understood what it meant to save until you can pay for what you buy. They used credit only for major life-changing purchases like a home and real emergencies, not for impulse buying in response to feelings of "I have to have that."

You too must understand how important behavior—what you *do not do* as well as what you do—affects your life, your money, and your future security. You must understand that programs like Medicaid, Social Security and Medicare, Supplemental Security Income and Welfare will allow you to live in the basement. But taking personal responsibility is essential to live anywhere between the first floor and the penthouse.

You and Your Money: A No-Stress Guide to Becoming Financially Fit puts all of this into perspective in a clear and riveting way. It underlines that you are in charge of your own well-being whether you like it or not, and it shows you how to become *successful*. From telling you about "The Right Stuff" and walking you through your own values to managing your finances so you can achieve your goals, this book will make a difference for every reader and their entire family.

Unlike my parents' day, or my own early years, we are now bombarded with "free" credit cards that carry high interest rates and gross penalties for being a dollar short and a day late. Ads push us to buy with no money down and no payment for months. Ads sell us on "low" monthly payments without mention of the total price, and they challenge us to "keep up with the Joneses." Even some politicians say it is our patriotic duty to spend so that the economy will grow. We get very few messages about how we could ChoosetoSave instead (see www.choosetosave.org). We see too few messages about how making financial fitness a value that drives our behavior can provide what we truly want and need to make us happy and secure. This book does those things. It provides a guide for independence and a roadmap for financial security.

My parents marvel at the fact that they are still alive: survivors of depression, poverty, illness, raising four children, World Wars, and so much more. Through it all, they lived according to their values, took charge of their own well-being, were savvy consumers, avoided debt, and built good credit when they had it. They committed to a savings plan, communicated about money, chose housing wisely, planned for life transitions, prepared for disasters, and found help when they needed it. They have made it to their 90s as a happy and independent couple, soon to celebrate their 70th wedding anniversary!

This book does not promise you a Diamond Wedding Anniversary, but it will guide you in ways you can lower your financial stress levels and increase your real happiness. It is all within your own control, if you reach out, believe in yourself, and grab hold of your courage. Like my parents and, perhaps, your parents too, you have "The Right Stuff" within. Let Lois Vitt and Karen Murrell show you the path to becoming financially fit.

Dallas Salisbury
President and CEO
Employee Benefit Research Institute

PREFACE

A movement toward increased consumer financial literacy is gathering momentum across communities, schools and colleges, workplaces, faith-based organizations, financial companies, the media, and all levels of government. Its message is clear: The key to success in the twenty-first century is within everyone's grasp if we embrace the concept of personal responsibility. To get ahead, we simply need to take charge of our own financial livelihoods.

Although consumers today have unprecedented access to financial resources through work, news sources, articles and books, seminars, and Internet offerings, there's more to the equation than just information. There are other complexities. More than just receiving information, we also need to understand the general economy, the capital markets, the health care system, and the details in the contracts we sign. If you are confused, you are in good company. Even noted Harvard University law professor and consumer advocate, Elizabeth Warren, complained on national public television that she found it difficult to understand all the fine print in a typical credit card contract.[1]

Typically, sponsors of financial education and published information believe that when people are given access to financial advice, they will automatically choose to be more prudent in their spending decisions. Financial information alone, it is thought, is enough to motivate people to plan ahead, save for emergencies, invest for future education costs and for retirement, and engage financial service professionals to help navigate the maze of investment choices.

Unfortunately, it isn't that simple. Financial information alone—no matter how skillfully it is presented—often does not resonate with most people mainly because the information is so voluminous and the changes in society are coming at us so fast that it seems we will never process it all.

The laws of motion as defined by Sir Isaac Newton and the great astronomer Galileo provide a framework for understanding inertia and momentum. Their wisdom indicates that a body at rest will remain at rest until moved by an outside force. The law of motion applied to understanding financial issues and putting them in practice—saving for emergencies, education, home ownership, and retirement—suggests that if people do little to plan for these life events (that is, remain at rest), they will make little headway.[2] Some outside force is necessary to provide the push to prepare for future financial security.

Unlike inert objects, however, we humans require some inner spark to generate the momentum that can propel us forward. In other words, the "outside force" of available financial information and education must be met by an "inner desire" to learn and to apply financial concepts. Partially due to how complicated we may think it is and how busy we are and partially due to our "buy now and pay later" culture, that spark may have been dampened. We may have fallen behind the curve of personal financial knowledge.

It doesn't have to remain this way.

As financial education researchers, teachers, and consultants, we've seen how the principles we write about in this book can turn even rank amateurs into competent money managers who enjoy the process of building financial security. *You and Your Money* combines our insights about today's changing societal realities, the character traits of people who have achieved success, and the financial basics. We show you four steps everyone can take to attain the promises of the *New* American Dream of the twenty-first century.

The first thing to realize is that we all make money from the inside out! Once we see the possibilities and realize they are within our reach, *then* we can achieve them. With this in mind, you can change your behaviors and spending and savings patterns and can implement a new strategy that will transform your approach to finances. Your savvy in this critical area can improve the quality of your whole life. You can be more confident about who's in charge of your financial well-being.

You are!

Lois A. Vitt　　　　　　Karen L. Murrell
Middleburg, VA　　　　　Silver Spring, MD
www.moneystudies.com　　www.higherheightsconsulting.com

ACKNOWLEDGMENTS

We extend our gratitude and best wishes to all those who have shared their personal financial stories with us in our research and for this book. You have given meaning to the ideas presented here by having lived them. We acknowledge the essential contributions of thought leaders, funding organizations, and financial educators who champion the cause of financial literacy education and investment education in schools, workplaces, communities, faith-based groups, and other organizations nationwide.

We express our deep gratitude to Jim Boyd at Prentice Hall for his patient and insightful shepherding of this endeavor over the long haul. We very much appreciate the helpful comments of our peer reviewers, Russ Hall and Susan Squires, and the magic of the production team that transformed our words into print. Heartfelt thanks to Joyce Thomas and Jerry Travers, who can always be counted on to come up with great ideas and ways of expressing them. Many thanks to colleagues, Lynn Gerlach and Jeanne Harnois, for helping us translate our message from the theoretical to the timely and practical. And we thank Kyle Meyer and Karen McMahon for their helpful reviews of our manuscript.

Lois thanks Jamie, Evelyn, and the Baker family for their considerable help in the office and on the home front, and most of all, she extends loving gratitude to Noel who makes everything possible.

Karen thanks Joyce, Levi, Yvonne and Joshua, as well as countless friends, who provided never-ending encouragement and support.

ABOUT THE AUTHORS

A former finance executive and now a sociologist, **Lois A. Vitt**, Ph.D. has been a life-long advocate of personal financial education. She began her career in mortgage finance and worked her way to top-level positions with major Wall Street firms. She also has helped inner-city, Native American, and Caribbean populations to access business and home ownership opportunities. She is founding director of the Institute for Socio-Financial Studies in Middleburg, Virginia, where she directs research and consults about consumer financial education that works. She directed Personal Finance and the Rush to Competence: Financial Literacy Education in the U.S. for the Fannie Mae Foundation and Goodbye to Complacency: Financial Literacy Education in the U.S. 2000-2005 for the AARP. She is Editor-in-Chief of the two-volume Encyclopedia of Retirement and Finance. Her most recent publication is 10 Secrets to Successful Home Buying and Selling: Using Your Housing Psychology to Make Smarter Decisions.

Her insights in the field of financial literacy education are informed by her personal life as well as her professional and academic experience. She raised and educated six children as a single parent. As an only child herself, she was a caregiver to both of her parents during their later years. She has experienced the disappointment and pain of business failure and personal loss, from which she learned the lessons of how to recover and begin again.

Karen L. Murrell founded Higher Heights Consulting and Training, Inc. to improve financial well-being and increase asset building opportunities for lower income consumers. She has a long, successful track record in the development of corporate and community initiatives to improve the lives of underserved individuals and families nationwide.

Ms. Murrell brings unique leadership and hands-on experience in the housing and financial services industry to her work. Her expertise has helped corporate clients and other organizations build community relations, develop strategic financial education programs, and create successful asset building initiatives. She also conducts train-the-trainer programs in these areas.

In the past, Ms. Murrell held leadership positions at Fannie Mae and the Fannie Mae Foundation where she helped launch initiatives that enabled millions of consumers to become homeowners. She developed financial education publications in nine languages and helped implement a public education advertising campaign in seven languages. Her work has involved building innovative key alliances with Fortune 500 companies, nonprofit organizations, financial institutions, faith-based institutions, and government agencies.

Part I

MAINTAINING A POSITIVE OUTLOOK

1

THE RIGHT STUFF

E very day you make financial choices. You buy morning coffee, take clothes to the cleaners, stock up on groceries, and get gas for the vehicle you drive. You might empty your pockets to give money to a child and then tap into an ATM to replenish your cash. On occasion you must cover the costs of an emergency. And once in a while, you make life-sized decisions—to change a job or career, move to a distant city, pay for education, or retire from the workforce. And all this in a constantly shifting societal environment!

Consider these recent challenges:

- Employers are terminating pensions for retirees and current workers at all levels. They are substituting 401(k) and 403(b) plans (you save your own money before any money is deposited by your employer) for traditional pensions (your employer deposited all the money in your account in exchange for years of work).
- Health benefits are continuing to cost more for employers, and these costs are increasingly being passed on to employees.
- Increasing numbers of Americans have no health insurance at all.
- Bankruptcy reform now limits a family's chances of starting over with a clean slate after a personal financial disaster.
- Political leaders talk about doing away with your all-important mortgage interest deduction.
- Politicians and lawmakers are proposing evermore "significant structural adjustments" to Social Security, Medicare, and Medicaid to deal with the nation's mounting budget deficit.[1]
- The IRS is more aggressively auditing individuals.[2]

In such a daunting environment, it is understandable that some people want to ignore the bigger picture. Others might claim that learning about financial management "is not their thing." But it isn't that easy; like it or not, we are already players in the financial game of life.

Consider all that you already know and grapple with on a daily basis:

You work and earn money, choose how you spend money, and borrow money each time you sign a credit card receipt. You make financial choices to save for emergencies and for your future security. Or perhaps you save little or nothing at all—letting life events "just happen," and then feel indignant, guilty, or depressed when they do. Granted, you might not always understand the subtle intricacies of the general economy, the capital markets, the health care system, or the fine print in the contracts you sign. Neither do most people. You might hate tackling personal finances and find even talking about finances a passionate turn-off ... but hold on! *There is a better way to think about personal finances.*

We can create a new model for living in the twenty-first century that shakes us from the complacency afflicting many in our nation today. And it starts with answering some big questions:

- What do I really value in life?
- What is my purpose?
- Am I living reactively or proactively?
- Am I honestly pleased with the way I am working to bring lasting benefits to myself and to those who depend on me?
- Do I "get involved" in the bigger picture and vote for responsible social and economic policies?
- Am I poised to achieve my biggest dreams?
- Am I even allowing myself to dream?

"The world makes way for the person who knows where he or she is going," wrote Ralph Waldo Emerson, nineteenth-century poet and essayist. But you don't have to go it alone. When it comes to finding your way on the road to financial security, you can look to another group for guidance, those who have achieved the status of living long, healthy lives. As we have discovered, whether you are on your way to a long and healthy life or to peace of mind and financial security, *the characteristics and habits of those who make it to their destinations are exactly the same.*

Following in Their Footsteps

Several years ago, Drs. Margery Hutter Silver and Thomas T. Perls (now Director of the New England Centenarian Study) presented findings to a group of gerontologists on a study in progress of the "oldest old" Americans. Silver and Perls were trying to discover the secrets of longevity from men and women who had reached the age of 100 and beyond. The results were surprising. No particular food or habit could account for the good living enjoyed by this lively group for over a century.

What the centenarians all had in common, according to these researchers, were the following four character traits: (1) they had a positive outlook; (2) they were engaged and active; (3) they had a social support system; and (4) they could cope well with loss. The nation's oldest old, it seems from these researchers' report, possess the "right stuff" for living through both good and tough times. They are the Americans who lived through the Great Depression, fought in World War II, worked hard, and pursued their dreams, all the while improving the American way of life for following generations.

The **Personal Characteristics** they possessed are the same as those you will uncover in yourself as you take charge of your life, plan for your future, and become competent in managing your everyday finances. You too will need

- to maintain a positive outlook,
- to be engaged and active in your financial affairs,
- to reach out to others for advice, education, financial resources, and financial help, and
- to learn to cope well with loss when you must.

Think this will be too difficult? Think again. When the people we interview decide to take charge of their financial affairs, they all say the same thing, "Why didn't I do this long ago?"[3] What most of them learned is that:

- You will naturally have a more **Positive Outlook** as you investigate what you really value, set goals, strategize, and periodically adjust your goals in anticipation of emerging trends and changing times.

In addition, you will find that as you learn and practice the basics, you will gain confidence and become encouraged to learn more.

- When you get more **Actively Involved** in your day-to-day finances, you will become curious and more aware of where your money actually goes. Soon enough and with less effort than you think, you will be engaged in planning your financial life—pro-actively.

- You will learn how to make wise saving, housing, and investment choices when you **Reach Out to Others** for strength, support, advice, education, and professional services. As you communicate more comfortably about your needs and preferences both at home and in the workplace, you'll find that caring people and financial resources are everywhere, and help to guide you along your way has never been more plentiful.

- The ability to **Plan for and Cope Well with Loss** can banish fear and help you recover quickly or change course in the face of adversity. No longer are you paralyzed when financial decisions must be made—you anticipate changes from time to time, and you go ahead and make them.

You and Your Money is more than a blueprint for building a secure financial future. It is also a powerful program to self-discovery. You can anticipate two results when you follow the steps we are suggesting: First, you will become a more aware and knowledgeable consumer as you practice the financial basics mindfully. Second, you will be on your way to a more personally fulfilling, happy, and secure life. During a recent financial education course attended by men and women in the Navy, these are the terms they used to describe "being in control of your financial life:"[4]

- Stress free
- High on life
- More confident
- More options
- Bigger savings account
- No fighting with your spouse
- No restless nights

Tapping Into Your Own Life Values

Would it surprise you to know that marketers often know your financial triggers better than you do? Wouldn't you like to understand your own motivations at least that well and even much better than their superficial tracking has revealed about you?

In the next few chapters, we help you focus on what really matters in your life. The Life Values Profile, explained in Chapter 3, "How We Decide," and Chapter 4, "Your Life Values Profile," will help you learn to wisely navigate the purchasing and savings decisions you face daily. You will find yourself on your way to building financial security as you:

- Become aware of your Life Values so you can interpret your impulses and use your new understanding to make smarter choices.
- Learn that your best financial decisions are always comprised of (1) financial behaviors in sync with what you really care about in life and (2) your knowledge of the financial basics.
- Enhance your understanding of your partner's and other family members' Life Values to minimize conflict and maximize harmony in your day-to-day financial life.
- Realize that wise financial choices today will anchor your entire well-being and the well-being of your loved ones in the future.
- Make routine money management practices and life decisions that will help you achieve financial competence and true security—whatever life may throw your way.

Getting Started

Financial competence is achieved by connecting the standards that guide you, the emotions that energize you, and the imagination that propels you so you will prosper *even when the future may seem uncertain*. In this book you will find guidance that we hope will help you become more at ease about managing money, skillful and confident about investing for your future, and surefooted in recovering quickly from any financial emergency. America is still a place where vision, dedication, and hard work can transform dreams into reality. Financial competence and savvy planning are essential tools for people who want to access opportunities and avoid pitfalls.

Think of it! Available books and magazines on money management, financial planning, and investing could fill a library. The Internet can provide you with thousands of answers, courses, self-help, and links to financial companies. Dozens of experts have written brilliantly about exactly how you should handle your money. We sorted through much of this advice to bring you the basics, and we have listed many resources in Chapter 19, "Finding the Help You Need," and in the Appendix, "Personal Finance Education Internet Sites," for you to check out for yourself.

We suggest five ways to interact with the information in this book: **ponder, daydream, experiment, practice,** and **plan.** The point of these processes is to help you *experience* the topics as well as read them. This is because real understanding happens, not only by reading about new ideas, but by "feeling" that they are particularly right for you.

PONDER

One expert family counselor, Rita Boothby, calls money "the root of all opportunity."[5] Is this a new idea to you? It was to us. Ponder this: Many people have been contaminated by the myth that money is evil, but according to Rita, people who believe money is about opportunity are likely to buy what's necessary and useful and leave the rest alone—*without guilt.* Some of their money circulates in the form of charity, and even if underpaid, they are likely to manage well and save what they can for the future. We marvel at the success stories of people from humble circumstances, but anyone—at any age or life stage—can develop the same habits and be successful as well.

As we present new ideas or what we believe are particularly valuable insights throughout this book, we collect them into "Points to Ponder" boxes. If you find them intriguing or important for your own situation, you might choose to close this book for a few moments to reflect on whether and how you can apply them to your particular life or financial situation.

DAYDREAM

Connecting with your dreams is necessary to release passion, have the energy to take on a task, and become excited about your goals. The key is uncovering your *ideal* self—the person you would like to be or what you want to accomplish with your life. And that starts with daydreaming.

Ninety-six percent of us, according to Jerome L. Singer of Yale, report having daydreams. Because you are allowing images to flow through your mind constantly, why not let your images work for you? You must be able to picture success before you can succeed at something; you must be able to imagine living in your own home before you are motivated to go out and buy it. And you must be able to see yourself as competent at managing all the business details of your life before you will gain the courage to try.

Using daydreams, you can rehearse how you will ask your boss for a raise and imagine his or her response. You can rewrite a scene where you wish you had behaved differently and prepare for what you might say or do the next time. You can envision yourself and your partner actually enjoying the time you spend together paying bills each month instead of fighting over them—or worse, one of you ignoring the bills altogether.

Sometimes we ask you to experience images while you are reading. When that happens, be sure you are comfortable, sit back, relax, and let the daydream inside your head unfold before you. Trust the flow of the imagery—it can guide you through a full script with characters playing out a drama.

EXPERIMENT

You will find mental and written explorations and exercises as you move through this book. All of the experiments are grounded in two facts of life: As a human being, you are influenced by your emotions, and where money is concerned, certain feelings can cause you or anyone else trouble. You can learn a lot about yourself if you study your emotional responses. You can also take action to distance yourself from troublesome feelings without reacting to them or denying them either. Most importantly, emotions are contagious, and for better or for worse, we humans take our emotional cues from one another.

If you are unable to acknowledge your angry feelings over a perceived slight at the checkout counter, for example, you can set off a chain reaction of negativity first to the checker, then to the next person in line, and on and on. However, those who have learned to recognize and confront such moments effectively won't let their distress impact someone else—and perhaps many others. Daniel Goleman, author of the bestselling book *Emotional Intelligence*, encourages leaders in many fields to take emotions "out of the closet" and acknowledge the importance of dealing with them.

Participating in the exercises in this book will expand your ability to integrate the material presented. They are intended to bring some of the subject matter to life as mini-projects. Some of them will surprise you, some will delight you, and others will allow you to take your own inner wisdom into the real world and try it out—to see what works and what doesn't work for you.

PRACTICE

No task or skill becomes routine and feels easy until you've practiced doing it. Watch any child learning to hit a baseball; with instruction and plenty of practice, he will eventually hit a home run. Interestingly, where finances are concerned, our parents and grandparents may have had more opportunities to practice. Take *Hamilton's Essentials of Arithmetic*, a book written in 1920 for seventh and eighth graders, for example. Here is a sampling of the table of contents:

- Investing Money
- Insurance
- Stocks and Bonds
- The Family Budget
- Running an Automobile
- Mercantile (Consumer) Problems
- Doing Business with Banks

Immigrants in the early 1900s were also taught how to handle money. In 1910, a "Guide to the United States for the Italian Immigrant" taught newcomers how to find work, travel safely, become a citizen, and handle and manage money—"il dollaro." For several months, a new arrival was visited twice a week and taught to practice "food preparation, buying . . . and discipline," until she became precise in recording all her expenditures, budgeting her resources, and laying a good financial foundation for her future life in America.[6]

As you read this book, you will find many pathways to laying a good foundation for your financial well-being and your ultimate peace of mind. As Italian newcomers learned nearly one hundred years ago, however, it takes practice.

PLAN

A few of you might believe you are lucky just to make it through each day. You might typically *react* to the events in your life and believe it impossible to turn things around or design and implement a plan. However, every noteworthy accomplishment has a plan behind it. Letting life "just happen to you" may spice it up some, but having no plan at all is a recipe for trouble.

What if the Egyptians had winged it when building the pyramids? Or if the astronauts had known only generally where they were headed? Financial consumer advocate, Bill Bachrach, asks these questions in *Values-Based Financial Planning.* He reminds us that great feats are achieved only as a result of people knowing what they want and then creating a strategy based on what is important to them. Olympic athletes, concert musicians, scientists, writers, artists, Nobel Prize winners, and many others accomplish what they set out to do only through planning. From modest to complex, *all goals need planning in order for us to achieve them.*

Although we listed "Plan" last, it is the most crucial financial activity of all. Creating a plan for the goals you want to pursue in life—even if you change them frequently—just makes sense. Otherwise you might not find your way, or you might become so caught up in stressful situations that you fail to take advantage of the many opportunities all around you.

Good luck on your journey to financial competence. Since you have gotten this far, we know you have the Right Stuff to succeed in achieving the *New* American Dream of the twenty-first century, including the freedom and opportunity associated with America's heritage, but based on a new sense of personal responsibility for designing a secure future.

2

THE "NEW"
AMERICAN DREAM

The American Dream is a way of living that includes having a job with advancement potential, owning a home, feeling useful, spending less than you make, and having a high degree of independence, autonomy, and contentment in later life. Throughout most of America's history, these values have served as a beacon for anyone willing to work hard and work smart. Its lure is one reason many people immigrated to the United States.

From all over the world, people came to the United States, filled with the promise that they could follow the "American Way" to satisfying work, a home of their own, and ultimate financial security. With persistence, they "made it" and passed both their wealth and their work ethic on to their children. It was a dream made possible by personal enterprise, the rapid expansion of the American economy during much of the twentieth century, and the "can-do" attitudes of those who played by the rules and flourished in this nation of plenty and opportunity.

Now here we are in the new Age of Technology, and the landscape is changing. Achieving the American Dream today seems more complicated and its future more uncertain. Outsourcing, deregulation, global competition, skyrocketing health care costs, corporate scandals, uncertainty in the markets—crisis seemingly follows crisis. Although most of them are not of our making, they all can and sometimes do impact our financial well-being.

We have seen the stories on the news; we have known friends, or friends of friends, or neighbors, fellow Americans who are skirting—or already living in—financial chaos or those who must rebuild their lives after a serious setback:

- Near-retirement-age couples whose life savings were held by employers that squandered or terminated their retirement benefits.
- Natural disaster victims who lost everything and must start over.
- Chronically ill people, the disabled, low-wage, and day workers who have no health insurance and cannot afford care.
- High school graduates without plans for college, unable to find living wage jobs and affordable housing.
- College graduates, burdened by high student loans, who will take years to repay the costs of their education.
- Employees who have lost good jobs through outsourcing or down-sizing and cannot find comparable employment.

If you believe these are rare occurrences, think again. These stories are signs of the changing times. The question is, "How can we adapt and thrive?"

Heeding the Signals of the Twenty-First Century

We need a new model for living in the twenty-first century that shakes us from our complacency. *Pro-activity is key.*

Already in numerous technical and manufacturing fields, skilled workers in India, China, and elsewhere are willing to do your job for a lot less pay! Are you prepared to go on to the next level of job or career if you are replaced? Or might you spend months, maybe years, looking for a job like the one you lost but that is no longer there? Outsourcing is just one of the signals of a changing economy and workforce. In addition, dropping wages, the eroded power of unions, and the decrease in skilled job opportunities are making it more and more difficult for many Americans to make ends meet.

Although you may be in your twenties or thirties, you should know how the nation's aging population is changing the economic and cultural landscape. And for those who are already (or nearly) retired, you need to understand how you may be affected by business inclinations and political infrastructure. Changing tax laws, the nation's health care issues, and legislation that impacts all facets of life quality are being debated and voted on almost daily. Each of us must look up from our too busy lives, take stock of our lifestyles, and become competent in the financial management skills of daily living and the unfolding future.

Character Traits of Financially Competent People

Those who master their destiny share many qualities, few of which are determined by society's definition of success—a formula that centers mostly on fame and fortune. Do you have what it takes? How many of these statements describe your principles and values? Individuals who will achieve their dreams in the twenty-first century:

- Say "I can."
- Commit to lifelong learning.
- Tap into their own (or a higher) consciousness—they go "within" as they deal "without."
- Have the courage to risk failure.
- Cope well with life's inevitable losses.
- Do not blame others for the circumstances of their lives.
- Seek the resources they need to make wise choices and decisions.
- Communicate clearly and calmly even when it feels uncomfortable.
- Stay tuned to the political and economic landscape.
- Vote to change what they do not like.

The fact is that for much of the past century, most of us entrusted our financial well-being to others—parents, financial corporations, insurance companies, employers, and the government. We handed over critical decisions about health care, job security, and retirement income, choosing to live comfortably in the present while "knowing" we would be just fine in the future. In the process, generations lost the knowledge needed about the role of money in our lives. We lost the skills to be financially self-sufficient and to make the life decisions that lead to real security. Some of us even lost the courage to try.

It is ironic that there are more people willing to teach courses about finances than there are people willing to take them. Ironic because there is more accessible information on personal finance topics than has ever been available to Americans before. The same corporations, insurance companies, financial professionals, employers, and government agencies on which we became dependent now want to teach people to become self-sufficient and financially competent. They are holding meetings, passing laws, and publishing information on the Web, in bookstores, at seminars, in courses, and in newspapers and magazines that exhort people to become "financially literate." Yet, too many of their intended audience are turning a deaf ear.

Other messages, however, also keep coming in loud and clear—messages like "Buy now and pay no interest" or "Pay nothing for one, two, or even three years!" This seductive communication from big business with its own agenda is drowning out the commonsense message of financial literacy. Whatever the product is, if it sounds free, it can begin to feel like a burning need. The idea of paying later is familiar and appealing because it has become a way of life—a really mixed up version of the original American Dream. In Chapter 19, "Finding the Help You Need," and in the Appendix, "Personal Finance Education Internet Sites," we offer sources of objective information that we hope will assist you in distinguishing between these contradictory messages.

American Life on the Edge and Beyond

Some people are living on the edge and do not even realize it. They believe they are getting by and will be "okay" in the future. Others are used to a certain standard of living—maybe even funding it by debt—which they could not keep up in case of a setback. Whether you are keeping up with your neighbors, struggling to get a new start, living the standard you see in advertising, or copying your parents' lifestyle, many Americans are wavering on the edge when it comes to financing their present and future lives.

The credit card industry presumes, based on happy past experience, that Americans will keep borrowing more money to support their spending habits. They count on consumers to pay down just enough debt to enable them to borrow more. But some families are smarter than that. They are stretching to pay down outstanding balances. Is your family one of these?

If so, credit card companies will intensify their advertising and marketing efforts to bring you back into the fold. So we all need to push back against these mixed up cultural messages: "Work hard, buy what you want, be happy, don't worry about the future." And when we do, the classic joke about too much month left at the end of the money will no longer be true for so many families.

We know that living paycheck to paycheck is worrisome, but try to think ahead about your future as well. Even though thinking about the consequences of a sudden illness, being in debt after college, unemployment, or being forced into early retirement may seem worse, the reality is that these are commonplace occurrences. After all, if you cannot even *think* about your future, you will not be able to plan for it either. Take the case of Tina who is part-owner of a small catering company.

For several years she stuck to her budget to make ends meet for her two young daughters and herself. Tina's ex-husband often was late with child-support payments, which put a crimp on any extras, such as going out for dinner or taking the children to Disney World. Still, she always made the rent payments when they were due and had enough to spare for the small pleasures in life—until the phone rang one night.

Tina's mom had suffered a massive stroke. Suddenly, she was partially paralyzed, unable to feed herself, and in need of full-time care. There was Sunny Meadows, the nearby nursing home, but costs were much more than Tina could afford. She spent days scouring the area trying to find an alternative but ended up back at Sunny Meadows. Her mom's Social Security check covered about a quarter of the monthly expenses. Tina, an only child, had to take over her mother's finances, apply for Medicaid, and cover the difference herself, including legal fees. Tina took on a second job to supplement her income. That meant putting her children in after-school-care programs, no more trips to Disney World, no dining out, and living on a budget so tight there was no room for extras. It also meant depleting her children's college fund as well as her retirement savings.

And then there's Dave. He had it all. Or so he thought. In his prime at 42, he enjoyed his job as a manager in the high-tech sector and earned a high income. His house was spacious with a hot tub on the deck off the master bedroom. The SUV and BMW convertible in his driveway were traded in every few years, and he and his family enjoyed twice-yearly vacations. Dave and his wife wore beautiful clothes and sported fine jewelry that impressed their friends at the country club. And Dave didn't skimp when it came to his kids either. They went to private schools and scored well in the hot-gadget category on every holiday occasion.

Yes, for Dave and his family, life was good. But one morning, his boss called him in to explain that thanks to corporate outsourcing, the division Dave headed was being relocated to India. It was unthinkable, but Dave, along with his staff, was handed a pink slip and two months' severance pay. Suddenly his carefully built American Dream was in major meltdown. His credit card balances were off the charts, and his astronomical payments that were easily met when his income was high, quickly ate away at his meager savings. Dave got himself right into the job market, but months of hunting in a changing employment landscape led nowhere. Dave and his family were losing it all, slowly but surely.

Despite their seemingly diverse lifestyles, Tina, Tina's mom, and Dave all had one thing in common—they had been living on the edge, lulled into the complacency of spending for today. None of them had really done anything wrong. They are all hard-working people who thought they were playing by the rules until their American Dream got swallowed up by real life. They were caught up in circumstances which they "did not think would happen." But these are not unimaginable scenarios for anyone who has the courage to look at life realistically and to plan for emergencies. Too often, the thread by which we hang our lifestyle is gossamer thin. In good times, we don't think much about it. But like the Wall Street fallout from the tech stock fireworks of the 1990s, the 9/11 terror attacks that wreaked havoc on whole industries, or natural disasters that can wipe out whole communities, bad times do come. When they do, we might find ourselves asking, "What was I thinking?" or "Why wasn't I better prepared?"

The "New" American Dream still has to do with freedom and opportunity. It also involves working hard at a job you love, earning, and living comfortably. But the twenty-first century version emphasizes a new approach to two traditional components: security and responsibility—or you can think of it as "response ability."

As the old, reliable social institutions of pensions, labor unions and Social Security are weakened, we are offered progressively less financial security. Instead, we have gotten BACK the responsibility for these aspects of our lives. Whether security from terrorists, job loss, changing climates and rules, or investment meltdowns, most of us are seeking a safe corner where we can make a life for ourselves and our families.

Given that many of us have no role models for how to manage these newly returned financial life components, we must become responsible again at a whole new level. This has added meaning for those of us who did not experience the Great Depression or the sacrifices of World War II. More than just a code phrase for increased health care costs and decreased value of employee benefits, the mantra of responsibility means that we must now take ownership and make choices pertinent to our personal and civic values in such areas as medical care and retirement savings. We must provide our own safety net and become much more aware consumers and citizens. *We must become involved.*

What Is Financial Competence?

At the core of the "New" American Dream is *financial competence,* and from this core springs achievement, resourcefulness, and financial security. You don't have to be a Wall Street wizard to be financially competent. Financial competence entails having a basic understanding of your relationship to money. Sure, it means understanding banking and credit, saving, investing, and practicing good money management. But it also means being able to talk about money and financial planning with your partner openly and without discomfort.

The husband of a friend, Susan, recently had to take a pay-cut with his company in order to save his job from being outsourced. She was frantic because he was still spending at his former levels. "We don't have to change our lifestyle yet," he told Susan when the pay-cut took effect. But time passed, and they began living partly on credit and rapidly sinking into debt. The couple was about to celebrate their 18th wedding anniversary the day Susan said, "You know, Phil and I have never been able to talk about finances. He gets very uptight."

If Susan and Phil were financially competent, they would have opened a dialogue with one another years ago. They might have saved and invested as protection against unforeseen emergencies. They may have been able to revise their financial planning and lifestyle spending in the immediate aftermath of Phil's pay-cut.

Financial competence is about factoring in future costs when making lifestyle choices and planning for contingencies. It is figuring out whether the freelance job you are considering will bankrupt you when you have to pay for your own health insurance. Or knowing exactly how much in student loans you can safely handle and for how long. It means understanding whether to refinance and take the money to pay credit card debt or to have some back-up funds for that left punch on the chin that life has a habit of surprising us with. It means understanding how to plan for and take ownership of the major events in your life, like education, career, buying a home, and retirement.

Financial competence also means looking at national and international events in a new way—realizing that these events may, in fact, impact your wallet. It means understanding that living in a global economy puts everyone at risk because when trouble in a country in another part of the world erupts, it can cause repercussions at home in terms of fuel costs, food and building prices, business, jobs, and investments. Or it means realizing that when companies pull up stakes and head to countries where wages are less and labor and environmental laws don't exist, our individual hopes and dreams can be suddenly deep-sixed, at least temporarily.

Thinking Clearly, Spending Mindfully

How many times in the past year have you made a purchase you really couldn't afford, but you whipped out a credit card and did it anyway?

Financial competence does not mean you can't behave that way; it simply means that you make educated choices and limit acting on impulse. It means you are aware of the full cost of what you are doing and have some contingency plans to balance your budget. Yes, anyone's financial life can go awry, but financial competence gives us the tools to pick ourselves up, brush off the debris, and build our financial foundation once again. However, we first must have the courage to face the financial facts of life.

While money is a necessary and important part of living, personal responsibility and pride in being responsible is the core that determines how we will live in today's complex world. Earning a living, raising and educating children, maintaining our health, giving care to aging parents or sick children, saving and investing for the future, and managing the other business-related aspects of our lives are all part of financial competence.

Unlike Tina and Dave, John *was* prepared for financial change.

John's mother lived alone and had just turned 76. She was living on Social Security and her salary as a part-time librarian, but John suspected that her finances were far from secure. Very soon her paycheck could stop coming, and Social Security would not be enough to cover the bills. In addition, she was growing frail and would no longer be able to live by herself. John decided to avoid a crisis by getting involved in his mother's financial affairs.

John's sincerity and concern persuaded his independent-minded mother to share her financial picture. Although her income was too small to pay for an assisted living facility, she had built up equity in her home, and that asset could contribute to her future living expenses. John convinced his mother to sell the house and move into an assisted living facility of her choosing. She not only had more care available, she could also serve as the facility's librarian. She was delighted. During the next two years, as she grew increasingly frail, her care needs were easily met. John did not wait until his mother's situation became a crisis. He approached his mother even though it had been difficult, helped her to think through possible lifestyle solutions, and then planned ahead.

Don't Worry, Get Educated Instead

When you are financially competent, you have made a commitment to lifelong learning and to the search for new solutions to handle changing life situations. You have learned when, how, and where to find the information you need to make choices. No matter what your age, sex, race, ethnicity, income, education, job, religion, or citizenship status, you can create a personal and social context for achieving your particular dreams.

The former Chair of the Management Department at a major graduate school of business told us that "everyone needs personal financial education." You wouldn't think that a person in his position would lack financial training, yet he had recently taken a week-long course on estate planning and was pleased with what he had learned.

Hundreds of courses are offered in every area of the United States today. Our research shows that American values—getting ahead, having work we love to do, setting goals, becoming a homeowner, getting a second chance, and becoming active in the community—are all motivators for the participants who choose to attend. Those people who can find the courage to seek out financial education, to require it of their employers, to organize it in their communities, and to use it in their everyday affairs will eventually transform their lives and their communities and even improve the way America does business.

Most people teach themselves by the seat of their pants the things they need to do day by day. They don't think about where they are headed until there is a problem—they get laid off from work, someone in the family becomes ill or hurt, or something happens in the economy that impacts them negatively. But what if, when these catastrophic events happened, you were ready for them? What if you had taken time to educate yourself so you knew how to cope?

Dave was living only part of the picture. He had not put together the simple truth that the American Dream involves having the courage to plan for the long term, not simply living for today. Tina was also living part of the picture. True, she had been blindsided by her mother's care needs, and she had to sit down and figure out how she would survive in her new circumstances. But financial competence also means knowing that life blindsides us sometimes, and we'd better have a contingency plan for when it does, so that we can quickly get back on our feet.

The Land of Opportunity

The American Dream has always been about having opportunity—and that means recognizing or reaching out for whatever situation or condition you can find or create that helps you attain your goals. It also means having a chance to improve your life and your prospects for self-advancement.

Today, the road to financial self-reliance can be bumpy, and it is no longer marked with familiar road signs. Until recently, we stayed loyal to companies and careers; employers took care of our pensions and health insurance; and even though government borrowed from Social Security, we "knew" it would always be there for us as it was for our parents.

Nowadays, we do and will continue to frequently change jobs, careers, companies, and even professions. Documents we do not understand offer us investments we find difficult to trust, yet our future well-being depends upon our ability to know how and when to invest. We pay taxes on forms we cannot decipher under codes we cannot fathom to federal and local governments that "have no money."

But even in this changed financial landscape, the opportunity to succeed is available to us all—as long as we can hold on to our deepest values, believe in ourselves, and navigate a new course of personal and civic financial responsibility. To do this, you will do well to remember the traits that breed success: staying positive, becoming active and competent in financial management, reaching out and becoming aware consumers and voters, and dealing well with loss if and when we must. This involves modeling our financial decisions after financially competent people's actions, aligning our decisions with our values, and crafting our own version of the "New" American Dream. And on the practical side, remember to check out all the helpful resources we offer to readers in the last chapter of this book and in the Appendix.

3

HOW WE DECIDE

Market research and advertising firms know we make spending decisions based on what we *value*. Insurance sales pitches focus on how much we value our families and are concerned for their future security. Automobile companies know that SUVs, sports cars, or mini-vans appeal to people who value power or social identity or family outings. Recognizing the coming retirement of the baby boomer generation, recent marketing campaigns have targeted boomer's values to sell them products and services. Trying to capture Gen Y's attention, marketers have discovered that what worked for boomers and echo boomers won't work for Gen Y consumers, because they have different values.

Whatever our age or life stage, what these marketing experts know is the simple concept that *our values influence our behaviors*. And by appealing to our values, they can convince us that we *need* or *really want* their products or services. Seen from this point of view, it is manipulative marketing. But if we turn this back to ourselves, we soon realize that one key to staying positive in life is consciously behaving in accordance with our own deeper values. As a bonus, we become marketing savvy and can more easily recognize advertising and selling techniques that try to—and too often do—influence our behaviors.

Connecting our values to our decision-making can make all the difference when we choose a home, make an investment, get an education, or interview for a new job. Understanding how values differ between spouses and among family members can help us to lessen, if not entirely avoid, the painful exchanges that can occur when conflicting values influence our emotions and our decisions. Uncovering our unique set of Personal Values takes a little detective work, but it will clue us into what motivates us to make our best choices, especially those that involve our finances.

We also can begin to understand what motivates us to make purchases we cannot afford, ignore good financial management, fail to save and invest for our future, or behave in other irresponsible ways by:

1. Learning where our values come from and how what we value influences our decisions.

2. Thinking carefully about what we value *most*.

3. Integrating our deeper values into our financial management.

Our Deeper Life Values

Values spark our desires, trigger emotions, and drive our decisions. How we channel our values shows up, not just in our character, but in how we handle our job or career, enjoy our social and intimate relationships, manage our lifestyle, and feel secure about what is in our wallets. For simplicity's sake, let's assume from now on that all of what you really care about in your life falls into four categories. They are: Personal Values, Social Values, Tangible Values, and Money Values. Collectively, we call them your "Life Values."

When Oprah inaugurated the "American Debt Diet" on her television show, her guest, Jean Shatsky, a regular on "The Today Show" and contributing editor to *Money Magazine*, emphasized to the audience that excessive debt—or the failure to value sound financial management—is not only about money, it's about all of life. So when the condo you love becomes available or the lawn tractor goes on sale or the stock you have been following drops, you will make a financial decision, but it will have only a little to do with your checkbook balance or your portfolio. Your decision will be made, in large part, on the basis of your four Life Values.

Check them out:

Your Personal (Inner) Life Values

- Security, identity, autonomy, and control.
- Spiritual values, including self-expression.

These are Personal Values such as your identity, the desire to achieve and to act as you please, your need for safety and security, and other aspects of the "real you." Such values reflect your desire for freedom and independence, your ability to control your everyday life, shape long-range goals, set your own priorities, and feel in charge. Everyone has a need to feel safe from perceived harm or loss, including financial upheaval. Real security is the feeling that you have the wherewithal to survive whatever you encounter, and it is based on deep-rooted confidence about your particular place in the world. Inner values also form the basis for finding purpose and meaning in life, the principles by which you live. Do you value your personal space? Need autonomy at home and at work? Do you value above all experiencing personal achievement and knowing the ropes? These are inner values, and they are rooted not only in how you see yourself, but how you believe others see you as well.

Your Social Life Values

- Spouse, partner, children, or family.
- Friends and extended family.
- Your larger communities of interest such as clubs, associations, and other networks.

These are "belonging" values that concern your spouse, partner, children, other family members, friends, neighbors, and community members. They include your living and working habits and involve your desires to be with others. They involve your tendencies to plan and budget for social events or allow them to be spontaneous, and your inclination to share financial information and responsibility. Do you share costs, pay bills, or provide for others? Are you generous about household expenditures and clear about joint budgeting? Do you enjoy a supportive lifestyle? Your unique financial history, habits, and cultural preferences are rooted in your family and social relationships. This history may be determining the way you handle money today.

Your Tangible (Physical) Life Values

- Your physical health.
- All of your external world, your material possessions, and your perceptions of comfort and beauty.

Tangible Values relate to the physical comforts and other tangible aspects of your environment. They include the amount of space you need around you to feel comfortable and the aesthetic stimulation you require to feel satisfied and fulfilled. Tangible Life Values involve your physical health and sometimes manifest as a search for the health benefits of a certain climate or activity. They include the general desire for beauty or specific features in your home, yard, or workplace. They trigger your inexplicable attraction to certain types of art and architecture, clothing styles, or vehicles to drive. Tangible Life Values are all about feeling physically satisfied and enjoying comfort and order in your surroundings. These values can reach far back into your childhood history, acting in concert with your Personal, Social, and Money Life Values—whether you realize it consciously or not.

Your Money (Financial) Life Values

- *Sufficiency*—Do I have enough? Do I earn enough? Save enough?
- *Sustainability*—How long will my money (or my payments) last?
- *Appropriateness*—Is my lifestyle appropriate? Is this purchase appropriate?

Money Life Values refer to all things about your finances. It is a subjective category—what you think or believe about money and your financial affairs. It represents how you value money or other material goods or investments, *not how much you actually have.* This value has nothing to do with your actual financial knowledge or education level. Everyone is concerned with the **sufficiency** of their finances, but the meaning of, "*Do I have enough?*" varies from person to person. In the same way, the urgency of **sustainability**—"*How long will my money last?*"—varies among individuals. A higher savings account balance usually indicates a person who thinks more about financial sustainability as opposed to the person who lives from paycheck-to-paycheck. Finally, the

appropriateness of our financial decisions—*"Is this right for me?"*—is often the key factor that keeps us in or out of financial trouble. Individuals who cannot or will not make decisions about the appropriateness of a purchase (or item, job, lifestyle, or vacation) in their lives are more likely than others to be ill-prepared to meet financial emergencies or to save for retirement.

Watching for Conflicting Values

Sometimes (such as when you think you are pretty good at managing money, but at the same time you are not saving enough or feel guilty about what you buy), your inner signals are contradictory. That's because your financial decisions, including earning, spending, investing, saving, and giving are about much more than money. *All four* of these Life Value categories, not just your Money Values, guide your everyday money interactions and influence your financial management style. You might be influenced by what other people say or do, by circumstances you can't control, by mindless habits, or by unanticipated events. Just when you need to stay cool and collected, you can become anxious and conflicted or misguided and over-confident. Foggy thinking and poor decision making are products of missing entirely or misunderstanding your own inner motives. Financial loss is all too often the unfortunate result.

When you get a handle on what you really value, you can more easily re-channel your impulses, your emotions, and your choices. You can shift the way you handle your finances into competence mode with a capital "C." You can clarify your thinking, make smarter decisions, improve your personal relationships, and get much better at making, keeping, and growing your money. You can say "goodbye" to guilt and anxiety and instead identify what real security is all about.

Learning About Your Life Values

The time has come for you to put pen to paper and start to learn more about the values that are guiding *you*. There is no point in crunching numbers until you have cracked the most important nut of all: How are *you* most likely to make decisions about personal finances?

Maybe you prefer not to know how you decide what and when to buy or whether and how to invest. You may be tempted to skip this section and move forward. But let's put your mind at ease; it is not about whether you do it the "right way" or the "wrong way." How you make your financial decisions is simply that—it's your method. It is what it is. Simply understanding what motivates you to buy and save and give and invest the way you do will put enough new tools in your financial tool-box to start you on the road to full financial competence.

DAYDREAM

It is not about whether your decision making is *right* or *wrong*. It is simply about understanding how you make financial decisions and then using that understanding as a tool to achieve your financial goals in the future. Take some time to dream about a financial decision you need to make soon. Think about the things that you value. Dream about the ways your values influence your decision.

Remember those marketing professionals we mentioned earlier? Recall that they track your spending habits right down to the titles of all the books you have purchased online in the past two years. They have your demographic information, but they know much more about you than your age, race, and sex. They have amassed enough data to predict where your hard-earned dollars are going next, and they even know why. What sales and advertising people realize is that for the most part, your financial decisions are really not about money. They are about your values and needs. All of us make decisions—about asking for a raise, participating in a retirement plan, or buying a new home—not only on the basis of their bottom line impact, but also on the basis of their social, psychological, and lifestyle implications, too.

There is a simple formula to explain all this, Everyone wants to be happy, right? And no one wants to be unhappy. In our efforts to feel comfortable and balanced in our lives, we actually juggle four sets of Life Values—our inner or Personal Life Values, our physical or Tangible Life Values, our Social Life Values, and our Money Life Values. When we make a financial decision, we do a quick and unconscious check of our values, perhaps something like this: "Will it make me feel safe and secure? Will it bring me the things that give me pleasure? Will it connect me more happily with others? Will it be appropriate, given what I (or my partner and I) can afford?" Yes, that last question is a purely financial question, but it's more about your Money Values and beliefs than it is about the bottom line.

When we do that quick check of our Life Values, what we really are doing is trying to keep everything in balance so that we experience a sense of equilibrium or, one might say, so we can sleep at night after we swipe our credit card. So each of us juggles these four values, but we each juggle in a slightly different way. While physical safety might be of greater concern to an individual living in a high-crime neighborhood, style and presentation might be more important to a successful executive with a lovely home and yacht and no mortgage. Those are extreme examples, of course, but these are the three points to keep in mind:

- We all have our unique needs and wants.
- Our needs and wants tend to shift and reconfigure over our lifetime.
- Our values, the core ideas upon which we set priorities and form preferences, are rather stable and are central to shaping our identity.

POINT TO PONDER

Do you know that your financial decisions are often not about money at all? They can involve your identity and personal needs, material wants, and social values. Even the "money" part of your reality is about *Money Values*, not about how much money you actually *have*.

Learning Secrets of the Marketplace

You may have some idea of the way you have been tracked, analyzed, and pigeon-holed as a consumer by the marketing industry. But what if you could learn those very same things about yourself, putting the results to work for you, to save your money and grow your assets rather than to convince you to overspend or make an impulse purchase? We are inviting you in the next chapter to use a tool similar to, but even more advanced than, those used by big-spending advertisers. You will be able to use a thoroughly researched, proven method that will help you understand your own financial decision patterns and motivations before you take out your wallet or credit card. You can do that right now by completing the Life Values Profile in the next chapter.

4

YOUR LIFE
VALUES PROFILE

By completing this profile, you will learn how your four Life Value categories influence your financial priorities. The Life Values Profile also can be an effective way of starting a conversation about finances with loved ones. Encourage your spouse, partner, and others in your household to create their own Life Values Profile. Together you can assess where your points of view are in alignment or where they collide.

Expect your values categories to overlap a lot, and keep in mind that there are no "right" or "wrong" answers, just preferences. Remember, too, that your answers are intensely personal—*do not answer what you believe someone else may want or value.* Quickly choose only one answer per statement, the one that feels most like who you really are. Then write the corresponding letter on a separate piece of paper so that your spouse, partner, or other family members also can complete the profile. Remember the results of your profile—this will help you later, because Part II, "Being Active In Financial Affairs," and Part III, "Building A Financial Support System," suggest how your profile influences your money management habits.

Your Life Values Profile

1. The most important priority in connection with my home is having:

    a) A place where I am part of a community and/or close to friends and family.
    b) A location that is private and allows me autonomy and security.
    c) A neighborhood that will appreciate greatly in value.
    d) A place that is beautiful, a real showplace with all the physical comforts.

2. An important objective for choosing the right health care plan is having:

    a) Access to preventive care and sports medicine for my active lifestyle.
    b) The maximum freedom to choose my health care providers in any location.
    c) Access to health care facilities in my community and good family practice health care providers.
    d) Evidence-based medical care—the best value for the money.

3. My decision about which vehicle to drive comes down to this main issue:

    a) My family members are on board with my decision, and the vehicle will serve all our needs as a family.
    b) I want a vehicle that is dependable and gets me where I'm going with the least amount of trouble.
    c) I'll weigh the costs and benefits of each vehicle and pick the one that meets my budget.
    d) I make enough to be able to afford the vehicle I love to drive even if the gas mileage is not great.

4. If I were to face an overdue account or bill that would have serious credit consequences, I would worry most about:

    a) My reputation and credit score.
    b) How this mistake could possibly have occurred and what I need to do to make sure it cannot happen again.

c) Where I could obtain the money to make this payment.

d) The impact this event might have on my partner or family.

5. When I think about changing jobs, my main concern is:

    a) Whether the new job would pay enough so I can cover the costs of my lifestyle.

    b) A place to work helping other people with colleagues I enjoy.

    c) The total financial package: pay, health care and retirement benefits.

    d) Having opportunities for personal challenge and fulfillment in my work.

6. In deciding whether to save, spend, or invest a sudden cash windfall, I would:

    a) Consider taking a trip around the world and enjoy myself thoroughly.

    b) Investigate a variety of investment possibilities, weighing the long-term return offered by each.

    c) Use it to fund a need, wish, or desire of a family member.

    d) Buy a new house with all the amenities and comforts I've always wanted.

7. Any decisions I would make (or have already made) about planning for retirement are based mostly on:

    a) The future needs of my partner and adult children and grandchildren.

    b) The retirement calculations that I have made, which have given me a benchmark number toward which to target my savings for later life.

    c) My desire to live an intellectually and physically fulfilled life as an older adult.

    d) My ambition to maintain a comfortable lifestyle in a beautiful place and pleasant community during retirement.

8. When it comes to "impulse purchases" of items not previously intended:

    a) I reflect on whether I've treated myself lately and then make my decision.

b) I recall the commitments I have made to others and consider whether I should buy the item or forgo it.

c) I tend to buy only what is on my list, unless the item offers serious savings on something I know will be needed in the near future.

d) I think about how well it will fit in with what I already own.

9. When I go shopping for holiday gifts for the family, I:

a) Tend to go overboard a little, because I like having something special for everyone and a few extra gifts for unexpected guests as well.

b) Value peace of mind after the holidays so I try to stay within my budget.

c) Seem always to budget too little because my decorating, and other options are more extravagant than I anticipate.

d) Consider my cash flow for the coming months, set a firm budget, and usually stick to it pretty closely.

10. In making vacation plans, I weigh the value and cost mostly in light of:

a) The opportunity to share the trip with people (or someone) I care about and enjoy being with.

b) The chance to see new places, architecture, cuisine, and lifestyles.

c) Fulfilling my desires of being able to do whatever I please during my vacation.

d) The likelihood that the enjoyment will be well worth my investment.

11. When the subject of financial planning comes up, my response is usually:

a) Keyed into the comfort level I have with my partner and other family members in discussing finances and our future.

b) Related to a "hook" that quickly suggests that I can live more comfortably if I plan carefully in advance.

c) Positive, interested, and determined to plan as well as I can.

d) Neutral but open-minded as long as the process incorporates my particular interests and foreseeable needs.

12. When people visit my home and see my lifestyle:

    a) They know that my family and community take priority in my life.
    b) They can learn a lot about who I am and what I care about.
    c) They cannot tell whether or not I am financially successful.
    d) They know I take great pride in the comfort and beauty of my home and its surroundings.

13. My most important spending goal right now involves having:

    a) Beauty and comfort that make my surroundings enjoyable.
    b) A clear plan for achieving financial security in later life.
    c) The means to spend more quality time with family and friends.
    d) The level of income I need to live life the way I want and enjoy.

14. When I hear the word "security," I automatically think of:

    a) A lifestyle in which I have what I need to be comfortable without worry.
    b) A diversified and sound investment portfolio, a 401(k), and a home that is not mortgaged to the hilt.
    c) Family and friendships and a sense of community that will last for a lifetime, no matter what happens.
    d) Having achieved a sense of self-esteem and the freedom to be who I really am.

15. When I balance my checkbook and get my current affairs in order, I am motivated by:

    a) The need to feel in control of my life and my affairs.
    b) The desire to maintain a reasonable lifestyle and have something left over to save.
    c) A desire to be able to cover my costs and pay my bills during the upcoming month.
    d) Memories of what my parents and grandparents did or said.

16. To feel satisfied and comfortable with my personal financial situation, I would need:

    a) A financial cushion as well as a long-range plan that is solid and realistic.

b) Control over my spending while knowing that I can afford what I want.

c) Enough money to maintain the wardrobe, car, and home furnishings that I enjoy.

d) The money I need to cover my children's school and other family expenses and plan some fun without worrying or feeling guilty.

17. To me a sizable savings account would mean:

a) The freedom to change jobs or maybe my career so I can truly "live my own life" the way I'd like.

b) Freedom from worry in living paycheck to paycheck and a chance to build future capital.

c) Spending more time with my family and giving back to my community.

d) The chance to join a gym, get a personal trainer, go to a spa, and/or treat myself to some attractive new clothes.

18. If I "fell in love with" a particular item that I believed would make me very happy, but it was beyond my budget, I would:

a) Adjust my budget and make concessions in other areas so I could have the item I desire.

b) Make a plan to be able to afford that item as soon as possible.

c) Pass it by and compensate instead with something else enjoyable, knowing I would feel too guilty about buying the item.

d) Consider whether it would make someone else in the family as happy as it would make me and then look for and find some way to pay for it if I could.

19. For me, the main purpose in investing is (would be):

a) Growing capital that I can tap into whenever and for whatever I choose.

b) An opportunity to build or preserve an appreciating capital asset.

c) The chance to fund a comfortable, enjoyable lifestyle in the future.

d) A source of security for my family, should I die an untimely death.

20. In my ideal financial position, I would have the freedom I need to:

a) Live my life independently, coming and going and doing as I please.

b) Share in the activities my friends and family enjoy without stressing my budget.

c) Keep my expenses under control while building financial security for the future.

d) Buy the things I like most and enjoy a comfortable lifestyle.

Scoring Your Profile Results

Now that you have completed the quiz, here is the key to determining which combination of Life Values tends to influence your financial decisions:

1. P stands for Personal Values

2. S stands for Social Values

3. T stands for Tangible Values

4. M stands for Money Values

Compare your answers to the following table and count the P's, S's, T's and M's you've chosen to determine your score for each Life Values category.

Table 4–1   Answer Code Listing

1.	a) S	b) P	c) M	d) T
2.	a) T	b) P	c) S	d) M
3.	a) S	b) P	c) M	d) T
4.	a) P	b) M	c) T	d) S
5.	a) T	b) S	c) M	d) P
6.	a) P	b) M	c) S	d) T
7.	a) S	b) M	c) P	d) T
8.	a) P	b) S	c) M	d) T
9.	a) S	b) P	c) T	d) M
10.	a) S	b) T	c) P	d) M
11.	a) S	b) T	c) M	d) P
12.	a) S	b) P	c) M	d) T
13.	a) T	b) M	c) S	d) P
14.	a) T	b) M	c) S	d) P
15.	a) P	b) M	c) T	d) S
16.	a) M	b) P	c) T	d) S
17.	a) P	b) M	c) S	d) T
18.	a) T	b) M	c) P	d) S
19.	a) P	b) M	c) T	d) S
20.	a) P	b) S	c) M	d) T

Evaluating Your Life Values Profile

A very high Life Values score (above 9) and a lower Life Values score (4 and below) reveal dominant and less important value priorities. When scores are fairly even across all categories, they suggest balance in all four Life Value categories.

Here is how these scores can generally be interpreted:

1. *Personal Values (Your "P" Score).* If you scored very high here, identity, autonomy, safety, and security are important to you. Are you protected if you suddenly lose your job? Taking charge of your personal finances now can give you the peace of mind of knowing your livelihood is secure. A very low P score might signal that you tend to see your financial decisions through someone else's eyes or that you are deferring to another's expectations regarding your earning, spending, savings, and investments. Perhaps you could benefit by becoming more active in your own financial affairs.

2. *Social Life Values (The "S" Score).* If you scored high here, some of your chief concerns probably involve caring for your family members. Would you like to ensure that you will have enough to provide for a child's education? Are you caring for a parent in his or her advanced years? A very high S score usually signals that you live—and finance—an interactive lifestyle, helping (or supporting) others in your life. A very low S factor may indicate that you live alone, enjoy your solitude, and prefer financial independence.

3. *Tangible Life Values (Your "T" Score).* If this is your dominant score, you are concerned with your health and physical sur-roundings. If you are not yet a homeowner, you dream about owning your own home. Or maybe you are even thinking about owning that vacation home you rent every year. Wise financial planning will allow you to maintain the comforts you now enjoy in your surroundings. A high T score also indicates that you are aware of your physical surroundings as you make financial decisions. While you like function, you also seek com-fort and beauty to the extent that you can afford it. A very low

T score could mean that you are a person on the go, efficient at settling in wherever you are and not all that interested in collecting material belongings that need your attention and care.

4. *Money Life Values (Your "M" Score).* If you scored high here, your value base is at least partially grounded in your financial management, or you are strongly inclined to becoming more effective in handling your finances. Learning more about personal finance will help you to maximize your knowledge and honor your values. A high M will trigger a need or desire to find a "good deal" when you shop. When you invest in a home, you seek a fair price and potential for appreciation above all. You are likely to care a lot about sticking to a budget, even if it is only a mental budget. If you scored a very low M, your home might be more of a haven than an investment. You probably care more about function or comfort than price tag, making decisions on a more subjective level, or even on impulse, rather than on any practical basis. Perhaps your purchase decisions are made either to nurture your sense of self or to lavish gifts on those you love.

Scoring Evenly Across Life Values Categories

Fairly even scores across all categories suggest balance in your Life Values. You value relationships and community as much as you value your privacy and independence. You may be ambitious to experience everything a career has to offer: income, benefits, good working conditions, and great co-workers, but you are usually willing to compromise on any one of those if you must. Your spending and saving habits tend toward balance too. If they do not, you may not be handling your finances as well as you would like. While you manage to meet your needs and those of your family, you would like to stash more away for future needs. Perhaps you have begun investing a little late in life, or maybe you have invested very cautiously, but you know and appreciate the importance of investing for future security.

If you are in a couple relationship, you might experience a shift to a different score for one or both of you as you work to understand and accommodate one another's financial values. But before you adjust your thinking to match or accommodate a partner's score, you should understand thoroughly the meaning of your Life Values scores and how they apply just to you.

Each Life Values category plays a role in your decision making. It provides a convenient inventory to help you discover for yourself how the dimensions of your life impact your financial choices. When you are true to your value system as you make your decisions, the probability of making the right decision is much greater.[1] If you attempt, however, to "force fit" your decision criteria to what the world tells you or to your spouse or partner's wishes or desires or to some other outside influence, your choices may end up being costly in both money and emotional outcomes.

EVALUATING HIGHER AND LOWER SCORES

If your scores are not fairly balanced, refer to Table 4–2 *Interpreting High Life Value Scores (9 and Above)* and Table 4–3 *Interpreting Low Life Value Scores (4 and Below)* to learn more about how you might be approaching your finances. Then, if you wish, check out the case studies that follow these tables to learn briefly how higher and lower scores play out in the lives of others. Perhaps they remind you of someone you know, or you can recognize your own Life Values at work in your life.

If your scores are balanced, your partner's scores are too, and you have a good grasp of the meaning of these Life Values categories, you might skip the following sections, and move on to the next chapter. Bookmark this page, however, and refer back to it later if you find that your Life Values and financial habits and decisions are not always in harmony. Do this especially if someone else is involved in your finances.

SCORING ON THE HIGHER SIDE (9 AND ABOVE)

As a general rule, the higher the score for a particular Life Value, the more likely it is to drive your financial choices. In Table 4–2 you might recognize some classic ways high Life Value scores play out in people's financial life as they approach earning, spending, saving, and investing.

Table 4–2   Interpreting High Life Values Score (9 and Above)
Your Likely Approach to Earning, Spending, Saving, and Investing

High P Score	High S Score	High T Score	High M Score
You have a clear sense of self.	You are probably attracted to a job because you like to help others. You also want to work with people you care about.	You seek work offering a pay rate that helps you achieve a certain lifestyle or standard of living.	You probably like your job most for its financial benefits.
You are likely to seek a job that offers personal fulfillment above everything else.			You particularly appreciate the pension plan and health care coverage.
You probably spend your money to achieve self-expression, a sense of identity, and a secure personal environment.	You probably spend money mostly to nurture relationships.	You like to spend money on material goods and pleasures.	When you spend, knowing you are getting a good deal gives you pleasure.
You save to fund your personal goals and dreams.	You save money while keeping the needs and well-being of loved ones in mind.	Your main goal in saving is to trade up and/or to enjoy comfort and beauty in your home and surroundings.	You save for long-term security and short-term goals.
You probably invest for your future security with little regard for others' needs.	You might invest because trusted individuals advise you to do so.	As you invest in your future, you are thinking of a comfortable retirement lifestyle.	You might very well enjoy "hands on" investing.
	Your investment goals involve family, friends and/or your community.		You also value accuracy, organization, and discipline.

High "P" and "M" Scores. Lowell scored highest in the "Personal Values" category and has a pretty high "M" score too. He is a single college professor who values his social relationships but values his personal time more. His lifestyle might seem a bit sparse to some, but the simplicity of his dwelling and the limits he has imposed on his collection of "things" afford him the freedom to come and go as he pleases. He pays rent for a loft that is perfectly pleasing to him, having made the conscious decision not to buy a house. His 7-year-old compact car fills in when public transportation falls short. Lowell's personal library is vast, and he has enjoyed economical sightseeing trips around the world. He has a very high net worth for a college professor.

High "S" and "P" Scores. Meredith, a college student in her early twenties, scored a very high Social or "S" score and a moderately high "P" score. She is popular, and her friendships are important to her. Meredith is known as a straight-shooter, if perhaps too generous to her friends. She shares her apartment with friends, and she shares charges for phone, utilities, and even groceries. She is confident her friends will never take advantage of her; she simply pays what she is told she owes at the end of each month. She is happy to make her car and clothing available to friends who want to borrow them, and she enjoys low-cost entertainment such as hiking and picnicking. Meredith works 20 hours per week in a university dining facility. Her friends tease her that it's time to move up the corporate ladder, but she enjoys the camaraderie of her fellow workers and the students she serves.

High "M" and "T" Scores. Sally has high "M" and "T" scores. When she shared that news with her mother and sisters, they were hardly surprised. Of her four siblings, Sally is the one who worked her way through college and managed to afford a car to take her where she needed to go. Today, Sally and her husband earn a good income and have adequate savings, but they still shop for bargains on quality furnishings for their beautiful home. In fact, they went without living room furniture for nearly a year, waiting to find the best quality for the lowest price. Sally's sisters wondered at Sally's empty living room, but they agreed later that the stylish furniture the couple finally chose would probably outlast their own by many years.

Lower Life Value scores offset high scores and continue the process of highlighting how you are ranking your interests and priorities. Check out the classic approach to earning, spending, saving and investing in Table 4–3 below and see the case studies that follow to further help you interpret your own scores.

Table 4–3   Interpreting Your Low Life Values Scores (4 and Below)
Your Likely Approach to Earning, Spending, Saving and Investing

Low P Score	Low S Score	Low T Score	Low M Score
You might value your job for the people, the pay, or the benefits, and you might stay even without job satisfaction. You spend your money on other people or to achieve a particular lifestyle. You might also enjoy finding a bargain. You save because your parents did and invest because you are advised to do so, although your plans for your future might be fuzzy.	You're probably a loner at work, but you seek good pay and benefits and enjoy what you do. Your spending is rarely related to the needs or wants of others; it might be guided by affordability, lifestyle, or the need for self-expression. You save for personal goals and security and invest for those same goals in the future.	You have little interest in material pleasures. At work, you enjoy the people or the work itself, even if you don't earn a big salary. Your spending is likely to focus on safety, self-expression, or the benefit of others. You might save for family needs or personal security, and you invest to take care of others or to face the future prudently.	You don't like budgeting, investing, or finances in general. You work primarily for job satisfaction and/or rewarding relationships. You might buy on a whim or to make a statement. If you save, it's probably due to automatic withholding or family influence. You might not be faithful at it on your own. You probably don't care to talk about money or to plan your financial future.

Low "S" and High "M" Scores.   Alan scored low on Social Values ("S") and high on Money Values ("M"). A graduate student, Alan lives alone in a one-room basement apartment where he is surrounded by the music and entertainment equipment he has worked and saved to purchase. He rarely has friends over, although his company is sought by others. He is a careful shopper and a reliable saver, even while living on a shoestring. Alan has spent many hours planning his future, and he has disciplined himself to make decisions that will ensure his future success. He definitely plans to have a nicer home in the future and a rewarding job that pays well, although he is not yet sure whether or when marriage and family will be a part of the picture.

Low "M" and High "S" Scores.   Paul scored very low in the Money Life Values ("M") category and high on Social "S" Life Values. A likable guy with lots of friends and a penchant for having fun, Paul is impulsive about spending. He and his wife bought a starter home a year ago, even though Paul's parents tried to guide them away from this decision. The house needs a serious makeover and worse, it is located in a declining neighborhood. But it is convenient to their work places and easily accessible to their friends, so Paul and Lisa bought the house anyway. Now they are talking about buying a new car, but this decision also may not be wise. The couple cannot afford the performance car they want and repairs to the home they just purchased. Paul, however, is unconcerned. He is not even worried that his checking account never quite balances.

Low "P" and High "S" Scores.   Anna grew up in a poor family that agonized over having enough money to pay the bills each month; anyone with plenty of money was believed to be unscrupulous or untrustworthy. Now, as a wife and mother, Anna is generous with her husband and children but finds it next to impossible to spend money on herself. She is faithful to her household budget and leaves most financial affairs to her husband. She has tried several times to find fulfilling work outside the home or a rewarding hobby, but she has yet to discover her source of inner happiness. She loves her husband and children but has no goals of her own. Anna has a high "S" and very low "P" score.

Shifting or Differing Life Values

High and low scores, while offsetting each other, can and do shift from time to time. They can also signal trouble in a relationship—especially if your partner or other loved one is uninterested in what interests you! Whatever your scores, be aware that if your finances seem to be causing the trouble between you, *it is not really all about the money*. The trouble—guaranteed—is more about your values differences than your finances. If you cannot take the Life Values profile separately and then talk with one another about the results, your relationship may need professional help. Take the case of Don and Melanie.

Don and Melanie are a couple whose opposing "T" scores have recently begun to wreak havoc in their married life. With a third child on the way, they agreed to search for a larger home. However, Don, with a high "T" score, insists on tangible benefits that mean little to Melanie, who scored low in the Tangible Life Values. Every time they go out looking at homes with their real estate agent, they spend the evening bickering. (Now they understand why!) Don is willing to pay more for pleasing architectural features in an older home that fails to offer either the housekeeping convenience Melanie seeks or the generous play yard she believes the children need. Don wants these advantages for his family, but not if he has to give up the porcelain tile bathroom and state-of-the-art kitchen he's had his heart set on. Melanie, for her part, wants simple, easy-maintenance living space to complement the on-the-go lifestyle she values. Now that Don and Melanie understand each other's Life Values differences, they have decided to attend a few sessions with a marriage counselor before committing to a lifestyle choice they might later regret.

Using Life Value Scores in Your Money Management

It might be helpful to date and keep the results of this Profile handy so that you can revisit it in the future. Your priorities can and do change over time, especially as you do some hard thinking about what really matters to you in life. You may want to retake the Profile before making any major life decisions: career changes, starting a family, retirement, or any planned or unplanned transitions. Periodically revisiting your Life Values Profile will ensure that your behaviors and values remain in harmony.

5

MOVING TO SECURE MONEY MANAGEMENT

Mention personal finance or managing money, and some people's eyes glaze over. They know it is necessary, but they would just as soon have a root canal than review their finances and plan for their future. Others may not believe it is possible to actually *like* the process of becoming good money managers.

The surprise about competent financial management is that the process of getting smart about money is usually full of fun and adventure, with some thrills as real for adults as a trip to any theme park feels to children. Adventure always requires curiosity and determination. So to enjoy the process of going from poor-to-secure financial management, you need to become at least somewhat *curious* and *determined enough* to learn how to make the system work for you.

The first key to competent money management is getting 100% committed to the process. Then you are open to the possibilities and discoveries you make when you embark upon any worthwhile journey. You may think, "Not me. I know I need to do it, but it is like eating brussel sprouts. Yes, they *are* good for me, so I'll have them tomorrow or next week, just not today." But managing money is not at all like eating your vegetables. It is giving yourself the gift of realizing how much you can accomplish, discovering an inner spark of excitement and then setting off a firestorm of achievement. It is about realizing, "Yes, I can do this!" And little else can be more satisfying than that—*except, possibly, managing money competently with your life partner.*

"Are we serious?" you may reasonably ask. "How can the biggest relationship destroyer of all time actually be enjoyable?"

Well, if you ever had a crush on a co-worker, a schoolmate, or the boy or girl next door, you might recall that however boring or difficult the project, working together with your friend or colleague or fantasy love-of-your-life-at-that-moment made it exciting, personally rewarding, and fun. Since the "household" has always been the basic economic unit in America, you and your partner and other family members are all stakeholders in your financial endeavors. It is up to you to decide how smooth you would like your family money management to be. You and your partner can choose to be sour about anything financial or to revive the excitement and pleasure of working together on one of the most important life projects you will ever undertake.

Motivating Yourself

Self-motivation in personal finances is not merely important, it is essential for your survival. Developing your abilities to manage money well can easily make the difference between experiencing near-or-actual poverty and enjoying a secure later life. In extreme cases, such as having no access to health care and little knowledge of how the political and medical "system" works for you in your particular geographical area, it can make the difference between life and death.

We know we are laying quite a motivational load on you, but self-motivation is all you have in the critical area of personal finances. There are no bosses to make sure you arrive at your desk on time to take on the tasks of budgeting and bill paying. There is no one but yourself to plot out near-term and long-range financial goals based on what you really care about. There is no one but you to search for the financial education classes in your community and to take the plunge that could change your level of belief in your own prospective competence, as well as your life and the lives of your loved ones perhaps for many years to come.

By getting 100% committed to the process of learning to become a competent money manager, we are hoping you will become motivated to use some "new-old" rules of the twenty-first century:

- Start now to think of yourself as becoming savvy about finances.
- Set aside some of your precious *time* to pursue education and excellence in personal money management.
- If you are in a couple relationship, take a deep breath and make these vows to each other: "to love, honor, and get real about money for as long as you both shall live."

Competing Values

Recall our previous discussions about how competing values are at play in our decisions to spend now or save for later. The same value trade-off is at work when we decide where to spend our limited *time*. For most of us, when we have finished work, we want to kick back, relax, or choose a way to have fun. And popular culture accommodates us with all sorts of possibilities for how we spend our time.

We are surrounded with images of carefree people sipping cocktails, sailing at sunset, and building sand castles on the beach. We are encouraged to watch the latest movies, join friends at trendy restaurants, or drive the vehicle of our dreams—at top speed—through fantasy city streets or mountain scenery. But if we look at where these messages are coming from, we find that most of our ideas of pleasure come from marketers intent on splitting us from our money. Ford, Bacardi, and the travel industry are not concerned with our well-being. They are Pied Pipers seducing us to come out and play.

It is easy enough to fall for these messages and to believe that material goods and indulgent experiences bring us the pleasure we crave and deserve. But wait. Maybe we could substitute learning to become "Captains of our own Financial Destiny" and find great pleasure in that. If you think about it, most of our ideas of fun are like empty calories in a candy bar. There is an immediate rush and then emptiness later. But when we begin looking at our financial chores as activities that can really bring us pleasure, and if we factor in personal satisfaction, we get the best of both worlds. By replacing that candy bar with a power bar, we satisfy our immediate craving and have the rush, but we continue to feel good later.

Looking for more personal satisfaction in our otherwise "boring" day-to-day activities can be incredibly rewarding. Billie Jean King, the grand slam tennis champion whose crusading efforts helped revolutionize the landscape of sports and society, won a huge honor when the U.S. Open complex was renamed the USTA Billie Jean King National Tennis Center. When describing in *Sports Illustrated* her inspiration to learn how to play tennis in the first place, she said, "It's about learning your craft. That's a wonderful thing—especially with today's consumerism and instant gratification. You can't buy that."[1]

Given that you are reading this book, you have made a decision to become competent about your financial management—to hone this all important craft. Tackling your spending priorities, bringing your goals in sync with your values, and learning to save and invest wisely are all endeavors similar to Billie Jean King's (and Andy Roddick's, Serena Williams', and the Pro's at your neighborhood tennis center). Watch them in your mind hitting tennis ball after tennis ball after tennis ball after tennis ball to become masters of their game.

In fact, getting on top of *your* financial game can be absolutely as rewarding as winning at any sport or activity you enjoy. It can be your "next wonderful thing." It all comes down to altering your definitions of "fun" by setting aside *time* to discover the more lasting pleasure that comes from knowing, "Yes, I can do this!" while building a solid financial base for the future.

Your Eureka Moment

Remember when you learned how to drive a car? You sat through drivers' education classes, went out on the road with a trained instructor, and practiced with a patient adult who guided you and offered encouragement. There might have been a few halting moments or times when you accidentally went into reverse instead of first gear. You might have heard gasps from the parent in the passenger seat, but one day you "got it," and you confidently maneuvered through traffic on your own. From then on, knowing how to drive has enriched your life in too many ways to count.

Researchers call the feeling of pride in accomplishment "self-efficacy," a hallmark American value."[2] Until we get to that point, however, another trait is also at work: *resistance*. We stubbornly resist change and experience negative attitudes about whatever it is we think we do not want to do. But the problem is that most people don't know what they don't know. They don't realize how much their lack of knowledge about financial topics is hurting their financial situation.

It is so natural for us to avoid change that before we actually try something new or different, we can stubbornly cling to the notion that we just don't like doing it! How silly is that? Peggy remembers that feeling all too well. Until she examined her relationship to her money and finances, Peggy was a person who, like many people, "hated all things financial."

Exactly why Peggy felt financially timid doesn't matter. When her finances were in trouble, Peggy assumed that she wasn't good at dealing with financial matters. She left the bills to her husband and refused to deal with financial matters or to even talk about finances. It was years before she decided that she wasn't being fair and started to pitch in. She was stunned when their finances began to interest her.

One day as Peggy pored over the family finances, she remembered that she had been very frugal when she was a poor college student. She stretched her budget so tight that she could hear her pennies scream. Remembering those days helped Peggy to take charge and get over her fear. Peggy knew she could always go back to being college-thrifty if she had to. Her "Eureka Moment" was just that simple.

Peggy decided to dive into the investment side of their finances. Newly competent and no longer afraid, she and her husband found a gifted advisor. They also hired a certified public accountant for tax planning. They found out quickly enough that two heads were better at planning a financial future than just one. Long story short, Peggy no longer had to stay on the sidelines of this essential part of their family life. She changed her poor judgment about her abilities and got back in the game—to her husband's relief and her own increasing pleasure.

You may be like Peggy, who built the idea of financial management into a chore that was beyond her ability, when in fact, she had known the basics all along. Perhaps it is something you have not yet learned that will lead you to your Eureka Moment. The best way to reach that Eureka Moment is to start small. You do not need to commit to extravagant goals. According to a study by the Fannie Mae Foundation,[3] if a task is perceived as difficult, it is seen as undesirable. A lot of people have the perception that managing money is difficult, that they are not good at it. But learning influences action, and learning also changes attitudes. After receiving even a modest level of education, most people realize it isn't rocket science and gain more and more confidence. Basically, what this means is that personal financial planning and managing money has gotten a bad reputation. But learning just a little bit will lead you to discover that, like driving a car, you *can* do it. And if you do, you will enrich your life in ways too numerous to count.

Learning Can Be Fun

It all starts with education—whether through taking a formal class, reading a book, or talking to a financial professional—to realize what you have been capable of all along. Successful financial management is not about how smart you are or how much income you have. It's about the decisions you make every day. We cover some basics in coming chapters, including committing to a savings plan and learning to invest, to get you started, but we encourage you to go further and explore the many generalized and specialized programs available to you.

There are a myriad of educational opportunities available today. The best-kept secret is that there are several professionals out there—bankers, financial planners, tax preparers, brokers—who want to teach you what you need to succeed. There are also many places to learn: workshops, books, employer-sponsored brown-bag lunches, online education, and adult-education classes. You can learn on your lunch hour at work, on a Saturday afternoon, or on a weekday evening. You can learn with friends, with colleagues, or alone, either in front of your computer or curled up by the fireplace.

Why all these choices all of a sudden? The ongoing trend in our nation is toward increased personal responsibility, and these professionals know that for *them* to be successful, *you* have to be successful. They also know that education is the key to your success. Education offers a side benefit: We like what we are good at. Once you realize that you can do something, you will develop not only confidence, but also a sense of personal satisfaction. This combination will stimulate quite possibly another Eureka Moment: that the more you learn, the more you want to learn because—guess what? You are enjoying the process!

Emily, 43, is single and has owned her own business selling women's accessories for over 21 years. "I feel that I can always learn more," says Emily who stays on the lookout for ways to gain knowledge from a variety of sources. She takes classes, attends workshops, listens to friends to find out what works for them, and reads a lot. The tip she most often shares with others: "Write down your goals." She carries her written goals with her so that if she needs a reminder—or a reason not to be parted from her savings—they are right there to review. So far, in part due to this technique, she has managed to meet all of her goals. Her first goal was to pay off credit cards, and she did. Next she established a retirement account, and finally she achieved her most important goal— to buy her own home. As Emily met each goal, she became more interested in personal finance, so she is currently looking for a class on retirement planning. Emily is relieved and happy that she has taken charge of her financial future. Managing her finances has become an activity she has learned to enjoy. So can you.

EXPERIMENT

Are you ready to get started on an education program? If you aren't sure where to begin, get started by following these steps.

1. Take an inventory of your money. Include bank accounts, investments, assets such as your car and your home, the piggy bank in the kitchen cabinet, and any other place you have money.

2. Ask yourself if you are happy with these categories and the numbers in them. Do you wish you had an IRA? Do you have a checking account but no savings account? Is your retirement account a little skimpy? Do you have an emergency fund?

---

3. Ask yourself if you have the knowledge to make any changes you would like to make. Could you put more money into your retirement fund? How could you create a savings account?

4. Make a list of the questions you have and put them into categories, such as Savings, Health Care, Retirement, Investments, Risk Protection, Education, Vacations.

5. Make a commitment to answer the questions you have. Using the tools in this book is a good start. You can also find specific answers using the resources in Chapter 19, "Finding the Help You Need," and the Appendix, "Personal Finance Education Internet Sites," in the back of the book or through a class or workshop.

Sharing Goals

If you are in a relationship, perhaps you are about to embark on a financial planning adventure with your partner. Maximizing the concepts discussed so far, finding your inner spark, and relishing a Eureka Moment, all involve learning and growing. Sharing this experience with your partner can lead to a deeper bond between you as you meet your goals together. One result of the demands of modern society is that most couples generally spend a great deal of time apart. Our work (even if one partner works in the home) takes us via different routes to challenges that can lead to divorce or to a state of isolation from one another. "We grew apart" is an all too common complaint.

Avoiding this unfortunate state of affairs takes patience and work. It involves taking advantage of opportunities that couples have to grow together, and nowhere can this be more rewarding than with financial management and planning. Since these activities involve setting and working toward goals, with couples, these goals are common and shared. Although you and your partner may have divergent philosophies, come from different backgrounds, and have your own sets of values, your ultimate goals are most often the same:

- Managing well
- Providing for your family
- Growing your assets
- Securing your future

By working together, you can also build harmony. If striving toward individual personal fulfillment is valuable to you, then working toward a mutually rewarding and fulfilling life with your partner can only be better.

Steve and Maria are engaged and plan to be married soon. Steve, 26, is a chef from Cambridge, Massachusetts, and Maria, 25, a native of El Salvador, is a banquet server. They talk about their finances regularly and can discuss issues comfortably. "If we're going to spend anything over $50, we have promised to tell the other," Steve says. They plan to have a joint account for their combined expenses but will maintain separate accounts as well. His is a "fun account" to be used primarily for nights out and movie rentals. Hers is a "hair and nails" account.

Although Maria wanted a festive wedding celebration, she wanted their own home more, so their wedding will be intimate and inexpensive. They are saving to buy a duplex to move into after their wedding, and plans call for rental income from the second duplex unit and more income properties after that. "It will be a good learning experience, and we have some good people behind us," Steve says referring to Maria's mother who also owns investment property. The couple has a shared vision of the future, and they are taking steps together to realize their vision. "A couple has to be on the same page," Maria says. "They have to work together if they really want to get ahead."

Communicating Through Differences

Not every couple has the strong sense of shared values and goals as Steve and Maria, and when life philosophies and values are different, tensions can mount over money. Couples often fight instead of talk, derailing any sense of adventure they might otherwise enjoy from their personal finance activities.

If you and your partner are misfiring in your attempts to communicate on financial planning matters, you are sabotaging a great opportunity to enjoy managing your money together. After you both complete the Life Values Profile in Chapter 4, "Your Life Values Profile," try this exercise.

First, compare the results of your test looking at not just the overall results, but where you have similarities. If you scored high on Personal Values and your partner scored high on Social Values, scan through your answers to find those in which your answer was "S." For example, suppose for question 6, which deals with how you would spend a sudden windfall, you answered (c) that you would use it to help a family member—a "Social Values" response. Carefully consider why you answered that way. Then use this insight to engage in a conversation with your partner. As you discuss the behaviors typified by that particular question, you will discover that you do have a common ground. You can then use that insight to explore how you are alike, and you can also use it as a springboard to better understand your partner's value system. Next, switch and consider a question where your partner's answer was aligned with your values.

What you value for yourself includes *everything in your life that really matters to you*, just as the values of those who share your life include *all that really matters to them*. Changing your focus from resistance to momentum, from reluctance to passion, involves taking that first step. It may feel like the stop-jerk-start you experienced when you learned to drive or your dizzying reluctance to jump off a diving board for the first time, but once you catch your breath, you will realize you have transformed your relationship as well as the way you both think about your financial future.

The Knowing-Doing Gap

Okay, you may be on board, you have even taken courses and *want* to move ahead, yet procrastination might be your particular habit: "I'll do it later," or "I'll get to it tomorrow," or "After the holidays." If so, you are not alone. Researchers have been studying this disconnect between what people know they should do and what they actually do. It even has a name: "the knowing-doing gap."[4] Like the question for company executives in Jeffrey Pfeffer and Robert I. Sutton's book, *The Knowing–Doing Gap*, you might have all the training and knowledge you need to manage competently, but *still* you do not take the actions you know you should. Just what does it take?

It turns out that most people are reluctant to transform knowledge into action unless they have some compelling reason. Kyle, for one, admits that he was a poor money manager until he and his wife took a home-buying course together. They enjoyed the class since it was something they could do as a team. Neither one was knowledgeable about financial matters, so they helped each other understand the concepts presented in class. Armed with new knowledge, they bought their home soon after and picked a mortgage with great terms thanks to the good advice they received. Kyle now says there is deep satisfaction in doing something he did not think he could do, and he and his wife are signing up for a new class on Investing.

Researchers speak of momentum as an "inner spark."[5] What might it take to get you to give up a night on the town to sit in the basement of your local YMCA and learn about budgeting, saving, home buying, or investing and then go home and put those lessons into practice? Your inner spark is a unique and personal experience—in Kyle's case it was a home of his own and the discovery he made that team learning and financial management with his wife were deeply satisfying.

Although we cannot predict what will trigger your inner spark—a new baby, getting accepted to the school of your choice, going for your dream job, obtaining credit for the first time, or buying a new home, we can suggest how to proceed once you feel it. Like the executive managers who succeed at turning knowledge into action, you too must develop a plan and follow it. You must analyze your spending, budget for the future, save and plan for your well-being, and inspire yourself to learn continuously, transforming that knowledge into daily action. According to authors Pfeffer and Sutton, executive managers that act on their knowledge also eliminate fear, abolish destructive internal conflict, and act in accordance with values that really matter to the firm. This can happen for individuals and families too.

If you completed the Life Values Profile in Chapter 4 and have gotten this far into our book, you are closer than you think to igniting that inner spark and generating the results that really matter to you.

6

A WORD ABOUT FEAR

The fastest Winter Olympic sledding event, the luge, involves an athlete (a luger) lying down on his or her back on a stripped-down sled and hurtling down an icy mountain, navigating hairpin turns at speeds sometimes as high as 90 mph. This sport definitely is not like taking your childhood sled to the park on a snowy afternoon! The prospect is scary enough as it is, even for a trained athlete. But add to that the pressure of competing with other top athletes for the Gold, and you really have a recipe for fear. For you and that luger on top of the mountain, there are two ways to go: Face your fear and fly down the mountain, or pick up your sled and go home.

What's the worst that can happen? Stand up to the fear, and you might take a tumble and get bruised and sore. Or you could do your very best and still lose to someone faster or more agile. But you also can experience the thrill of overcoming your fear and achieve the biggest victory of your life. Give up, and you will never know what you could have accomplished. For Italian Armin Zoeggeler who won the Gold at the Olympic Games in Turin, Italy, facing his fear paid off, and it can pay off for you too.

Do not think for a minute that we believe there is no *basis* for many people's fear of tackling their finances. Powerful institutions, especially, can be intimidating, overcharge us, capitalize intentionally on our vulnerabilities, or simply hide the truth in masses of what marketers and their lawyers call "mouse print," meaning of course that only a mouse could get close enough to read it. In addition, the mean-spirited and unfair universal default provision has been widely adopted by credit card companies. Universal default is a clause included within most credit card offers and agreements, which says if you are late with *any other creditor*, you are considered late with your credit card issuers. This not only negatively impacts your credit card interest rate, which can suddenly zoom skyward if you are late paying a telephone or any other type of monthly bill, but it also will adversely affect your credit score.

The message of this chapter, like those before it, is that we can no longer afford to roll over and play dead. We must stand up to meet the financial tasks before us, become much more familiar with the game, and play to win in spite of our fears. It is also wise to become familiar with the politics of personal financial issues and vote to change those we believe could be holding us back. If you fall victim to an unfair financial practice, complain to your congressional representatives, to your news sources, in blogs, and to anyone else who will listen to the unfairness of powerful financial interests against ordinary working consumers. Your complaints will be heard, and in the process, your *actions* will help lessen your fears.

We talked in the last chapter about beginning to actually *like* managing money, especially about steps that can change your resistance into momentum. If you still feel reluctant to start, you may well be blocked by fear. Like a strong narcotic, fear can smother or sabotage even our best intentions. It is an insidious emotion because it stifles our ability to take action. It just mires us, as if in quicksand. Contrast this with love, which compels even the grouchiest soul to be kind-hearted, propelling him or her forward. The feeling that we have been treated unfairly also can energize us, compelling us to do something to resolve the situation. *But fear can stop us dead in our tracks if we let it.*

Scientists who study sleep have identified the period when we first wake up, before becoming fully functional, as "sleep inertia." This sluggishness causes us not to hear the alarm go off or to make faulty decisions, perhaps until we have had that first cup of coffee. Sometime after 10 minutes (and up to two hours according to sleep scientists), we cross that threshold where we feel "awake" and ready to face the day.

This same kind of inertia is at play when we are fearful. Our psyche shuts down, and we become emotionally paralyzed and unable to act, even though we realize intellectually that it is in our best interest to move forward. We literally are drowsy about the object of our fear, and we procrastinate or refuse—consciously or unconsciously—to deal with the situation. That is how fear works: *it gives our power to the object of our fear*. And unlike sleep inertia, fear can hang around, not for 10 minutes or two hours but for as long as we are unable to break its spell and wake up and face the day.

Fear also can be an isolating emotion. It is easy to feel that we are alone—that everyone else, if faced with a similar situation, would have an easier time of it. But the contrary is true. Fear is universal. At some point, everyone gets that sick feeling in the pit of their stomach or the sweaty palms that signal unease. But the good news, and the lesson we can learn from the Olympic athletes, is that it is controllable. As athletes follow the advice of coaches and sports psychologists to re-pattern behavior to overcome fear, we can also train ourselves to overcome our fears of financial management, or lack of money, or planning for the future. But to move past fear—to recapture the power we have traded away—we may first need to understand what is causing that fear.

Generalizing Our Financial Fears of the Past

We all bring money beliefs, habits, and anxieties into the way we deal with our everyday finances. Our value standards and behaviors about money affect not only us, but also the people we love. Any unchecked control issues that play out over money can derail relationships and even impact the lives of those we care about after we've passed on. Following are ten money myths that underlie some of our greatest fears or our cherished-but-wrong-headed beliefs and habits. If you want to take a new path to financial competence that is proven, easier, sound, and even enjoyable, follow along as we help you become more open-minded about your personal financial present and future. First, though, let's dispel the following myths:

The Top Ten Money Myths[1]

1. *Having money means fewer worries and ease of living.*

   It is tempting to believe that people who have money are wise, self-disciplined, self-confident and untroubled. Yet having money does not by itself lead to feelings of security, and at times not even to feelings of *financial security*. How you feel about life and how comfortable you are about money management is not determined by the size of your bank account, but by your values and priorities. Taking responsibility for your financial well-being means setting life priorities and making choices each day in the service of those priorities.

2. *Financial matters are too complicated to understand and master.*

   Financial competence is like most life challenges: The fundamentals are mastered *one at a time*. We begin by learning the financial basics and the practical steps we must take to resolve the financial concerns in life. To succeed, we must patiently explore our own needs and values and be willing to seek appropriate guidance from skilled partners, family members, friends, or professionals when advice is needed. We need to know our discomfort levels and when it is time to back off completely from making a financial decision. This can make the difference between being vulnerable to slick advertising and feeling in control of our spending impulses.

3. *Financial planning and investing should be left to an expert.*

   We all need to take responsibility for our patterns of spending, difficulties with budgeting, and willingness to plan, save, and invest for future life events. We need the courage to communicate with partners and other family members. Then we are in a position to choose financial experts wisely and deal most constructively with them.

4. *Genuine love and true commitment will conquer all, including money problems.*

   Too often anxiety over money matters gets rationalized when we are in love, but this is romantic rather than realistic. We are really setting the stage for painful disillusionment that is as predictable as it is unnecessary. What genuine love and true commitment *can* do is help us establish a dialogue with our partners. This must include the honest expression of our feelings about money together with the time and mutual respect needed to resolve our money issues with one another.

5. *Better quality costs more.*

Quality and cost are not always linked, but the image of quality portrayed by elaborate packaging and advertising is linked to cost. What organizations pay for prestige, brand, and advertising are as important as materials, labor, and other basic costs. They all are factors that impact the prices we pay for goods and services. Be a money conscious consumer—refuse to be drawn into *illusions* of quality. This goes for nearly everything we consume: education, housing, clothing, recreation, transportation, food, and even good wines.

6. *Credit and debit cards are convenient devices that make purchasing easy.*

Yes, if only in the ironic sense of being *too* easy. With credit and debit card use, one side of the exchange transaction is missing—the act of consciously paying money for goods or services received. All during recorded history, the exchange of valued items formed a basis for human interaction, which in turn fostered communication among peoples despite language barriers. Although no one wants to return to primitive living, we benefit by consciously planning our everyday purchases and limiting impulse buying to a budgeted amount each month.

7. *Money is a substitute for love or spending time with someone.*

Few would agree that this is true, but our actions speak louder than words. Money is a symbol of success, power, and control. Too often it is substituted for other types of investments in relationships, such as time, energy, thoughtfulness, and empathy. While most of us would like to deny doing this, it is amazing how amply we invest our relationships with material gifts while giving little thought to this underlying irrational principle.

8. *Financial security is determined by the amount of our accumulated capital.*

Security is never determined by quantitative measurement alone, but rather by our ability to live fulfilling lives, our relationship to others, and attitudes about life in general. Real security is the sustained feeling and belief that one can handle unforeseen challenges as they arise, whether they concern our financial affairs or not. Money should be a tool for positive growth and possibility in our life. However, for many people, money or the lack of money causes anxiety and stress instead.

9. *Money management should be handled by the partner most comfortable or skilled in financial affairs.*

Both partners in a relationship should be actively engaged in, or at least knowledgeable about, *all* aspects of the couple's finances. Challenge any assumption you might have that money management is a chore to be avoided and reconsider whether two heads could be better than one at improving your joint financial well-being. Working with a loved one on the business affairs of your marriage or partnership can be fun and personally rewarding and not just in the area of finances.

10. *A lot of money is the best gauge of success in our society.*

While this myth forms the basis for much of society's interactions, it is nevertheless a myth. Yes, the accumulation of money is one driving force. When we really look at the sad (and sometimes tragic) lives that have been governed by wealth, however, we can see its uselessness as a primary success indicator. Even opinion polls disagree with this widely held notion about the power of money. They show *"life satisfaction," "a happy marriage,"* and *"feeling in control"* as more cherished signs of success than *"a lot of money,"* and these values win out by a very large margin!

Myths persist because we have a need to cover the truths they hide. If we want to stop believing in myths, we are required to put aside the fears that got us where we are in the first place. We need to think differently, take responsibility, and connect to our loved ones in common effort that can bring us riches—not only in terms of our finances, but in all of our relationships too. That means asking the difficult questions that heal us and offer hope for real change because the route to healthy money and interpersonal relationships is paved with answers from the past. The clues are always in our feelings. When our buttons are pushed, when the pouting begins, or the anger wells up, or that familiar pit-of-the-stomach sick feeling attacks us over some financial matter, something from the past is influencing us. You can count on it.

The Power of Revisiting the Past

Financial fears usually do not stand alone; they are rooted in more deep-seated anxieties. Some people fear loss, being wrong, being embarrassed, or failing. These fears may be rooted in our childhood, or we may have been conditioned to them over time. Still others get that gut-wrenching feeling because they believe they are "bad with money" but actually have had great difficulty with arithmetic. Or they are intimidated by people in financial institutions because they really dread the possibility of rejection by authority figures. Whether you are guided by deep-seated behaviors or general uneasiness, these fears can manifest themselves as indecision and doubt—attitudes that are counter-intuitive to developing a sound financial plan. Fear kills enthusiasm and thwarts action. It destroys self-confidence and limits creative imagination. It also exaggerates negative imagination until even a small occurrence can become the trigger for a major panic attack, as in the story that follows.

Nancy recently left her job at a law firm to start a new business as a freelance paralegal and researcher. She successfully launched the business and acquired several new clients. Everything seemed right on course, and Nancy was happy to be on her own at last. Then, one day, Nancy received a check for $3,500 from one of her new clients. She deposited the check and paid bills with the money before waiting for it to clear. Unfortunately, the check was returned by Nancy's bank for insufficient funds, leaving her without the means to cover the checks she had already written. Although Nancy thought her new client would replace the check, she went into a full blown panic anyway. The situation was inconvenient, and creditors to whom she had sent checks needed to be called, but Nancy treated the matter as a disaster instead of the learning experience it really was. She came close to returning to the security of her old job, but a colleague helped Nancy overcome her panic by reminding her of the determination she had mustered to start her own business in the first place.

Replacing Fear with Curiosity, Determination, and Focused Passion

Nancy's situation is a classic example of a fear blown way out of proportion to the event. The risks of such small events permeate all of our financial management—the financial world today is just too complicated and too multi-faceted to assure us of smooth sailing all the time. We can make errors in calculations, inadvertently pay a bill a few days late, be turned down for credit because of an error on our credit report, or receive a notice from a tax authority based on incorrect information. Any of these events can cause one's heart to skip a beat, but there are steps you can take to overcome your initial tendency to panic:

1. Do not stuff a notice or letter bearing "bad news" into a drawer or into some other place where it could remain hidden.

2. Read the notice or letter over and over again, until you are certain you understand what the communication is saying.

3. Do not jump to any conclusions until you thoroughly investigate the situation—the reality could be far different from what the letter or notice indicates.

4. If you need help, *ask for it and do not feel ashamed*. Chances are the person or persons you ask have experienced the same or a similar situation before.

5. Replace your fear, first, with the curiosity you need to get to the bottom of the situation; next, with determination to take care of it; and then with the focused passion you bring to any new set of circumstances that you must resolve.

6. Finally, do not procrastinate. Get going instead.

These are the very same steps to follow if you are fearful about applying for your first home mortgage, trying to pay down excessive debt, investigating a new job or career path, or just beginning to invest for your future. The alternatives to transforming fear into constructive action are simply not acceptable whenever our finances are involved. Even when we are afraid to try, we must try anyway. Even if we think we may lose what we already have, we must learn to invest anyway. Even if we are barely getting by, we must learn to make the changes that can improve our standing, our health, and our future. In other words, in this day and age, we cannot remain stuck in the status quo—fear or no fear—so learning to transform our fears is the best lesson we might ever learn.

Transforming Fear

Transforming fears into other, more constructive emotions, will not only improve your financial situation; it will improve your life situation. But how does one live a "fearless" life? If you want to create a financial future that is different from your current situation, it will be necessary to give up some familiar behaviors and take that necessary step into the unknown. If you try and find you cannot break free from fear, find a good counselor and resolve to uncover and dissolve your fears. Consider these words by Ruben Gonzalez, a three-time Olympic luge athlete and world champion, *"Every time you do something you fear, you gain strength, confidence, courage, and faith. You must always stop and look fear in the face and do what you think you cannot do."*[2]

The good news is that you don't have to hurl yourself down an icy mountain; there are less physically demanding techniques that can help you conquer your fears. By identifying your fear, you can take positive steps to overcome it. What are you afraid of? Thinking about your fear in a constructive way demystifies it. When you can put your fear into words, "I'm afraid I might fail," or "I'm afraid I won't understand," or "I'm afraid because I don't know what to expect," it gives you something you can tackle. It is no longer the unknown; you have taken the first step.

While fear is a universal emotion, our triggers can be intensely personal. What are you afraid of? Take a few moments to write out your answer (or answers) to this simple yet complex question. Once you see your answers in black and white, and keep questioning "why" you are afraid, what you will be able to discover is a harmless reason for your fear and the strength to resolve the real problem that is causing it.

****

Here is one example:

- I am afraid of answering the telephone because it might be a creditor. Why am I afraid of talking to a creditor?
- I am afraid that he/she will be angry over the telephone and demand payment that I do not have. Why am I afraid of the creditor's anger in the face of the truth about my financial situation?
- I am afraid of being in trouble. Why am I afraid of being in trouble?
- I was punished for being in trouble as a child.
- Today, however, I am an adult and no longer can I be punished for having financial trouble that, with help, I can resolve. While I may still feel a little nervous about answering the phone, I will face the creditor and tell him/her the truth.

****

Congratulations for taking the simple steps that will always tell you "why" you fear what you do. By shining the light on what you really fear, you will have taken the first step in transforming it and turning the monster under the bed into the teddy bear it usually is.

Continue by identifying what triggers your fear of financial management, investing, or financial planning, asking yourself one more question, "What's the worst thing that can happen?" Is the worst-case scenario something you can handle? It usually is. The awareness of the worst-case scenario eliminates the fear in you, fear that holds you back. Famous TV psychologist, Dr. Phil McGraw, refers to it as "the power of the what-if." In other words, once you know the "what-if," you will discover that it is not that difficult to be decisive and take action. And once you make that choice, you will suddenly find that you are unstuck.

The secret to overcoming fear, no matter what that fear is, is to just do it. Once you do, fear's power is gone, replaced by, as Gonzalez said, "strength, confidence, courage, and faith." Not a bad trade.

When asked recently about fear, many Olympic athletes and coaches talked about the various ways athletes deal with pre-event fear. They reported various strategies—from isolation to listening to music and even to crying.[3] But when it is all over, the only tears are of joy or relief. For both the winners and the losers who faced their fear, there are no regrets, only satisfaction.

To get beyond her fears, Nancy examined the source. She realized that she was not afraid of a temporary financial setback but was very fearful of having her new business fail. Once she took the mystery out of her fear, Nancy felt empowered to take action. The inertia was gone. She called the creditors with whom she had made agreements, explained the situation, and asked for extensions. Because she had resisted the urge to avoid the problem and do nothing and instead acted quickly, her creditors were understanding. She then carefully examined her financial situation. She calculated how much of a reserve she would need to pay for her basic expenses, and she made sure she always kept this amount in her general savings account. Nancy made a conscious decision to stop worrying and let go of her fear. Within a week, the bounced check was replaced, and she was in a much more comfortable financial position. After weathering this storm, she realized she could handle anything. She replaced her fear with confidence, and her business flourished.

Overcoming fear is largely a matter of changing your belief—moving from a halting, sluggish one to a positive, energizing state of mind. It is also a choice. We have spoken already and will continue our theme throughout this book of making choices. You can choose to confront your fear, and once you do, it will lose its hold over you. The inertia and paralysis will be gone, and in its place will be a rush of clarity. Just as the luger feels as if he is flying faster than the wind, you, too, will be in *the zone*.

Remember you are in control as long as you believe in yourself and keep up your spirits. A positive attitude springs from believing that "I can do this!" or "I can do that!" Believe that you can do it, and you will maintain the positive attitude that is the first step to achieving financial competence.

Learning to face our money fears head-on is the beginning of financial empowerment. When you are no longer hiding from your money fears, you can begin to fulfill your financial dreams. So take a deep breath and move forward. You'll be glad you did.

Part II

BEING ACTIVE IN FINANCIAL AFFAIRS

7

WHO'S IN CHARGE OF YOUR FINANCIAL WELL-BEING?

Do you pursue happiness through the "things" and "services" you buy? The answer is most likely "yes" for most of us—at least up to a point.

None of us can altogether escape the marketing messages that bombard us as we watch TV, read a newspaper, look over our mail, go to the movies, or simply answer the phone. Credit card offers pour into our mailboxes. We are offered new, low-interest loans to "pay off" debts we still will owe. Sales pitches greet us to buy new vehicles, clothing and sporting goods, computers, electronic gadgets, TVs, and furniture. They are *free* today, and we can pay tomorrow, or next year, or even the year after that.

Here is where the results of your Life Values Profile can be helpful. With more clarity about your own Life Values, you can learn whether your purchases and other financial habits are in sync with what really matters to you. Take the environment for instance. Do you value a clean environment and the conservation of natural resources but drive a gas-guzzling SUV for the fun of it or because all your friends drive SUVs too? If so, you might be experiencing an inner clash of values. Unintended inner conflicts can pile up from habits that override our deeper values. The anticipation of a shopping spree, the impulsive love of a "good deal," or any number of material substitutions can cover up

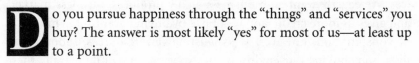

inner needs to love or be loved, to care for the earth, to play or create or imagine, or to work for a better society. In the long run, our "surface decisions" to go shopping for inner joy can lead us to a lot more emptiness than we realize.

The "buy today, pay tomorrow" mentality is a part of daily life, and it is ingrained in our culture, our government, businesses, shopping habits, even our travel plans. Famously, after 9/11, President Bush advised us to go shopping as usual. After all, that's been the American way for most— if not all—of our lives. We spend, and our spending, in large measure, drives the economy and maintains what many of us regard as the quality of our life.

As a result, some of us want everything ever made, and we want it now. We want it on sale and in more than one color. We and big business are locked in the cycle of creation and consumption of products and services. We eagerly want, and business gladly produces. Business markets and gives us more credit, and we oblige by buying over time. This dance of consumption, however, is exhausting our resources, sapping our lives, and spoiling our environment. Now, because quite literally there are so many of us, it is threatening our livelihoods and our future financial security. Because we have become so materialistic, we even seem to have neglected those less fortunate than ourselves—to our own detriment.

In studies conducted around the world, researchers have correlated people's attitudes toward money with their ethics or values. Some results have suggested that those who had lower expectations of money tended to report having happier and less stressful lives.[1] Attuning your finances to your Life Values is the key. Living in tune with your deeper values helps you to:

- Buy only what you can really afford.
- Resist the dance of consumption.
- Ignore the wider culture of revolving credit.
- Become a steward of what you already have.
- Care for the less fortunate if you can.
- Save and plan for your future.

Instead of passively following the crowd, you watch yourself make financial decisions, take back control over your buying habits, spending decisions, and, ultimately, your financial well-being. Chances are excellent that you will be happier too.

We shape the marketplace, and the marketplace, in turn, shapes us. When we want what we want NOW, business will break records getting it to us. One woman in a recent study captured this idea perfectly. She said, "*Saving is something people are interested in, but in reality, people want to enjoy what they can have right now.*" What this example of a value tradeoff means is that the urgency to have "stuff" and "pleasure" now may be valued more than the discipline of saving for emergencies or for longer-term life events. The problem comes when business knows our all-too-human predispositions, escalating and easing the way for us to satisfy our never-ending wants—indeed, even creating evermore wants—the newest fashion, the biggest TV, the up-to-the-minute computer, the larger house, the faster car, and on and on.

The next chapter, "Becoming a Savvy Consumer," has some practical ideas to follow as you interact with the retailers and grocers and health care providers in the nation's vast marketplace. But for now—*before* you buy your next latte or CD, or even go to your favorite supermarket or movie theatre—let's check out how the marketplace takes charge of anticipating your wants and needs.

How Advertisers and Retailers Target You

Your deepest urges, innermost longings, and lifestyle patterns are of intense interest to market researchers. Big companies budget lavish amounts to learn what motivates you to buy all sorts of products and services. They use market surveys and focus groups, track your Internet shopping habits, accumulate sales register data, and employ increasingly sophisticated techniques to learn about your lifestyle and spending patterns including your health habits, eating patterns, the clothing you buy, the vehicle you drive, and that dream vacation you are longing to take. They collect information on your purchases and the way you pay your bills. They pool information from grocery stores, retailers, insurance companies, health care providers, and financial services companies, to name just a few.

Their research is used to target you with savvy advertising that taps right into your inner motives. Their number one "Power Research" tool is *observation of your spending behavior*, and chances are good that they know more about the details of your spending habits and lifestyle patterns than you do. We believe it is time for you to do your own Power Research about how you behave, to observe *yourself* making purchases and other lifestyle and financial decisions.

If you completed the Life Values Profile in Chapter 4, "Your Life Values Profile," you know yourself better and understand how your values and attitudes drive your behaviors and habits. Now we will introduce you to tools similar to those used by big advertisers. This combination will help you develop a clear picture of what motivates your financial decision-making activities as you:

- use your unique Life Values Profile to help you gain insight into what you really value in life and why,
- begin to observe your spending habits and payment patterns the same way market researchers do, and
- recall your "Money History" (later in this chapter).

We want to help *you*—not advertisers, retailers, financial companies, parents, spouses, partners, children, close friends or casual acquaintances—*gain conscious control* over how you allocate your hard-won resources. Your Life Values Profile is a crucial step on your way to becoming financially savvy and enjoying the resulting peace of mind, self-esteem, and inner sense of security that financial competence bestows.

See for yourself how you might fare in the following exercise about rational decision making in the context of a routine spending decision. What choice would you be most likely to make? And how can you adjust your thinking to become more active and engaged in your purchasing decisions?

OBSERVING A ROUTINE SPENDING DECISION

Imagine this.

You are standing in front of a display of bedding, HDTVs, or riding lawnmowers, whichever strikes your fancy. There before you is the exact bedcover, TV, or lawnmower you have been wanting lately, and today it is on sale for half its usual cost. The problem is that you don't have the cash to buy it. And you have promised yourself to halt credit card purchases and pay down your balances. You feel a little *uncomfortable*: Should you charge this purchase or not? You tap quickly—more or less unconsciously—into your decision alternatives as you think about whether or not to buy the bedcover, TV, or lawnmower. Here are your possible decisions:

A. You decide to keep your promise not to make credit card purchases and don't buy the item.

B. You initially decide to keep your promise not to make credit card purchases, but on your way to the parking lot, you can't get the bedcover, HDTV, or lawnmower out of your mind.

C. You decide to buy the item and charge it to your credit card as a convenience. You promise yourself that you will still whittle down your outstanding credit card balances and that you'll pay the full cost of this purchase on top of your regular payment when you receive the next bill. You will worry about exactly how you will do that later.

D. You override your promise not to make any more purchases on credit, and you go ahead and buy the item you want. You decide that the purchase is "worth" the extra time it will now take you to pay down your balances.

If you were to confront such a choice, which of the following spending behaviors would be most familiar: **A, B, C,** or **D**?

Spending Behaviors and Decision-Making

If you made **Choice A**, you understand that your purchase would bring only temporary gratification. The good feeling you have about keeping your promise to yourself will more than offset any regret about not purchasing the item. Your sense of self-esteem is heightened because:

- You have had the self-control that keeps you from being seduced by the marketplace.
- You lived up to standards you set for yourself.
- You made a decision based on actively weighing the purchase against your financial planning objectives.

If you made **Choices B, C,** or **D**, you have more decisions to make:

- In **Choice B**, you must run through your alternatives again until
  1) after thinking more about it, you decide the choice you made to forego the purchase was the right one, and it then becomes **Choice A**, or
  2) you decide to return to the store to confront your purchase decision all over again, which brings you back to *square one.*
- In **Choice C**, you have changed (and complicated) the rules of your promise to yourself. In addition to paying down the credit card balance, you must still decide how you will pay for the item you just purchased. You have simply deferred until later the risk of breaking your original promise to later if you cannot make the additional payment.
- In **Choice D**, you *rationalize* your decision altogether:
  1) You think up reasons why it is okay that you broke your promise to yourself and bought the item you wanted.
  2) You convince yourself that your reasons are "good" reasons.

If someone else is involved in your routine purchase decision, navigating **Choices B, C,** and **D** is more complicated. Not only must you think through the wants, financial goals, and promises you have made to yourself, you must also address the promises you may have made to, or with, the other person.

Let's recap some of the influences, both outer and inner, that are at work in our example. As you read through these, reflect upon the "inner" conversations that might have been going on if you were involved in this transaction.

First, let's notice the marketplace (outer) incentives put in place by the retailer:

- The item you want is on sale.
- It is half price if you buy the item *today*.
- Payment is easy and quick—a swipe of your credit card, and the item belongs to you!

Now take a look at the (inner) incentives that may influence your decision to purchase the item. Note how they correspond with the incentives put in place by the retailer:

- You are getting a really good deal.
- You must decide quickly because the opportunity won't last.
- You can think about the consequences of your purchase decision later.

If you made **Choice A**, you are out of range of this retailer's influence, and you have a head start in being engaged in your financial life. If you made **Choice B, C,** or **D,** there is some inner work for you to do in the area of committing to the goals and promises you make to yourself.

POINT TO PONDER

Rationalizing choices means offering "reasoned" explanations for your choices and decision-making behaviors. You use these explanations to

- give yourself or others permission to make a choice or
- defend or explain a choice you've already made.

If you have been skeptical about the inner and outer influences at play in your financial choices, we hope this imaginary purchase

---

decision exercise has convinced you to put aside your judgments and plow on. Our hope is that you now have a better picture of how these influences might be at work in your life and how you can temper them to gain better control of your finances.

One of the biggest mistakes almost every one of us makes is to presume that his or her spending and other financial decisions are rational and objective without any *feeling* component or unconscious influence. As you begin to observe your inner motivations and feelings, and how these link up with your actual financial behaviors, you will be able to sharpen your understanding of how and why you handle money and finances the way you do. This knowledge should not only enlighten you, but should also give you pause about whether or not you are on the track to meeting your goals and being true to your Life Values.

Searching for What You Really Value

In the exercise you just completed, you acted according to what you wanted *most*. In other words, you either decided to keep your promise to yourself or to buy the prized item, according to your inner priorities. Did your decision square with what you really value in life? Maybe it does; maybe it doesn't. But if you decided to push down the desire to keep a solemn commitment to yourself or to someone else and caved in to a spending desire instead, you may be overriding an important inner Life Value.

Why are values so important? Yes, we know that the word is often overused and sometimes abused. The fact is, though, what we *value* determines our attitudes and beliefs about the way things are, judgments about the way things should be, the choices we make, and the actions we take. We develop our deepest values through the experiences of a lifetime, from childhood through adulthood.

The values we were taught when we were young—by our parents, secular and religious teachers, culture, and society—often still underlie our attitudes, and ultimately, our choices and our current lifestyles. They are also a driving force behind our major decisions, such as whether to move, get an education, change jobs, buy a new vehicle, or save more for the future. Whenever we make choices, we engage, consciously or unconsciously, in a process that matches our values to our decisions. In other words, we think and *feel* our way through the choices we make—to have fun, be safe, enjoy privacy and independence, please someone we love, be more attractive, improve our surroundings, take pride in an accomplishment, or achieve other such standards we have set for ourselves.

These inner needs and wants form the basis for the Life Values we discussed in Chapter 4, and we can use them to *frame* our thinking about the decisions we make. Without a clear understanding of our values and how we develop them, we would plunge into the decision process with little thoughtful preparation and then react with surprise to our own, a partner's, or a child's strong feelings about this choice or that one. When this happens, there has been a *clash of values,* an event that can have damaging effects for us and for our loved ones. In most financial decision situations, it is possible to do much better. With "values-focused planning," you can cut out the noise and end up much closer to getting what you really care about.

In Chapter 6, "A Word About Fear," we spoke briefly about how your childhood helped to form your money habits today. Now let's take a closer look at your family history to explore how your values may have been formed in childhood.

How Childhood Dreams Become Adult Habits

Your family history influences your decisions today. Dreams and fantasies about wanting toys, clothes, and other possessions (material and intrinsic) begin in childhood and stay with us more or less over the years. The dream of getting the "treasures" we dream about is both symbolic and literal for children, and the dream endures for many of us throughout adulthood. When you examine more closely your unique money history, including your dreams and fantasies about the way your parents taught you to value money and the things money could buy, you will better understand your own patterns about making meaningful financial decisions today.

Whether spending money, managing money, or making other financial decisions, you can unwittingly reenact your original family culture without being aware of why you are doing it. In fact, you may be imitating a parent's behaviors *even when you do not like those behaviors.* When you establish a relationship with a partner that will involve joint finances, you now are dealing with the family patterns and cultures from *two* distinct pasts. Identifying your childhood relationships to money will help give you insight into what you value (or hate) about your financial life today and will allow you to shed the behaviors you have outgrown. The goal is a smooth functioning system that fully reflects your adult values rather than the needs and wants mired in your childhood.

Your Unique Money History

With only a few minutes of serious reflection, you can record vital information about your childhood that will help you understand your relationship to money today.

Step 1: Think carefully about what went on in your childhood and how you interacted with your parents and siblings when it came to your allowance, discussions (or fights) about money, silences when you asked questions, the purchases you made, the "things" that you wanted, how and whether you got them, and the purchases and decisions about money that were made for you.

Step 2: Write a brief description of your most positive childhood memories about money and finances, or the things that you knew that money could buy. What did you enjoy? What were the special features? What made it "special?"

Step 3: Write a brief description of your most negative childhood memories about money and finances, or the things that you knew that money could buy. What did you most dislike? What experiences related to money and finances made you unhappy when you were a child?

Step 4: Now, compare your childhood experiences with your positive and negative financial habits as an adult. Do you recognize any childhood patterns or preferences brought into adulthood? If so, are they compatible with your adult values and lifestyle, or do they cause disharmony?

It is time to claim your own values without ever again having to look back in time.

The Payoffs of Becoming Financially Competent

The payoffs of learning about these influences on your current money behavior patterns can be huge. Ask your partner to complete these exercises too, because the issues you will uncover can help smooth the way for improved communication and mutual understanding. In fact, the relationship benefits that will emerge are immediately transferable to the other personal and professional choices you will make in life.

To begin to use your money history to gain insight into your current behaviors, here are three crucial questions to ask yourself before you approach the checkout counter on your next shopping trip:

1. Why do I want to buy this/these items?

2. How do I make spending decisions? Am I actively engaged or passive and reactive?

3. Does my decision-making approach help me or hurt me?

As you become a seasoned observer of your financial behaviors, the answers to these three questions will sharpen. Focusing on these three questions will help you further hone your understanding of your spending patterns. You will discover which purchases are habit-driven or based on satisfying leftover childhood desires, and which ones are truly values-driven, and you can use this insight to purposefully navigate your way through the financial decisions you face every day.

8

BECOMING A
SAVVY CONSUMER

This is not our parents' (or grandparents') financial marketplace. Only a few decades ago, we were faced with far fewer financial decisions than today. Savings were still invested in passbook accounts and U.S. Savings Bonds, mortgage rates were fixed, most goods and services were purchased with cash or checks, a college education was affordable, Social Security and Medicare were taken for granted, and employers provided health benefits and retirement funds in return for years of loyal employment. All of these combined required little financial decision making from most of us.

Today, there are many available options, and the trend is toward more personal involvement and responsibility for payment. We must take charge and actively manage the decisions we encounter on a daily basis. There is no room for passivity. Instead, the key is to become accountable for, and actively engaged in, our own financial success. The theory of personal accountability extends to all things financial, not just investing and saving for retirement. It extends to how we shop, what we buy, how we vote, how we educate ourselves and our children, and how we manage our health and well-being. As if that were not enough, along with the many financial decisions we now must make comes the necessity to protect ourselves from such things as scams and identity theft.

We seem to have less money left over and more financial demands than our parents and grandparents, and it is easy to become overwhelmed with all the responsibilities we are expected to shoulder. How in the world can we educate our kids, help our parents through their later years, and help ourselves save and plan for a healthful and secure retirement? Difficult as it may initially seem, it is only by seizing and maintaining *control* over our choices that we can get back to the basics and finally accept the fact that navigating our financial life in good times or bad always *starts* with one simple concept. Yes, we know, you have heard it many times before. But just as eating fewer calories to lose weight is true, so is the recognition that we must always spend less than our income if we want to realize our financial goals.

Your first, and perhaps greatest, challenge is to get control of your spending. Like Kathy and Ed in the following account, we must all become savvy consumers:

Kathy and Ed describe themselves as solidly middle class. They have steady income from stable employment that allows them to provide for their two teenage girls. Their combined income is average, but Kathy has figured out how to stretch the money they make. With the mortgage paid off, she and Ed recently took out a home-improvement loan to increase their living space, upgrade their home and maximize its value. They shop wisely and try to get the best deals on clothes, food, vehicles, and other items. They read *Consumer Reports* before committing to big expenditures. They are conscientious about the quality of the goods and services they purchase, their health habits, and their political choices. They are savvy consumers—and savvy is what it takes to survive in today's financial environment.

Choosing to Spend Wisely

Being a consumer involves more than going on a shopping spree at the local mall on a Saturday afternoon. We are consumers every day, and the choices we make are more complex than spending versus not spending. We also make choices about where we spend our money, how we feed and clothe our family, where and how we educate our children, what we do for entertainment, and if and where we go on vacation. These are choices that we make regularly. In addition, there is something we call "spending creepage" that comes into play in our routine spending choices—choices that impact every facet of our daily lives.

Let's follow Joe as he goes through a normal day. He could be your neighbor, your colleague, or he could even be you. He is married to his childhood sweetheart and has two teenage daughters. Joe is an engineer, and his wife teaches second grade. Like many Americans, they live paycheck-to-paycheck and have little or no savings besides the 401(k) plans to which they contribute as little as possible.

Every weekday morning, Joe leaves his suburban home and drives 45 minutes to his city job. He parks at a nearby garage, stops on his way to the office for coffee and a donut, and picks up a salad at the corner deli for lunch. Pretty routine stuff. But already, just a couple of hours into his day, Joe made three spending choices based on convenience and by cruising on autopilot.

Joe has a high P (Personal Values) score. Even on the way to work, he is focused on his job, which brings him great satisfaction. Coffee, donuts, and his luncheon salad are irrelevant to his job satisfaction, so Joe does not take those purchases seriously. They are conveniences to him, so once he thinks about what is really important to him, he may be able to improve his debt-ridden personal bottom line. Let's find out.

If Joe started thinking as a savvy consumer, he might make different choices by exploring his actions from a financial perspective. He could look first at his commute: He now pays for fuel and to park, but since he has regular hours, he could carpool or take public transportation if it is available. He could think differently about his coffee-and-donut habit: That $3.50 expenditure may not seem like a big deal, but as you may have guessed by now, it can add up over time. In fact, it costs Joe over $900 a year. Coffee and a breakfast bar at home would cost only a fraction of that amount and be a more healthy alternative as well. Finally, by not stopping for his daily gourmet salad, Joe would avoid his other miscellaneous purchases and perhaps learn to brown bag it for lunch—at least part of the time.

Picky, picky you might be thinking, and we do not blame you if you believe this is an inconvenient, restrictive, unrewarding way for Joe to have to live. But it isn't really, not if you look more closely at Joe's financial aspirations. For one thing, Joe really wants to send his girls to college but worries about where the money will come from. He is already in debt and finding it difficult to meet all his credit obligations. He and his wife, despite being close friends, cannot discuss retirement without fighting, so that topic is off the table for now.

If, however, Joe and his family really want to accomplish college for their girls and retirement for themselves, they must all four do away with their current spending and credit card habits and start planning for what is important to them in life. It is their everyday small choices that are bleeding their resources, and they have no choice but to become savvy consumers. They have to start somewhere, and *it is from the little things now* that they will raise the money and reap the future rewards from affordable college educations and retirement security.

Being a savvy consumer means doing this type of analysis and making smart choices in every corner of your life. It means being engaged in all of your purchasing decisions, large and small, and being willing to spend a little time and to plan ahead. Now let's meet Phil.

Phil bases his decisions on the belief that he works hard for his money and wants to keep as much of it as he can. When Phil leaves the house in the morning, he picks up the newspaper from the front porch and also sticks an energy drink in his briefcase. (Phil doesn't drink coffee and picks up his energy drinks in multi-packs at the supermarket, paying a lot less per drink.) Phil does pick up his salad at the deli on the corner because he does not have time to prepare lunch at home. But he looks for ways to fine tune and streamline his spending habits. Phil has a high M (Money Values) score and finds pleasure in managing his finances wisely. He saves the maximum he can in his 401(k), and he walks the two miles to work each day. Phil is not yet married, but he owns his home, has investments that are life-cycle appropriate, and he meets regularly with a financial planner to fine tune his personal long-term goals and planning. Phil also carefully checks the credentials and voting records of his congressional representatives and lets his consumer preferences be known.

Maneuvering through the marketplace of goods and services involves more choices than decisions. We can easily make it through the decisions. Do I buy or not buy? But this is only the beginning of the process. We must make smart choices too. Here is an example:

You know you want to have lunch; that is easy enough to decide. If you stop thinking about it at that point, however, you have made a *decision*, but you have not explored your *choices*.

1. Do you make lunch at home and brown bag it?

2. Do you grab a burger at the local fast food counter?

3. Do you walk a block to the local deli and buy the lunchtime special for $5.75?

4. Do you go to the corner bistro with a friend and splurge on sparkling water and a cassolet for $20?

POINT TO PONDER

Being a savvy consumer is about making both decisions and choices. Decisions are often black and white: "yes or no" or "stop or go." Choices, on the other hand, come in shades of gray and offer us many alternatives. If we *decide* not to consider the alternatives, however, we no longer are exercising the power to *choose*.

We make financial choices every day. Our choices involve satisfying routine daily needs, such as stopping by a convenience store or going the extra mile to the local supermarket. They include planning ahead or buying on impulse—usually without a list. Still other choices can bind us for the longer term and cause real financial harm, like making major purchases (an appliance, car, even a house) in a split second with no real forethought, investigation or planning. In contrast, the savvy consumer knows to plan for satisfying both short-and-longer-term needs and desires. Shopping excursions are planned in advance helped by a list of *affordable* needs and wants. They are informed by a good understanding of *why* a particular purchase is being made, plus knowledge about pricing and fair service and retail practices.

Kathy, who we met earlier in this chapter, is one such shopper. She seems to know when major stores run sales and is there when the doors open for the early-bird specials. You may think, "I don't have time for

---

that." But if you are not making your choices by factoring in your financial plans, you may be saving time, but at what expense? Consider this: Kathy usually has all of her Christmas shopping done in October at a savings of hundreds of dollars. So by the holidays, she has time to bake and decorate her house and is rested enough to enjoy the look on the faces of those lucky enough to open her beautiful gifts. (And, yes, she is there for the after-Christmas sales, buying her wrapping paper and other necessities for the following Christmas—at 75% off!)

Kathy had an S (Social Values) score of 8 and an M (Money Values) score of 7. She has clearly recognized her need to cultivate relationships and she enjoys spending money on loved ones. However, she is also a disciplined shopper and has developed good spending habits over the years. She is savvy because she has worked to achieve balance in these two values drivers.

When you embark on a pattern of smart spending, you will not have to give up all the fun purchases you make. But you will have to make choices! And you will need to recognize and manage your particular passions. Remember Maria and Steve, the young couple we met in an earlier chapter who are planning a wedding and a first home? They know they must save and spend carefully to meet these goals, yet Maria really enjoys her trips to the beauty salon, and Steve loves video games, so they have set aside a certain amount from each paycheck to indulge in these passions.

What is your passion? For Maria and Steve, it is beautiful hair and video games; for others it could be books or antique markets, music CDs and concerts, new shoes, day trips, or even spa days. When you make smart choices about expenditures you are passionate about, you will plan for what you can afford. These indulgences are important and will help keep you focused on good financial management. When you look at the new leather jacket in your closet or the movie you purchased that just won an Academy Award, you can be inspired to continue to meet long-term financial goals without resentment. A well-planned splurge is like having just a taste of chocolate, not indulging in the whole cake. So pick your passion, and figure out how to indulge it so it does not break the bank.

Such advice is especially important to anyone having a very high score (9+) in Personal, Social or Tangible Values. If you are strongly committed to personal goals and self-expression or to indulging loved ones or to achieving an ideal lifestyle or standard of living, you know you can be blind to the important Money Values in your life. You may need to actively seek balance in your spending habits. Budgeting to address those strong values drivers, while reining them in, is your savvy move. Plan to have only *some* of what you want, *some* of the time because your M (Money Values) score is dangerously low.

Being Engaged

To fully navigate your marketplace choices, you also need to rev up other behaviors. Part of the personal responsibility mantra means being assertive and engaged in your purchasing activities. So how *do* you switch from being a passive consumer to becoming an active, assertive, smart consumer? Here are some suggestions:

- Be engaged *before* you shop: Know your needs and wants.

  - Window shopping can be as tempting as grocery shopping on an empty stomach. Do not go looking for what might be available— go looking for what you need and want. Arm yourself with knowledge about the product you are seeking. Know its important features, and avoid substitutes with bells and whistles you might never use.
  - Stop and think before sealing the deal. *Do I really need this?* Think about the things you already own and never use.

- Be engaged *while* shopping: Seek the best price every time.

  - Compare prices from news sources and information from Web sites. Make an effort to investigate costs, and do not overlook warehouse stores, outlets, and discount shops. Friends and relatives can be helpful to shop with if they are price conscious; if not, better to go it alone.
  - When you think you have narrowed the field, do not cave in and pay a price beyond your means or expectations. Bargaining might not feel comfortable for you, but get your courage up and ask a

few candid questions: *Will this item be going on sale soon? Can you give me a discount, considering the large size of my purchase? Will you match the price I found at XYZ Outlet?* (Of course you will have to bring proof of the competitor's lower price.)

- Remain engaged *after* the sale: Be willing to change your mind.

  - No matter how delighted you are with the purchase at the moment, inquire at the point of sale about the store's return policy and any restocking fee that might be imposed. Keep your mind open to the possibility of returning the item for a full refund if you are in any way dissatisfied or if you later realize you have made an unwise purchase.
  - Once you get your new purchase home, keep the tags intact and save your receipt and the packaging. Maintain the new item in sellable condition as you ponder your decision. If you think you have made a mistake, you probably have, so return the item, and you are likely to get a full refund to go with your feeling of relief.

EXERCISE

KEEPING AN EXPENSE DIARY

Practice making smart choices. Carry a notebook with you and keep an expense diary for one week, recording every expenditure you make. Don't be shy; include every expense, no matter how large or small, and even one-time expenses. Then go through the list and determine what type of expense each is, if it is necessary or extravagant. Look at the choices you made or could have made regarding each expense. Could you have gotten it on sale? Is what you spent commensurate with the value received? (In other words, did you get what you paid for?) Look to your routine expenses and do the math, determining how much you spend on that particular item or service per month or per year. Is it still a smart choice? Looking at your expenses in depth like this will help you identify particular patterns and habits—you may be surprised!

Managing Your Own Health Care

Just as we need to be smart about our purchases, we need to be particularly informed about purchasing and managing our health care. Current trends in health coverage and care are mirroring personal financial management trends by following the consumer "accountability model." That means you can expect to increasingly face the requirement by health care providers that you participate responsibly in your own care. You should also expect to absorb at least part of the spiraling costs of health care as well.

In the old model, most working Americans were provided employer- or union-sponsored health insurance as an earned benefit. Employees picked their doctors and depended upon them to tend to the health care needs of their families. The health insurance company paid the doctor bills, and if hospitalization was needed, it paid for hospital care as well. Hospitals usually were community-based or university sponsored, and most were operated on a nonprofit basis. In striking contrast, the health care field today—from doctors to hospitals, to pharmaceutical companies, to health financial corporations, to consultants, to Wall Street—is big business. It got that way over many years, and our nation should have prepared better for the costs and complexity in human and social terms of what was to come.

Today, those of you who are still fortunate enough to have sponsored health care coverage, but also those of you who are not, are nevertheless all "consumers of health care." As consumers, you must be savvy enough to pick the health plan that is right for you if it is offered and to incorporate health care into your financial planning. If you do not understand your plan, you must pester your employer or union or coverage provider until you do; if you are uninsured and unable to obtain coverage for whatever reason, *you must pester your politicians to change your access to health care.*

The new health care models are called "consumer-driven health care," and theoretically, they are founded upon sound principles. The nation's employers, their consultants, and the health care industry "burned out" from the consumer backlash over health maintenance organizations (HMOs). So, they created consumer-driven health care (called CDHC for short)[1] to give us more choice about who provides and coordinates our care and what our care will consist of. The newer plans are less structured and more varied, giving us more choices but also requiring more payment responsibility from us. These health benefits models anticipate that if we pay our own health care bills or a large part of them anyway, we will make healthier choices: not to smoke, not to abuse alcohol, to choose healthful meals, and to exercise regularly. Our healthier choices, goes the theory, will result in savings—for us, for our employers, and for the health care industry—because we will not *use* so much health care. As consumers, we will naturally need less health care and be rewarded by paying less for the care we consume. Our employers and the health care industry, meanwhile, can then cap their out-of-control health care expenses.[2] They will also have an easier time continuing to generate the profits that Wall Street and their investors expect to remain competitive in a global economy.

What's Wrong with This Picture?

Aside from all the loyal employees and other consumers who already are suffering from chronic illnesses, the health care industry and our nation's employers are setting themselves up squarely in opposition to the vast fast food, entertainment, tobacco, and many other industries that want us to keep right on living the sedentary lifestyles that most Americans do. After all, they want to remain profitable too. In addition, generations of consumers have been taught that doctors are trained specialists (and authority figures) who know better than they what treatment is best and which remedy costs what. Do you know how to "shop" for the best value in an appendectomy in the 12 hours you have before your emergency operation? Do you feel qualified to suggest to your care provider that a CT scan might cost less when he or she has just ordered an MRI?

Being a savvy consumer in the health care arena means first, understanding the term, "consumer-driven health care" and the hype that surrounds it. If you are not noticing any difference between the policing that is going on by your health coverage plan today and the old-style HMOs, then you are sensing—correctly—that you are really not in the "driver's seat" at all and therefore cannot be driving your own care. What may be changing for you dramatically, however—and perhaps forever in the U.S. unless our politicians can be persuaded to go to bat for consumers—is your share of the costs for health coverage and care.

What You Can Control

Because the remedies available in our nation are still among the best in the world, let's now concentrate on what you can control to change the odds in your direction as a savvy health care consumer. If you have health care insurance coverage, you are somewhat limited by the benefits spelled out in your policy. However, you can exert control over your health care costs at many points. These five steps can save you significant money:

- Plan ahead to devote pre-tax income to health care.
- Choose your care providers prudently.
- Negotiate fees for care when necessary.
- Direct the discussion yourself when visiting a health care provider.
- Be proactive about your prescriptions.

First, before anyone gets sick or injured, study the benefits package provided by your employer to see whether you are offered a flexible spending plan. If so, you will want to take advantage of this opportunity to set aside pre-tax dollars from your paycheck to fund medical expenses over the next year. You will have to decide in advance how much you want withheld for the total year; guesstimate this on the basis of your out-of-pocket expenses from recent years. Look carefully at exactly which procedures are covered, and then be sure to file the appropriate paperwork (with receipts) to withdraw funds from this account. In this way you are still paying out-of-pocket expenses, but you are avoiding taxes on that money. Every little bit helps.

When it does become necessary to seek care, stay within your insurance provider's network. In fact, familiarize yourself in advance with the list of available doctors, hospitals, and other providers. Be aware that many services initiated in the office of your primary caregiver are outsourced. Try to ensure that your films are read by a radiologist within the network, your lab results are studied by a member pathologist, and your anesthesia is administered by a network specialist, or the fees for each service provided beyond the network might well be denied by your insurance company.

When you simply have to go beyond your insurance network, negotiate the fees. Don't feel at all uncomfortable inquiring of the insurance company the total coverage for the service you need. Then tell your out-of-network provider what that limit is and ask them to honor it. If the business manager gives you a flat refusal, speak directly to the doctor about it at your next opportunity. Doctors routinely "write off" or "adjust" charges not covered by insurance.

And speaking of discussions with your doctor, form the habit of being proactive about that too. Direct the conversation in the examining room. In most cases, health care providers are delighted to care for patients who report their symptoms willingly and come prepared with a list of relevant questions and concerns. Ask burning questions early on, while you have the provider's full attention, and do not excuse the medical professional until you know everything you need to know. Do your part, of course, by preparing a list of all your medications, including dosages. On that same paper, list worrisome symptoms and questions you want answered. Far from taking up too much of the doctor's valuable time, you will find that the entire process is more focused and purposeful and actually saves time.

Once your physician has sent you on your way with a few prescriptions, you have a further opportunity to control your health care costs: Be smart about your prescriptions. Pharmacies do not all charge the same price for the same drugs. Find a reputable licensed pharmacy that offers a lower drug price in general. While all medications have a generic name, the generic version is not readily available in all cases. When it is, your out-of-pocket cost can be a fraction of the price for a brand name drug. Frequent a pharmacy that readily offers generic drugs, and remind the pharmacist that the lower-priced alternative is your preference.

When You Don't Have Health Insurance

It is a disturbing fact that, in our advanced and wealthy country, great numbers of families and individuals remain totally uninsured or under-insured. Health insurance costs rose 87% from 2000 to 2006, putting health insurance benefits beyond the reach of some employers, especially small companies. Families unable to bear the full financial burden of insurance find themselves without coverage. Ironically, hospitals, clinics and pharmacies generally charge the uninsured more than those with coverage—sometimes four or five times as much as they charge insurance companies! All is not lost, though. You still have some control.

Tell the hospital or care provider that you are uninsured and ask for a discounted price. If it is not forthcoming, try to find a provider who will offer a discount. Meanwhile, research your options for free health screenings by your local health department or nonprofit agencies like the American Heart Association or the American Cancer Society. The Veterans Health Administration (877-222-8387) offers free or reduced-price services to military veterans. You might qualify for Medicaid, even if only temporarily. Call your local public health or social services agency to inquire about your eligibility, or research the topic online at http://cms.hhs.gov/medicaid. If you require a prescription you cannot afford, ask the pharmacist how you can contact the pharmaceutical company directly to request a price break, or call 800-762-4636 for help. You might be surprised at the assistance extended to you.

When you do find yourself confronting a medical bill simply beyond your means, do not panic, and do not automatically reach for a credit card. Ask the provider to help you establish a long-term payment plan. Even if the provider charges some interest, it will be well below the rates your credit card company would have imposed.

Making sound purchasing decisions involves how you pay for your purchases. Besides the credit limits imposed on you by others, think about what else you need to consider before you absent-mindedly just say, "charge it." Becoming engaged and active in your financial affairs is about taking control and practicing personal accountability as you navigate your way through the number of choices that are available to you as a consumer. By spending wisely and staying in tune with your Life Values, you will be rewarded with more money in your pocket, and you will have become an aware, savvy, and engaged consumer.

9

GETTING AND KEEPING GOOD CREDIT

Mastering the marketplace includes questions about *if, what, and when* to buy. Having good credit reflects how we choose *to pay* for our purchases—cash, check, credit card, debit card, or other stored value card. Using payment methods to our advantage involves making deliberate, planned choices. Even among payment cards, there are many choices: Some cards act like cash or checks; others act like loans. Still others are "hybrids," a combination of both debit and credit, and always are attached to terms and conditions, fees, and/or rates of interest—sometimes extremely high rates of interest.

Most people know the major difference between types of payment cards. We use one or more of these cards to make routine purchases in person, over the phone or the Internet, to give as gifts, and make prepaid phone calls. Not all types of payment cards, however, build good credit. The following brief review describes only the basics, and there are endless variations and exceptions in all of the following categories. Making certain you know exactly what type of card(s) you are using and their specific terms and conditions means reading the fine print in your contract and the bills you receive every month. If you need help, go to one of the educational Internet sites given in Chapter 19, "Finding the Help You Need," or listed in the Appendix, "Personal Finance Education Internet Sites," of this book.

Credit card issuers make money from you and also from the merchants who accept their cards for payment of goods and services. When markets change, or when they perceive a dip in your credit status, they can and do change the rules on you, sometimes without your knowledge and nearly always without your permission.

Later we discuss how credit benefits you and some new reasons why having good credit is so important in today's uncertain consumer environment. After you become familiar with this chapter, maybe you will be motivated to take a class on credit management. If you do, you will probably never again look at the cards in your wallet in quite the same way.

Credit Cards

Credit card approval is really "loan approval" by a credit provider to you, the "borrower." You may make purchases using the card up to a pre-established credit (loan) limit at a pre-determined rate of interest. The amount of credit is "revolving," which simply means as you know, that you are required to pay a proportion of the bill by a given due date, or you may pay off the entire balance owed and spend/borrow again. There are many terms and conditions of the credit card or cards you may be using, and you need to know all of these details. The point to remember, however, is that each time you swipe that credit card you are using *borrowed money, not extra cash.* Some people even tape this reminder to their credit card, so they will not forget this crucial fact in the rush of making unintended purchases.

Charge Cards

Certain American Express cards, Diners Club, and some merchants issue charge cards that are similar to credit cards. They act like short-term loans, and cardholders must repay all charges in full each month. No part of the balance, unlike revolving credit, may be carried forward. The two types of cards are often interchangeably called "charge cards" to describe any card that can be used as payment or for credit. In return for an annual fee, most people use charge cards for convenience and to keep track of their expenses.

Debit Cards

Debit cards immediately signal the withdrawal of funds from an account into which you have previously deposited money. When you pay with a debit card, the store clerk checks electronically to make sure you have enough funds in your account. Merchants prefer that you use debit cards instead of credit cards because the fees they pay to the card issuer are less for debit card payments than for credit transactions. A debit card does not accumulate and push up the amount of debt that you owe because you use only the amount you have on deposit.

Hybrid Cards

A hybrid card is a debit card with "overdraft charging privileges." If your bank account balance is less than the item you wish to purchase, you will not be denied by the card issuer. You will be able to debit your account directly and to charge the balance, or even your next purchase, up to your credit limit, of course. Be sure to understand any fees associated with overdraft charging privileges before you use this service.

Stored Value Cards

A stored value card is a catchall phrase used to describe a whole family of payment cards. They all use magnetic strip technology to store information about funds that have been prepaid. Payroll cards, government benefit cards, prepaid debit cards, gift cards, and telephone cards are examples of stored value cards. There are two main types of stored value cards in the marketplace: single purpose cards such as prepaid gift and telephone cards, and multipurpose stored value cards, an alternative to checking accounts, for people who usually do not deal with banks.

Multipurpose stored value cards can be used to make debit transactions at a wide variety of retail locations. They can receive and store new deposits, like a bank account, and cardholders can use them for withdrawing cash from ATMs. Some multipurpose cards are branded by Visa or MasterCard and can be used wherever those brands are accepted.

Our Credit Society—A Way of Life

It is predicted that before long, our nation will be a "cashless" society. With all the variations of charge, credit, and stored value cards that exist now, it is true that cash is a disappearing form of payment. But *credit* is not disappearing. In fact it is growing exponentially. In the U.S., the number of major credit cards in use increased from 213 million in 1990 to 566.8 million by the beginning of 2005.[1] The dollar amount of debt owed by American consumers grew from $154 billion in 1990 to $805.5 billion by the end of 2005.[2] And when it comes to credit, that old cliché, "there's no such thing as a free lunch," could not be more true. Credit is not free.

Credit is, however, a very valuable consumer resource, and *good* credit is essential to buying a new home, financing a business venture, or funding higher education. Abused or overused credit, on the other hand, can threaten your budget and your good name before you know what you did to incur the penalties that can jack up your costs to obscene levels. So learning—and understanding—the basics of getting and keeping good credit is yet another critical ground rule for becoming competent at financial management.

From frills to necessities, the uses of credit are virtually limitless, and its wide availability for some is an all-too-inviting trap. The friendly smile of the salesclerk who asks, "Debit or credit?" and the ease with which many of us answer "credit" might well be numbing some of us to the real financial impact of that deceptively simple question. If you are among those answering "credit," you are not alone as the numbers are plainly showing.

In addition, the marketplace gives a certain cachet to credit, and credit card companies can be brutally competitive. To get us to spend more, we are urged to use our cards for everything from cash advances, to incidental expenses, to more luxury purchases which we might not consider buying if we had to pay cash. We are invited to earn miles, shopping points, and free dinners, if we will only spend more on credit.

These messages, however, come from the very companies who benefit from our every purchase or cash advance transaction. These companies have *their profit margins*, not our financial well-being, in mind as they extol the virtues of buying on credit. It is easy to forget that the purchasing ease of credit is seductively convenient, and when we pay on credit, we are really creating debt, debt, debt. Sometimes we remember this too late, and our debt load has climbed to heights we did not anticipate. Worse, debt is expensive, and once incurred, debt can become difficult to repay.

The Upside—and Downside—of Credit

On the upside, credit is convenient and even necessary. Many of us keep a credit card in our wallets for necessary purchases and in case of an emergency, like a tire blowout that needs to be repaired immediately when we don't have the cash. Credit cards can save money on your purchases by allowing you to be spontaneous and take advantage of special sales, but sale balances should be paid off quickly before the advantage of the sale is lost through added interest and fees.

Planned credit is necessary to good financial health. In the form of a positive credit rating, it enables you to acquire assets. It communicates to lenders, insurance companies, and even to prospective employers that you are a good credit risk and that your personal affairs are in order. When you apply for the mortgage on your first (or next) home, your lender will not have to guess whether or not your payments will be made on time—you have a track record. When you apply for insurance on your home or personal belongings, your credit standing tells companies that you are not likely to try to cheat the system. And your prospective employer who relies on a credit report is assured that you will not lose time at work, at least dodging creditors, and that you are likely to keep your promises in the workplace as you have done with your creditors. Those who have never used credit do not have this history and must build it if they want the benefits that good credit bestows.

On the downside, available credit encourages impulse purchases, and this is the problem that everyone is now facing. With costs and rates climbing, accumulated unplanned debt can be a significant drain on personal resources, making it extremely difficult—if not impossible—to build and sustain savings and assets.

When you are savvy about credit, you control your financial destiny instead of being "used" by credit companies. You are exhibiting these essential qualities of competent personal financial managers:

- The wise use of credit has a positive effect in your life.
- You are engaged with banks and other credit card issuers and can negotiate to obtain their best terms and conditions for your future financial benefit.
- You can expect to receive credit on the best terms and conditions as you consider your housing, education, investment and/or retirement options.
- You have one or more sources of credit to smooth out temporary cash shortfalls or time lapses in your earnings.

The trick, then, is not to avoid having credit cards, but to make judicious use of them. But before you use your card for any reason, ask yourself if the use you are considering is something that will benefit you more than the debt may hurt you.

DAYDREAM

Pretend you have been thinking about buying a new jacket for the coming winter season. You walk through the mall on another errand, and there is an elegant store offering a one-day-only sale—20% off winter jackets. Before you plunk down your credit card, you stop and think: "Am I sure I want to splurge on an expensive jacket from this particular store? Or could I find another winter jacket I might like just as well from a designer warehouse? Will the price of *this* jacket, plus interest on my credit card, end up doubling what the initial discount would be?" See yourself resisting the siren call of "on sale today only," and then buying another great-looking jacket on terms you can really afford.

All of your purchases, especially your larger ones, should be made through the lens of your Life Values Profile. Think through your purchase decisions instead of buying on credit *just because the card is there.* Many people rationalize their impulse buying to cover up the truth that they could easily have done without the item. If this happens to you, try getting into the habit of thinking through to the consequences of your purchases: "more stuff, higher debt, tougher to meet monthly payments," *before* you start planning your next trip to the mall. And try this: If your credit card is burning a hole in your pocket, then turn that old familiar American Express commercial on its head, and "*Do* leave home without it!"

Beware of Credit Traps

Not all credit cards are created equally. When choosing a card, pay close attention to the beginning interest rate and the terms and conditions under which the rate can rise. In addition, look carefully at the features offered—especially if you are paying a fee to use them. Consider the following traps when managing your credit card activity.

Be cautious about using a card based on its perks or special bonuses. You might be tempted to charge more just to get a bonus, like frequent flyer miles. Unless you pay off your balances every month, most bonuses do not pay off. Interest costs and fees can be more than the value of the bonus, or the bonus could go unused.

Be sure to read the fine print and understand the terms of each card. Unless you looked for it, you would likely miss the fact that many credit card companies have the built-in "universal default" clause we talked about earlier, allowing them to raise your interest rate if you're late making a payment—even to another creditor.

Avoid paying too high a rate for your credit card purchases. Always check the fees and interest rate on cash advances before you actually borrow cash from your credit card. Check with your bank to see whether you might obtain a consumer loan instead. Do this also when you are thinking about a large purchase. If you can borrow the same amount from a bank or credit union at a lower rate of interest, you can avoid this all-too-common high-interest trap.

Do not pay for extras like credit card insurance or gold or platinum status. There are almost always lower-price or free alternatives to these services. Even if you are worried about protection from credit card fraud, do not purchase insurance. This might be tempting to you if you have a high P (Personal) score and are particularly vigilant about personal security. Instead, photocopy all of your credit cards and indicate next to each card on the photocopy the number to call if your card is lost or stolen. Keep one copy in your safe deposit box and another one at home.

From Poor Credit to Good Credit

Poor credit results from making late payments, borrowing too much money in relation to your income, or charging to the limit ("maxing out") your credit cards. When you have marginal or poor credit, you can experience difficulty getting a car loan, a place to live, or your ideal job. You can be turned down for an insurance policy, and a bank can decide you are not a worthy customer, *even if you want to open a bank account and deposit money with that bank.* Although you eventually may be approved with marginal credit, you will pay higher rates and fees than someone with good credit. And poor credit can take years to fix.

Life is full of maybes and possibilities. You may meet the man or woman of your dreams and decide to settle down, or you may be offered the ideal job across town, but you need to buy a better car if you are going to accept it. Your credit rating can make a difference in whether or not you pursue these possibilities. Then there are life's little surprises. Your plan to start a family eventually may suddenly accelerate by an unplanned, but happy, pregnancy. Or your father may have a stroke and suddenly be unable to care for himself, forcing you to shoulder some of the burden. Your credit rating can help you roll with life's punches, or life's punches can roll over you. Being prepared to manage and cope with sudden loss is an important part of having the "right stuff."

Understanding Credit Scores

As almost everyone knows, our credit-worthiness is based on credit scores that are tallied from information accumulated from credit reporting agencies and other sources. Lenders use credit scores to help them decide whether to give loans or credit cards to applicants, and if they do, what their credit risk is likely to be. The most widely used credit scores are FICO® scores, calculated by Fair Isaac, the company that created the widespread use of credit scoring. Although some banks and financial institutions use their own credit scoring, FICO scores are widely used and are based solely on information in consumer credit reports maintained at the three major U.S. credit reporting agencies: TransUnion, Equifax, and Experian.

In addition to FICO scoring, many financial institutions and banks calculate and maintain their own credit scoring system, and a few newcomers are vying to compete with FICO in the future. All scores, by whatever company calculates them, use complex formulas that compare certain factors in your credit reports—your pattern of repayment, how close you are to your credit limit, the length of your credit history (not your age), your credit mix, and the number of inquiries made by companies to whom you have applied for credit—with the rest of the population.

What this number does is to allow creditors to see at a glance whether you are a good credit risk or not. The ease of using this number, as opposed to reviewing your entire credit report, makes it easier for creditors to make quick decisions (such as those "instant credit" offers at the cash register). It also creates uniformity throughout the financial marketplace. Most creditors create ranges of what they find acceptable or of what interest rates they will offer, and they simply compare your number to their ranges.

Getting Your Credit Report and Score

Your credit report is available free of charge and your score is available for a nominal fee. To protect yourself from identity theft or mistaken identity and other reporting errors, you should make it a point to review your credit report from each credit reporting agency at least once a year. This is essential if you are thinking about making a large purchase such as a home or car. You can request your credit report by phone, mail, or request it online by using the contact information below.

Annual Credit Report Request Service
P.O. Box 105281
Atlanta, GA 30348-5281
1-877-322-8228
https://www.annualcreditreport.com

How to Review Your Credit History

Your credit report is a record of how you have paid your mortgages, car loans, credit cards, and other loans. It shows how much debt you have, if you have made your payments on time, or if you have not paid back some loans at all. Credit reports contain the following information:

- Your social security number, current and previous addresses, nicknames, spouse's name, year of birth, and current and previous employers.
- Records of loans, credit cards, bank accounts, and retail store accounts.
- Public information on bankruptcy, tax liens, or legal judgments against you.
- Names of companies that have obtained copies of your credit report within the last six months (or two years for employment purposes).

Negative information stays on your credit report for seven years—ten years if a bankruptcy is involved—it is automatically deleted thereafter. Seven to ten years can be a long time if you want to move forward on a life goal and find that negative credit information is holding you back. Some negative information like tax liens and other judgments can remain indefinitely on your report unless they are satisfied in full and released from the public records.

Correcting Errors

Credit reports very frequently contain errors, so review your credit report at least once a year for errors or outdated information, which can affect your credit score and your ability to qualify for a loan at a competitive rate. This is simply being actively engaged in your own financial affairs, another of the four essential characteristics of good financial health.

No matter how they developed, or even whether or not you realize they are there, errors in your credit report are your responsibility. While it may be argued that in certain cases ignorance is bliss, this is not one of those cases. It is up to you to be proactive and recognize and fix any discrepancies. Errors, even small ones, take time to fix. In addition, a review of your credit report can indicate if you are a victim of identity theft—a crime that can go unnoticed for months, or even years, until you access your credit history. We suggest that you approach your annual credit review the same way you do your annual physical. Just as your routine physical can uncover problems while they are still minor and can easily be remedied—for example, if your doctor notices your cholesterol is creeping up, you can make changes in your diet and lifestyle that can prevent a heart attack—finding an error (or identity theft) in your credit report can give you time to fix it before it becomes an issue and you find your mortgage application stamped "DENIED."

If you uncover an error or inconsistency in any of the areas discussed here, simply send the credit reporting agency a letter notifying them about the error. Detailed information on how to do this is included in the report. And if you access your report online (www.annualcreditreport.com), you can even submit your inquiry request through the Web site. The agency is required to investigate the complaint within 30 days and respond with its results. If the agency finds that the information in the report is inaccurate, the creditor must notify the other major credit-reporting agencies of the error. If the credit reporting agency does not find an error, but you still believe the report is inaccurate, you can contact the creditor directly to resolve the problem. You also have the right to submit a written statement of up to 100 words that will appear on your credit report explaining your side of the dispute.

Establishing a Credit History from Scratch

Some people simply don't have a credit history. You may have never used credit or, perhaps, were recently divorced and all of the financial activity during your marriage was in your partner's name. You may be young and just got your first job. While it is great to have no debt, it is not so great to have no credit. As we discussed earlier, one of the factors the credit bureaus use when calculating your credit score is the length of your credit history. What this means is that, all other factors being equal, a 25-year-old with a credit history of five years will be considered a better credit risk than a 50-year-old with no credit history. (Actual age is considered irrelevant in calculating your credit score. That's right— while age may give you wisdom, experience, confidence, and laugh lines, it doesn't improve your credit score!)

It will take some time to establish a credit history. So if you have gone through life without ever using credit, or if you are just starting out in life, make it a point to establish (and then maintain) a solid credit history by following the steps below. (The laugh lines will take care of themselves.)

- Open a secured credit card account. A secured credit card is basically a prepaid card that functions much like prepaid cell phone minutes. You pay in advance and then "charge" up to that amount.
- Apply for one or two credit cards at local department stores. Use the cards for some purchases and be sure to make payments on time each month to show that you can manage credit effectively.
- Obtain a small loan from your bank or credit union and pay it back promptly or ahead of time. You'll want to confirm that the bank reports transactions to a credit bureau so this information will be included on your credit report.
- Apply for a bank credit card. Use the card for some purchases and be sure to make payments on time.

If you are married and are not the partner who controls the finances, make certain that you work to establish your *own* independent credit history.

Maintaining and Restoring Good Credit

Andrea and Will's lives were turned upside down when Andrea was unexpectedly laid-off from her corporate job at a major telecommunications company. The couple's annual income plummeted from

$120,000 to $40,000. They did not have any emergency savings to fall back on. During Andrea's unemployment, the couple relied on credit to make ends meet. It took Andrea eight months, but she ultimately found a fulfilling, good paying job. However, by then, the two of them had accumulated $30,000 in debt and had damaged their credit rating because several bills had been paid late.

Now that Andrea is once again gainfully employed, the couple is working to restore their credit rating. Andrea received a $5,000 signing bonus and used it to pay down some of their credit cards. This will free up $100 a month that can be used to pay off other creditors. Andrea and Will are also establishing an emergency fund so they will be better prepared for unforeseen life events that could happen in the future.

Most people do not set out to destroy their credit rating. Sometimes it is due to the folly of youth or carelessness. Sometimes early struggles to establish a livelihood, and unexpected illness, or unemployment (as in Andrea's case) can curtail your ability to pay your bills on time. Unfortunately, whether the reasons are understandable or foolish, bad credit is still bad credit. But you can do something about it. It is hard work to rebuild your credit rating, but it can be done, and it is well worth the effort.

Depending on how serious your past and present credit problems are, it may take time and patience to achieve good credit, but you don't need a "credit-repair" clinic to do it. Most charge a healthy fee, but that doesn't mean that they have any special tricks up their sleeves. There's nothing they can do for you that you can't do for yourself—for free. Just use the following tips:

- *Pay bills on time.* You can begin to improve your credit history immediately by making at least the minimum payments on time. Within a few months it will be obvious that you are managing your credit responsibilities better, and a new, stronger credit report will result.
- *Talk to your creditors.* Most creditors are willing to work with you to get the debt paid. If you have large medical bills, for example, you can arrange for a payment plan that will allow you to pay a reasonable amount each month, avoiding collection agencies and negative reports to credit bureaus.

- *Use credit sparingly.* A general rule of thumb is to spend no more than a third of your income on all debt, including mortgages, credit cards, and consumer loans. Try to use credit cards only for purchases that have long-term value, such as furniture, or for emergency situations, such as repairing a flat tire. Don't depend on credit cards for everyday frills like dining out or entertainment.
- *Pay more than the minimum required.* Minimum payments generally amount to a small percentage over the interest added to your account for the month. So if you only pay the minimum, you won't see your balances go down significantly. What you will see is that you end up paying a lot of money in interest charges. For example, if you have a card with an 18% interest rate, it will take you more than nine years to pay off a debt of $2,000 if you pay only the minimum balance due each month.

PLAN

Plan to pay off your debts: If you have significant debt from credit cards or other loans, follow the steps that follow to pay off your debt. Begin by reviewing the number of credit cards you are using, the interest rate of each, and the amount you pay annually for fees. Do the same with any loans you may have. Once you are armed with this information:

1. *Make a list of your outstanding debts.* Here's a case where knowledge is definitely power. The first step in trimming your debt is to figure out just how much you really owe. Include: educational loans, home improvement loans, checking account overdrafts, passbook loans, personal loans for insurance, taxes, or travel, rent-to-own agreements, and other installment purchases.

2. *Prioritize and decide which debts to pay first.* Sort your list in order by interest rate, putting the account with the highest interest rate at the top of the list. Start paying more than the monthly payment for debts at the top of the list, which have the highest rate of interest, then move down the list. If you have several accounts with smaller balances, you can choose

to pay off bills with the lowest balance due. This may not make the most financial sense, but it will help from a psychological sense as you will begin to see immediate progress. In either case, once you pay off a bill, add that monthly payment to the payment for the next creditor on your list.

3. *Shop around for credit cards and loans with the lowest interest rate.* Lower interest rates are available for good customers, but you have to request it. Ask your credit card company to consider lowering your rate. If not, then start shopping around for a card with a lower rate. Switching from a card with 21% interest to one with 14% could mean saving $50 or more per month, and you may be eligible for an even lower rate. If you decide to transfer your outstanding balance from a high-rate card to a low-rate card, ask the new bank to waive the transfer fees, and be sure the new card's low rate is for more than just a few months. Check www.bankrate.com for a list of credit cards with low interest rates.

A combined strategy of paying off your debt and developing an outstanding credit rating will put you in a solid position to maintain control of your finances. Streamlining your credit picture and making savvier purchasing decisions go hand-in-hand with developing a savings strategy that will maximize your wealth and improve your overall financial well-being. As you shift from paying off your debts to increasing your savings, you will find that you have stopped looking over your shoulder and are instead looking ahead. And with a solid savings plan, the future is bright, indeed!

In moving into the next step in building your financial support system, you will come to realize that you are not in this alone. As you begin to put your financial plan into action, you will want to develop a network of resources: a support system comprised of not just family and friends, but also community resources and professionals. Building this network starts with communicating about money—both talking and listening. When it comes to your personal finance conversations, you will discover that silence isn't always golden.

10

STAYING AHEAD OF SCAMMERS AND THIEVES

New scams surface more frequently these days, but attempts to defraud unsuspecting consumers are nothing new. Our great-grandparents were seduced by "snake-oil" salesmen and worthless "miracle" cures, unless they had been alerted to these deceitful practices. Today, thanks particularly to the Internet, scams and the risk of identity theft are becoming both commonplace and ever more sophisticated. According to the Better Business Bureau, the average identity fraud case costs consumers $6,383. While most banks and credit card companies offer protection against fraud, most consumers nevertheless end up footing the bill themselves, while they must take the time and spend their own money just to have the case investigated.[1]

Why Do We Fall for Fraud and Scams?

Scammers appeal to the best and the worst in each of us. Some appeal to our generosity, others to our desire to get rich quick. They know these ploys will work at least some of the time, and that is good enough for them to profit.

They also know that no one wants to be left out when the lottery jackpot is high and seems almost within reach. Sophisticated offers from all sorts of unsavory promotional companies and individuals arrive by telephone, email, and snail mail that are cleverly disguised to sound and look very real. Scammers seduce us into believing we actually have a chance to cash in, and we don't want to let what could be a "sure thing" slip away.

Our contemporary lifestyle itself makes us ripe for the picking. Sometimes we cave quickly just to end an annoying phone call and move on. At our hectic pace, we can easily be confused by scam artists or miss important details. Sometimes, though, we are victimized simply through intimidation or, even more sadly, through our natural tendency toward altruism—a chance to reach out, give to the needy, or be a good citizen.

Telephone and Internet con artists don't miss a trick, as explained all too clearly on a Web site called www.CrimesOfPersusaion.com. If you are solicited by Publishing Clearing House, for example, will you notice they don't have the name quite right? It's Publish*ers*, not Publish*ing*, but that particular ruse has fooled many already. If you get a call from the American Kidney Foundation, will it immediately register that the real organization is the American Kidney Fund? And how many people give to the American Cancer Center, which is not a bona fide charitable organization but a scam, thinking they are donating to the American Cancer Society?

Scams That Have Stood the Test of Time

HOME IMPROVEMENT SCAMS

Many of the worst scams involve predatory home improvement deals. Predatory lenders, sometimes working with contractors, strip owners of their home equity through a series of high-cost loans that consumers are all too often unable to repay. Or contractors hired directly by a homeowner disappear after taking the homeowner's money without making the repairs they agreed to make. If you are considering home improvement work, work only with a licensed contractor and be sure to check all the contractor's references.

CREDIT REPAIR SCAMS

Alleged credit-repair services claim the ability to erase bad marks from a consumer's credit history or to create a new credit identity, which is illegal. Do not believe such offers that poor credit can be magically wiped away. Credit repair companies can do nothing for consumers that consumers cannot do for themselves for little or no cost. The very act of correcting credit errors is a learning experience that everyone should have a direct hand in doing on their own should that become necessary. Do not be sucked into giving this task over completely to anyone who indicates "they'll take care of everything—not to worry."

TRAVEL AND VACATION SCHEMES

Travel clubs promise free travel certificates that come with steep, undisclosed costs. Or, as a novel twist, a vacation is offered (and actually awarded, sometimes) as a prize. However, the travel involves so many terms and conditions, it is more often than not rendered useless. That "dream vacation" is for the off-season only and includes no airfare. To make matters worse, the recipient of the "prize" has often been persuaded to pony up an "advance fee" of some sort to win the travel or vacation deal, and the fee or product purchase required generally exceeds the value of the prize or gift.

TELEMARKETING FRAUD

Many Americans have protected themselves against the talons of telemarketers by entering their phone numbers on the National Do Not Call Registry (www.donotcall.gov/). Still, for those not enrolled and for those whose aging parents or young adult children are not enrolled, it is worth the time to gain a better understanding of fraudulent telemarketing practices.

Telemarketing and legitimate survey research are not fraudulent practices. However, be aware that the telephone also is used to dupe the unsuspecting. Scam artists call to announce that you have just won a fabulous prize. (Of course they cannot release the prize to you until you pay the taxes and transfer fee, "that's the law—everything gets taxed, you know.") The first thing to remember is that your taxes are between you and the U.S. government. Yes, you must pay taxes on a lottery jackpot or sweepstakes prize, but you pay them directly to the government, not to anyone else. If you are asked to pay any amount up front, be very cautious: The gift or prize might be nonexistent or might never find its way to you. The telemarketer on your line is probably targeting you to collect the "fee" or "taxes" and will never be heard from again.

What if the offer you hear over the phone sounds legitimate and you want to go ahead with it. STOP and THINK! A legitimate "good deal" or "special offer" or request to "give to a charity" is not good for *you* if you a) cannot really afford it or b) are being pressured to decide quickly or to pay immediately. Ask instead for the caller to mail you a solicitation or offer, and tell the caller "you do not respond to telephone requests for money." If the call is fraudulent, expect to hear an abrupt dial tone. If it is legitimate, the caller will agree to your request.

Never give your credit card or bank account information to an unknown caller, and never send money in advance for an item you did not order or have not received. These con artists can make very attractive (but bogus) offers. If you have a high M (Money Value) score, you might initially want this "great deal or bargain." Or if the product or prize is just the item your high T (Tangible Value) heart needs to complete a favorite collection, you might be tempted but *resist the offer anyway*. Everyone is vulnerable to fraudulent telemarketers. Being aware of your Life Values Profile can help make you less so.

BUSINESS SCAMS

Some scam artists target businesses with phony billings or sell substandard office products. Always check credentials and references before you switch vendors. Ask all callers who target businesses with requests for donations to charities or upcoming civic events to put their requests in writing. Large corporations generally have their advertising/donation budgets planned for the year and simply decline these offers, so small businesses are more at risk. Does the charity actually exist? Is the civic event really scheduled to take place in your area? Can you see a copy of the program or flyer from previous years? Again, if you are asked to decide in a hurry, just say no.

SWEEPSTAKES

Probably the best way to fall prey to a scam is to make a habit of entering sweepstakes. Some are legitimate, but still they are huge money-making machines, collecting far more entries than you might ever believe. In fact, the odds of winning any major sweepstakes prize are said to be 1 in 50,000,000.

When you enter a sweepstakes, do you feel obligated to purchase a product? Many consumers are unaware that the U.S. Supreme Court has made it illegal to require a purchase to be entered in a sweepstakes. Would making the purchase improve your odds of winning, though? Publishers Clearing House claims that 23 of their 30 millionaire winners did *not* order a magazine with their entry.[2]

And how tempting is that non-negotiable check you find in the envelope, made out to you, suggesting you might have won $500,000? Actually, sweepstakes companies are prohibited from mailing those non-negotiable checks unless you have actually won a prize, so that "check" might be your first indication you are dealing with a fraud.

Getting into the habit of entering sweepstakes is dangerous, but, when the sweepstakes is combined with fraudulent telemarketing, things can get dicey. If a great offer comes by phone when you least expect it and is promoted by a highly trained, skilled persuader, you become much more susceptible to the con.

As in any telemarketing scam described here, the caller is usually calling to inform you that you have won a prize. Don't even consider investing in this scam. Chances are very good there is no prize whatsoever. Even the product you're ordering is likely to be inferior or never show up. The company itself might be bogus. This caller could very well be simply collecting checks in a postal box and getting rich by duping hopeful individuals.

It gets even worse, though. The con artist might ask for your credit card information because the company is offering a special gift for those willing to pay immediately, over the phone. This can be tricky because some bona fide fund raising companies do make such legitimate offers at times and actually do send the free gift. How will you know whether to give out your credit card information? The rules are simple: If you have *any* doubt at all, don't do it. And if you feel pressured or hurried in any way, don't do it.

Recovery/Reload Scams

That term might sound unfamiliar, but if you have entered numerous sweepstakes and never won a big prize, investing a small fortune and left feeling like a loser, you've probably heard from a reload scam artist. These are the best of the best telemarketing cons, and they're out to take advantage of your embarrassment, frustration, or even desperation. *They track the results of previous sweepstakes scams, so they know exactly how much you have spent in fruitless attempts to win a major prize.* As far as they're concerned, you are ready for a real trip to the cleaners. In fact, they even refer to you as a "mooch."

You will get a call advising you that, since you've been a faithful player or purchaser, you are now eligible for an "executive prize," or perhaps your name has advanced to the "winners' circle." All you need to do is make one more purchase, and this time you really will be a winner. This call will probably be recorded, and the con artist will get you to admit that you are sending money to buy a product, not to qualify for a prize; this will protect the scammer if you decide to take him to court in the future.

People who enter these contests repeatedly often win small, enticing prizes to keep them on the hook. They are gambling on the big win and, like any other form of gambling, this can become addictive. If the subject lives alone and has little social contact and no real support system, such behavior can actually become a kind of social life. For elderly people who have gradually frittered away their savings, with no chance of recouping it, the need to keep going and win big becomes a matter of pride or desperation. How pleasant, then, to receive the "reloading" call, which promises that this is the last purchase you'll have to make before your ship comes in! Ninety percent of such fraudulent calls are made to people over the age of 70!

Fraudulent Telefunding for "Charity"

Every day bona fide charities call citizens to solicit donations or assistance with fund raising. It is sometimes difficult, then, to recognize a bogus request for a "charitable donation." Even worse, such canvassing can take a third form: the hired fund raising company that truly is raising funds for a good cause, although little of the money they collect will go to that cause. So a savvy consumer, especially one with a high S or P score (likely to fall prey on the basis of a strong social conscience or strong personal ideals) must first distinguish among the three types of calls and also consider whether contributing is in his or her best interests at this time. Again, the best course is to ask the caller to mail you a solicitation form or donation request—unless you are very sure that the call and caller are completely legitimate. *Be aware though, that sometimes your "State Troopers" or other calls for help from familiar "civic organizations" or other "authorities" are really trick calls.*

- If you are sure this is a bona fide charity conducting a well-known fund raiser (e.g. the March of Dimes "Mother's March"), your decision must be based on how well that request matches your current financial posture and long-term financial goals.
- If you are not sure whether this is a legitimate cause, you can either end the conversation (with no need for future remorse) or get enough information to verify the caller's authenticity and, perhaps, report a scam.
- If you are confident of the legitimacy of the campaign and that it really gives its proceeds to a good cause, first decide whether it is a good match for you. Then ask the caller what percentage of your donation will go to the firefighters or police or homeless children. While the caller is not obligated to disclose those figures, he or she is required to tell you *where* you can get that information.

POINT TO PONDER

SMART GIVING

If you plan to donate to charity, it is advisable not to leave this altruistic behavior to chance. Make charitable donations a part of your long-term and short-term planning. Choose your charities and stick with them. And realize that when someone calls or knocks on your door to ask for a donation, no matter how good the cause or persuasive the solicitor, this is your money being requested. You need feel no guilt about saying "No," and don't feel a need to explain. Be proactive in every aspect of your financial oversight.

These offers usually come by postal mail or email (more of that unwanted spam). They offer you an opportunity to try a product and keep it if you will simply give them some feedback about how you liked it. Or, they offer you an opportunity to eat at all the finest restaurants in your area and get reimbursed for all or part of your expense, if you just file a little report afterward. Some of these offers are legitimate; most are not. Be especially wary of the offers that require you to join a "mystery shoppers club" or in some other way pay dues or send money in advance. Even with legitimate mystery shopping (which some consumers actually enjoy and feel has benefited them), you will have an obligation to file reports, sometimes extensive, time-consuming reports. Know what you are getting into and never send money in advance.

The Newer, "Improved" Scams

SPAM SCAMS

These are Internet offers that come to us through email. Every day we are besieged with several offers for miracle drugs, fake watches, even fortunes from war-torn countries. You know the kind: a poorly written email message from some hapless citizen of a foreign nation, struggling nobly to write in English because he/she has been left holding a fortune overseas and there is solid evidence that you are entitled to a big share of it. You are asked to kindly provide your bank account information so said foreign benefactor can deposit your fortune for you. A word of advice: Do not open these emails or follow any links, no matter how innocent or enticing they appear—just hit DELETE.

IMPERSONATING A GOVERNMENT OFFICIAL

If you receive notice of a windfall or prize being held in your name and it comes from an official sounding source, check it out before responding. Organizations that have successfully bilked people out of bogus "taxes," "duties," and other advance fees include "Internal Monitoring Services," "Cash Awards Bureau," and "U.S. Entitlement Services." Find out whether such a government agency exists before trusting them.

MISREPRESENTING A CONSUMER ASSISTANCE ORGANIZATION

Some of the most pathetic and dangerous scammers actually pretend to be working on your behalf. Two that come to mind are HELP which stands for Help Elderly Live Protected and SCAT: Senior Citizens Against Telemarketing. Both are fraudulent, but either one might easily fool a senior citizen into a very expensive trusting relationship.

FOREIGN LOTTERY OFFERS

If you are invited to join an exclusive, can't-lose lottery organization that will provide you with numbers most likely to win a foreign lottery (for a fat upfront membership fee on your part, of course), you need know only one thing: It's against the law for anyone to sell tickets for a foreign lottery in the U.S. Forget it!

AFFINITY INVESTMENT FRAUD

This type of fraud preys on identifiable social groups that usually have strong bonds of trust and respect: religious groups, ethnic communities, professional membership organizations, or senior citizens. The con artist often convinces a respected leader of the group to embrace the fraud, which appears to be legitimate, who then recruits other members of the group to get behind the effort, i.e., invest their money too. Because the group is tight-knit and probably based on long-term relationships, it is easy for them to convince each other to put their money on the line.

To safeguard yourself from such fraudulent investment, do not take the word of even the most respected and trustworthy member of your group unless you can verify all the information independently. If your friend makes the deal sound good, remember that someone made the same deal sound good to him or her; anyone can be fooled, especially the good-hearted. And remember the old saw: If it sounds too good to be true, it probably is. No investment is without risk; be extremely wary of "guaranteed" returns or "can't-lose" schemes. Never invest unless the particulars are presented to you in writing, and be very suspicious of any "secret" deals you're asked to keep under your hat. Avoid the promise of "once-in-a-lifetime" deals, especially if they seem to be hush-hush.

Identity theft is a serious crime, and it's growing at an exponential rate. Identity thieves are also growing more sophisticated and can get your private information through a variety of sources, from hacking into secure databases or through forays in your trash, among other methods. You can avert problems by shredding your trash and closely guarding your social security number. No matter how careful you are, consider this: Four out of five victims have no idea how an identity thief obtained their personal information. And once they get this information, identity thieves frequently open new accounts in your name and change your address to avoid detection. They apply for new credit cards using your information, make charges, and leave the bills unpaid. People whose identities have been stolen can spend months or years—and thousands of dollars—cleaning up the mess thieves have made of their good name and credit record. Some consumer protection agencies, most notably the nonprofit Consumers Union, publisher of *Consumer Reports*, are lobbying Congress to pass a federal law permitting citizens in any state who suspect their credit information has been compromised to freeze their credit files quickly, before identity theft has occurred.

If you think your identity has been stolen, take the following steps.

- Contact the fraud departments of any one of the three major credit bureaus to place a fraud alert on your credit file. (See also Chapter 19, "Finding the Help You Need," for helpful resources and check out the Internet list in the Appendix, "Personal Finance Education Internet Sites.") The fraud alert requests creditors to contact you before opening any new accounts or making any changes to your existing accounts. As soon as the credit bureau confirms your fraud alert, the other two credit bureaus will automatically be notified to also place fraud alerts, and all three credit reports will be sent to you free of charge.
- Immediately close the accounts that you know or believe have been tampered with or opened fraudulently.
- File a police report. Get a copy of the report to submit to your creditors and others that may require proof of the crime.
- File your complaint with the Federal Trade Commission (FTC). The FTC maintains a database of identity theft cases used by law

enforcement agencies for investigations. Filing a complaint will help them learn more about identity theft and the problems victims face so that they can better assist you. Visit www.consumer.gov/idtheft/ for more information and other tips on protecting yourself from identity theft.

Is Anyone Looking Out for Your Interests?

To avoid the ever-growing plethora of scams, we must become our own investigative reporters. We have to ask the tough questions and do our homework. However, we do have allies in the Federal Trade Commission, the Better Business Bureau, the Securities and Exchange Commission, and many other organizations. The Better Business Bureau (BBB) has tips to help consumers avoid scams and unscrupulous deals. While we have touched upon many of them already, you cannot be too careful, so we summarize this important information for you in the following section.

BE AN EDUCATED CONSUMER: KNOW THE DANGER SIGNALS OF SCAMS

(Adapted from the Better Business Bureau)

Be alert for these red flags:

- A deal that sounds much better than any being advertised by firms you know to be legitimate—offers that are "too good to be true."

- A promoter who is not based locally, provides no telephone number, and uses a PO box or mail drop, rather than a full street address.

- A promoter name and/or logo that closely mimics that of a respected brand or business.

- Pressure words, such as "urgent" or "final deadline," sprinkled throughout the sales literature.

- Pressure, threats, or harassment, either in writing, during a phone call, in an email message, or in a personal contact.

- Immediate request or demand for a check, money order, or cash to be picked up by a courier or to be sent to a mail drop or PO box.
- Vague answers or none at all to key questions you ask about the offer.
- Insistence that you finalize a deal orally or provide personal financial information (such as your social security number or credit card number), without a written contract or other documentation in writing.

Protect yourself with the following tips:

- Take your time deciding; be firm in the face of pressure.
- Protect your privacy. Provide personal information only if you know who's collecting it, why, and how it's being used.
- Read before you sign. Fully understand the contract, and make sure it matches what the salesperson told you.
- Don't believe it just because you saw it on the Internet. Obtain the company's physical address and phone number and check the company out with your Better Business Bureau.
- If asked to purchase goods sight unseen, compare the prices and warranties with those offered by local firms. Remember that you run a risk of getting inferior merchandise when you order products from unfamiliar businesses without being able to inspect them first.

For more information on how to protect yourself from schemes, scams, and fraud contact your local Better Business Bureau (www.bbb.org).

In addition to the Federal Trade Commission (FTC) and the Better Business Bureau, the Securities and Exchange Commission (SEC) is also at work to protect consumers from fraud. The stated mission of the SEC is to protect investors, maintain fair, orderly, and efficient markets, and facilitate capital formation. To that end the SEC maintains an Office of Investor Education and Assistance as well as a Web site filled with information and advice: www.sec.gov. That office invites reports of suspected email scams. Simply forward the suspicious email, without responding to it, to www.enforcement@sec.gov. Another site serves people who feel they have already been victimized by a fraudster: www.sec.gov/complaint. Recognizing the particular vulnerability of seniors, on July 17, 2006, the SEC hosted its first-ever Seniors Summit to examine how regulators and others can better coordinate efforts to protect older Americans from investment fraud and abusive sales practices.

Finally, in addition to the wealth of resources we provide in Chapter 19 and in the Appendix, any consumer who wants to know more about fraudulent practices and how to protect against them can visit the Consumers Union Web site at www.consumersunion.org. As you navigate the shark-infested waters of saving, spending, and investing, remember that it is your own responsibility to safeguard your wealth and your good name. Your Life Values Profile will help you identify your likely areas of vulnerability so that you never fall victim to scams and frauds.

11

COMMITTING TO A
SAVINGS PLAN

While looking through an adult education catalog, we discovered that out of eight course offerings in personal finance, only one included learning how to save.[1] Does this mean Americans know most of what there is to know about saving? Or is there not wide enough interest in the topic?

A study of rates of personal saving across nations might be indicating a lack of interest in the U.S. The amount of money that Americans saved each year recently dipped below 1% of their annual income. However, the Japanese, on average, saved 6.5%, Germans, 10.6%, and the French, 11.4%.[2] Should we be concerned about this?

If you consider the current trend toward personal responsibility in retirement planning and the uncertain state of Social Security, the answer is definitely "yes." And if the reality facing many mid-life adults is any indication, we can no longer afford to have a cavalier attitude toward savings. People are living longer: Today, a 65-year-old can expect to live to about age 82 ½ and by 2070, life expectancy at age 65 is projected to be 85 ½ years.[3] We see the evidence of this longevity everywhere. You might have noticed it in your own family. Many Americans approaching retirement themselves have aging parents who could one day need their financial assistance. Helping out can be an enriching social and familial experience, but in some families, when older parents outlive their retirement assets, difficulties for all involved can also result.

By sheer force of numbers, as the Baby Boomer generation is aging, many longstanding assumptions are also being challenged. Bald is beautiful, and you can actually trust people over 30 and even over 40. Celebrity figures such as model Lauren Hutton (62), actor Morgan Freeman (69), and actress Susan Sarandon (59) provide uplifting evidence for anyone who is worried about aging that maturity and experience are attractive. So most of these assumptions are positive; but some of them are not.

Boomers, unfortunately, have proved by their miscalculations that to neglect careful saving and planning ahead is not without consequences. Only about one-quarter of the Baby Boom generation has saved responsibly and is ready for retirement from the workforce. The remaining three-quarters are alarmingly unprepared for retirement, and many are planning to work through their later years.[4] No problem, if that is what is *desired*. The lesson is that we cannot afford any longer to live just for the moment. We must start thinking more clearly about our tomorrows too, so that whether we stay longer in the workforce, or enjoy more leisure during later life, is a matter of personal *choice*, not need.

When "Trouble" Is Our Teacher

For some people, "trouble" might be the only teacher they actually listen to where saving money is concerned. Not the trouble they are warned about in the financial news and by friends, or financial advisors and educators, but the trouble they encounter first hand. Others might remind them that they need to save more, spend less, budget, or learn how to invest for the future, but they prefer to think more pleasant thoughts and ignore the warnings about rainy days or illness or the possibility of a lost job or derailed career. Then the unthinkable happens, and trouble steps in to become their teacher. Here is what happened to Anne:

Anne was an actress who never made the big time but enjoyed steady employment until she turned almost fifty. Bouncy and fun-loving, she was not prepared for the day she was sent home because she was "too old" for a part in a commercial. As casting rejections became more frequent and the income declined, Anne realized she was in for some major life changes. She returned to the nursing career she had abandoned for acting and moved in with other student nurses. In addition to a mid-life career change, however, Anne had another important priority to face: learning to manage her financial well-being.

With drastically reduced income, plenty of debt, no savings or health coverage, school loans added to her financial load and her anguish about living on the edge. She made it, but her struggle to re-establish herself took nearly a decade. At age 58, she was finally free from debt, able to afford her own small home, and had started an IRA. Why, she wondered, had it taken her so long to arrive at a place of financial stability? What income security could she possibly build for her approaching retirement years? Would she be able to retire at all?

The good news is that everyone can look at this example as a call to action—to return to the basics and save now for future needs. To do this, we have to understand where our apathy comes from and then move from inaction to action. We must move from a grudging attitude toward savings to a more positive one. In Anne's case, she loves nursing, and her sunny disposition will serve her well during what promises to be an extended second career. While she is already blessed with a positive outlook, she has learned as well to appreciate her newfound ability to save for future uncertainty.

It Is All About Attitude

The concept of saving money is actually quite simple: *Spend less than you make.* We all inherently know this. So why does it prove to be so elusive for so many? Why are Americans so bad at saving our money?

The quick answer, the one that pops into everyone's mind right away, is that they would love to save more, but their expenses are too high. After the bills are paid, they have nothing left over. But a more complicated answer may lie in our lifestyles. Have you ever noticed that no matter how much salary you earn, once you get a raise, your expenses go up as well? As our incomes increase, we typically use the extra money to buy things we want or believe we need. We live our financial lives for the moment, often worrying about paying our bills, providing for our families, and feeding our various cravings. While we do not come right out and say it, we are following the example of Scarlet O'Hara in the classic, *Gone with the Wind*: "Fiddle-dee-dee, tomorrow is another day."

It is this attitude that can have us in the red instead of in the black when retirement comes around. Where does this attitude come from? There are many issues that influence our money-saving mindset. One of these influences, of course, is the way our consumer-driven society encourages us to spend our money. Through advertisements that show people enjoying new cars, tropical vacations, and lavish homes, we become convinced that happiness is a late-model mini van or a week in the south of France. However, these outside influences—marketing and peer pressure—are only part of the picture. There are other, more personal reasons why people choose to spend rather than save. The first step to achieving a positive money-saving mindset is *to uncover the real reason why you spend as much, or more money than you make.*

Many spending habits can be traced to behaviors ingrained in childhood. If spending money freely without a disciplined saving strategy was typical in your family, you may have just never learned solid money-managing skills. Or you may have grown up in a family where money was tight and luxuries were few. You may have vowed, as Scarlet O'Hara did, never to go without nice things again. Your childhood experiences might have led you to personal values focused on tangible things, and you now have a high T score on the Life Values Profile. So often, despite our best intentions, a variety of personal and emotional obstacles can get in the way of making sound financial decisions.

But we cannot blame parents, siblings, or childhood experiences for our own inability to live within our means and to save. Instead, we must leave our childhood baggage at the door and take responsibility for our own financial future. It can be difficult to deal with emotions and temptations that affect your financial decisions, but when you deal with these feelings, you will soon discover and begin to understand the real reasons that you avoid saving.

There are three underlying reasons behind our resistance to developing a savings attitude. Once you do the soul searching, you will likely find that, for you, it is one or a combination, of the following:

- You just do not get it. You find finance and money matters confusing and alien, you have convinced yourself that you just aren't good with numbers, or you cannot be bothered—tomorrow will take care of itself. You have a low M (Money) score.
- You are confused about needs and wants, from a material perspective. You are convinced that you *need* that new high-definition TV or that European vacation. You have earned this or that pleasure and beauty in your life. You have a high T (Tangible) score.
- You know what you want out of life—to educate your children, take care of your parents' needs when they are older, travel with your partner during later life—and you are pretty certain that it will all fall into place, at least that is what you are praying for. Your S (Social) and P (Personal) scores may dominate, but your M (Money) score may not be very high.

Once you understand your motivations, you can decide if they are still serving you or if it is time to adjust your behaviors and take ownership of your financial future by getting back to basics and learning how to save.

Goals—The Perfect Attitude Adjuster

Change is 80% attitude and 20% action. The best way to change your attitude is to break through resistance and discover a reason you want to change. Your dreams can be your first big step to developing a positive savings attitude.

DAYDREAM

We all have fantasies where we win $20 million in a lottery. In these fantasies we quit our jobs, travel, set up charitable foundations, and spend, spend, spend. Of course, these fantasies are relatively short-lived since we know that it is unlikely to happen. But even without the $20 million, what do you want out of life?

Daydream constructively and spend some time fantasizing about where you see yourself at various stages in your life: turning 30, 40, 50, or 65 or when your children turn 18 and are ready to head out into the world. When do you want to stop working, or maybe you envision a career change? In this exercise, you're limited only by what you can imagine—certainly not by age anymore!

Your goals are your dreams defined, and they are often driven by your Life Values. When do you want to retire, and what does retirement mean to you? Are you just starting out and planning to have a family or buy a home? Do you have children and want to be able to pay for a wedding or college or help them get started on the fulfillment of their own dreams?

Defining goals makes them more real and concrete, which can have a powerful influence on changing your behavior. Doing this *requires* you to daydream and to create a plan of action defined by time and money. Based on when you want to achieve your goals, break them down into three types: short, medium, and long-term goals. Now comes the challenging part. You need to assign a dollar value to each of your goals. If they are short-term goals—for example, if you would like to buy a house in the next year—how much will you need to save to achieve that goal? By looking at real estate prices in your area and investigating how much of a down payment you will need, you can come up with a realistic picture. Defining your goals in this way will put you on the path of achieving them. You can literally make your *daydreams* come true. Remember the example of Janet in Chapter 5, "Moving to Secure Money Management," who wrote down her goals and carried them with her. Pen and paper is not the same as etched in stone. Just as your Life Values can change, your goals can change over time, so don't be afraid to change them if you need to. Set a date to review your goals regularly, at least every few years or as you experience major life changes.

Education—You Can Never Be Too Smart

We talked earlier about learning as a method of breaking free from the trap of being uncomfortable with numbers. Education can also be your key when it comes to developing a savings plan, including helping to make sure that you have laid out your goals in a realistic way. There is a wealth of information to be gleaned by reading the financial pages in the newspaper, watching a financial news show on television, or reading a personal finance magazine. Remember, the first two steps in achieving financial health are developing a positive attitude and actively engaging in your own financial affairs.

Consider taking a workshop or a class or even consider taking several courses. Employers, faith-based organizations, and your local YMCA offer brown bag seminars and workshops on personal finance at little or no cost. Some of these require very little time commitment as well—usually a lunch hour or an evening out. For more in-depth classes, look to your local adult education center or community college for courses in personal finance, wealth building, or investing.

To activate the third essential quality for personal financial health, the ability to reach out to a network of supportive resources, think about hiring a fee-based financial planner. These are planners who earn their income from the fees they charge, not from broker's commissions. In other words, their financial stake is in you, not an investment product. They tend to have a broader base of knowledge, and they can be very helpful in guiding you through the maze of financial decisions that you must make to become financially secure. They can be especially effective at helping you to quantify and acid-test your goals.

Education will not only make you a smarter saver, but, as we discussed in Chapter 3, "How We Decide," learning increases your confidence and enjoyment as well. Not a bad bonus!

Analyze Your Expenses

Of course, in order to start saving, you need to have money to save. Guess what? You already have it. The trick is to look at what you're spending and figure out what you can trim or cut out altogether.

Keep an expense diary and write down all of your expenses every day for one month. Record every purchase, even every cup of coffee. During this time, make no effort to change your spending habits, just write it all down. Carrying a notebook is key. If you rely on memory or cleaning out your wallet every night or week, you may misreport or miss some expenditures altogether, especially those without receipts. Also make sure to include credit and debit card charges. At the end of the month, transfer your expenses to a chart summarizing each expense by type. Avoid being too general—try not to lump incidental expenses into "miscellaneous." Instead, use categories that are relevant to you—mortgage/rent, utilities, cable TV, food, entertainment (such as movies or dining out), insurance, donations—you get the idea. Then multiply that by 12 to get your annual costs for these items. Add to the list those expenses that you only incur once or twice a year that may have fallen outside your sample month.

You now have a reasonably accurate list of your annual expenses. Are you surprised by what you see? Most people are.

Go through this list carefully, and now armed with the savvy shopping skills we explored in the last chapter—part of becoming engaged and active in your financial affairs—look at whether these expenses are "needs" or "wants." If they are truly needs, ask yourself if the amount is practical or if there is some way to economize, perhaps by shopping at an outlet or waiting for sales? If they are wants, are you making savvy choices or indulging in random whims? Look at your wants in detail. It may seem innocent to go to the movies once a week, but what if you are also dining out twice a week and regularly buying books and CDs? Cutting down your wants will reduce your expenses, freeing up more cash to add to your savings. If you think about it, is it really worth seeing the new blockbuster release weekly in the theater (as opposed to renting it six months later when it comes out on DVD) if, instead, it means that you can tour Asia later with money you have saved to have that or another daydream come true?

It does not have to hurt. Some of your cost-saving measures can be relatively minor but will still add up in a big way. Take the case of Deborah, who regularly stopped at a local coffee shop to purchase a cup of coffee and a muffin for $4.95 every morning on her way to work.

When Deborah began tracking her expenses, she realized that having coffee and a muffin every morning added up to quite an expense—more than $1,200 a year. Looking at her habits in this new light helped Deborah realize that by simply giving up her daily coffee and muffin she could move that much closer to her savings goals.

Developing a Spending Plan—The B-Word—As Part of an Overall Savings Strategy

Throughout this book, we have been looking at financial planning through the lens of our individual values. By marrying our Life Values with our financial behavior, it becomes apparent that personal finance is, indeed, personal. By making choices that are in line with our Life Values, we can work toward our goals in a constructive way.

Now that you have defined your goals and have a clear picture of your expenses, you can turn to developing a spending plan. If it sounds like a budget, you are right. But it's really a "budget-plus."

Most people are reluctant to set a budget because they don't want to confine themselves; they get claustrophobic thinking about the restrictive aspect of a budget that encourages simply cutting down expenses. A spending plan, on the other hand, is a financial road map that will help you reach your savings objectives. The purpose of a spending plan is to see clearly where your money is coming from and exactly where you would like it to go. It will help you not only anticipate expenses and guide your spending, but also meet your savings goals.

Using a spending plan worksheet or a computerized spreadsheet program, such as Excel, record your monthly income, targeted expenses, and how much you will set aside to meet your savings goals. When recording your expenses, use the insight you gained from the tracking exercise to make any necessary adjustments. Your total income needs to equal your total expenses and savings, so you may have to do a bit of juggling to get the numbers to work out. But when you are done, you will have a realistic and workable plan.

Don't just file this away. Your spending plan needs to be a living document. By tacking it onto the refrigerator or placing it in your daily planner, it will be easy to refer to it regularly. Also use it to try to uncover more opportunities to cut back expenses and save. This may be a hard process at first, but you will find as you regularly review your spending plan that you are actually meeting these goals. What better incentive could there be for sticking with your plan?

Your Home as Your Savings

Many Americans who are fortunate enough to be homeowners regard their *homes* as their real source of savings. They build up equity with regular monthly payments and sometimes watch home values grow with little or no effort on their part. During times of price appreciation, some homeowners have been able to get a "jump" on accumulating savings for unforeseen circumstances, or for education, or retirement, by borrowing home equity and moving the proceeds into accounts where their money could be accessed when needed. If you regard your home as your *real* savings but left your equity untouched during the price appreciation of the recent past, take heart. It is not necessarily gone forever.

Like all markets, the housing market fluctuates. With the housing market, however, history teaches a lesson that most of us must keep relearning: Home prices are likely to rise over time regardless of how high we think they are today or how low they may drop temporarily. Yes, a temporary drop can last for a few years, but our homes are not like the Capital Market. We live with our family in our housing investment, maintain forced savings through ordinary living expenses, control the daily management of our equity, and we can almost always look forward to the day when a "down" market is finally over.

A "correction" in rising housing prices that reduces your ability to use home equity also gives you the opportunity to begin accumulating savings from other sources. Everyone needs to develop the habit of spending less than they make, find other ways to create additional earnings, and/or save the maximum allowable in retirement and health care saving plans. We all must also learn another very valuable financial life lesson: *We need to commit to a saving plan that is not exclusively tied to our housing.*

Compound Interest

As you begin saving money, you will want to find ways to make the most of your savings. Putting money into an account that bears compound interest is an easy, hassle-free method to make your money grow.

Albert Einstein reportedly once called compound interest "the greatest mathematical discovery of all time," according to several sources,[5] but this quote appeared enough years after the great scientist died to raise questions as to whether he really said it. Whether he said it or not, you don't need to be an Einstein to understand the magic of compound interest. When you save money at a financial institution, interest is added to your savings at regular intervals. The interest is added to the balance in your savings account, and you then start earning interest on your interest, as well as on amounts you continue to deposit as savings. This mushrooming effect, compound interest, has an exponential result—the earlier you start saving, the more time there is for compound interest to take effect. Over long periods of time, regular saving of even small amounts can build up to large sums of money.

Compound interest is the guiding principle behind not just basic savings accounts. This principle also underlies retirement savings, health savings, college education savings and other investment vehicles which offer compound rates of interest. By understanding how compound interest works in your favor, you learn how to compare savings vehicles, including tax-deferred savings at even higher rates of return. By understanding how the compounding effects of interest work in favor of your lenders, you will grow very motivated to shave years off your mortgage, whittle away your credit card and other debt over time, and learn how to grow your investment portfolio instead. These are subjects you will eagerly take on once you flip your attitude to the positive side of saving to achieve your financial goals.

So far, we have discussed the importance of developing a positive attitude toward personal finance in achieving your goals. We have also looked at how to stay positive and active in your financial affairs, even if you haven't felt very positive in the past, and even if you have been blocked by fear. You can use your adjusted attitude to commit to a serious personal saving plan, and pretty soon you will start to enjoy watching your savings grow.

As you have discovered, the key to financial competence lies in the dual understanding of both financial knowledge and your own Life Values. There is no magic formula. Financial fitness is achieved by using the synergy between your knowledge and values to turn your dreams into reality. We explore this relationship further in the coming sections as we continue with the steps needed to develop financial independence and control, starting with Step Three: Building a Financial Support System.

Part III

BUILDING A FINANCIAL
SUPPORT SYSTEM

12

COMMUNICATING ABOUT MONEY— COUNT THE WAYS

T here is an axiom in newspaper writing that the seeds of the ending are in the beginning. The idea is to let readers know early on what the story is about so they won't be disappointed at the end. We can use this same guidance for relating to others, in what we say to them and how we interpret what is being said to us. If we communicate our expectations clearly and listen carefully to what others are saying to us, we can save ourselves a lot of disappointment later.

A personal finance student shared with class members this experience about the consequences of poor communications at work. Tim was employed by a well-known firm for 28 years before he was asked to take early retirement at age 57. His polite farewells covered up his surprise and anger over the "puny" retirement benefits he was due to receive. Tim's retirement *from* the company, though, had followed the pattern of his employment *with* the company: satisfying work, strong friendships with coworkers, nods of approval from superiors, and avoidance of any discussions related to money. Tim had never inquired about a promotion, training, or transfer to increase his income. He had never consulted with the Human Resources department to go over his benefits package, and he had not voiced his frustration at having to use his own vehicle for company business without reimbursement.

Tim ignored outreach attempts by company benefits educators to update him on the performance of his retirement portfolio. He tossed the forms he was given to estimate his income needs during later life. For Tim, all things related to his finances were better left unaddressed, unsaid, and avoided altogether. He passively expected "everything to turn out all right" by the time he was ready to retire at some unspecified age. His supervisors had no idea he felt underpaid, and the HR director assumed he was at ease with his benefits explanations. No one was aware of the extent that Tim used his personal vehicle for the company's benefit, so, of course, he received no reimbursement.

Tim left the company feeling that he had never achieved the level of compensation he deserved. His later reflections, however, about what had gone wrong all those years finally taught him late—*but not too late*—how to communicate (and to do so with less and less discomfort). First, he enrolled in a post-retirement Life Planning Seminar, and several of the exercises were all about communication—with his ex-colleagues, his spouse, parents, and children, with financial advisors and later life career consultants. Then he practiced communicating every chance he could. Tim hated it all at first, but he soon realized that he had no choice but to learn how to reach out and interact with the myriad numbers of social contacts he needed to adapt proactively (and productively) to his new daily routine. What can Tim's story teach us?

So far, we have discovered that:

- With a positive attitude we can take charge of our life and become competent in all of our financial affairs.
- Successful financial management involves waking ourselves up to what is going on at home, at work, in the neighborhood, the nation, and the world.
- We make choices about our financial life every day, *and failing to choose is a choice in itself.*
- Our financial decisions are much less about money than we had ever imagined.
- The new emphasis is on "personal responsibility." No one is watching out for our interests today—not the government, not our employer, not our banker, broker, hairdresser or bartender.

Here is the next thing to remember: Unless we speak up and let our needs be known, like Tim we will be understandably ignored, perhaps until it really is too late. Be particularly concerned about your need to communicate well as a parent, partner, employee or colleague, and especially as a consumer today because *it can mean the difference between life and death.* If Tim had fallen ill suddenly and his failure to communicate was with health care providers, instead of his employer, heaven help him.

The Three R's and the All-Important "C"

How did we become a society of communication wimps? Were we born that way? Or did it happen somehow along the way? If you find it difficult to communicate with others comfortably or to ask for help with what you want or need, these might be some of the reasons:

- When we are children, we are taught to "be seen and not heard."
- Many teachers reward conformity, not curiosity, and call that "good behavior."
- Many employers also reward conformity and call conformers "good employees."
- Our culture conditions us to "go it alone" and to "look out for number one."
- We admire the "strong, silent hero."
- Complainers do not top our popularity lists.
- Questioning "authority" can get us into big trouble.
- Criticizing "authority" can get us into even bigger trouble.
- At least half of the time, we do not know how or to whom we should complain.
- We may be afraid that speaking up to someone will offend her or him, and we do not want that person to dislike us.
- Or we may have learned that speaking up is just a waste of time.

Although American independence is part of our national heritage, we have done our citizens no favors by teaching them reading, writing, and arithmetic, but ignoring the one skill we need above all to really succeed in life: communication.

We established our nation on the ideals of freedom, independence, and self-sufficiency, but these ideals do not mean that we must go it alone. Looking to our example of those who live long, happy, and healthy lives, we find they grasped this idea and actively reached out to others by building a strong social support system. You can bet that they did this primarily by talking, sharing, and listening closely to what others had to say.

Communicating and Interacting About Money

The first step is honing your communication skills, which you can do at any age or life stage. All it takes is practice, practice, practice, practice, practice until you finally feel comfortable. How important is this skill? Communicating our expectations about money was always an important issue. Today it is the critical factor in becoming financially competent and improving our future well-being and the well-being of those we love. It involves:

- Speaking up about our needs and wants.
- Requiring clarification of contract "terms and conditions" that we deserve to know up front *before* we sign.
- Clearly expressing our expectations and preferences.
- Requesting assistance through verbal and written means.
- Registering our protest of questionable "authority" no matter how scary it seems to us. (Our Constitution guarantees us this right.)

These are all examples of expressive communication. Just like Tim, however, many individuals hesitate or refuse to express themselves, especially where money is concerned. Incredibly, they also believe everything will turn out all right in the end—without any (or little) effort on their part.

In fact, a majority of workers (55%) believe they are behind schedule when it comes to planning and saving for retirement, according to the *2006 Retirement Confidence Survey* recently released by the Employee Benefit Research Institute (EBRI) and the American Savings Education Council (ASEC). Almost 70% of workers have saved for retirement, but many have saved less than $25,000.[1] Yet most workers surveyed who expect to retire within 15 years say they, "hope to travel, pursue a broad range of interests, visit children, and give presents to grandchildren after retirement." This is not just optimism; it is magical thinking![2]

All communication, including communicating about finances, is also about:

- Receiving and deciphering messages.
- Reading with comprehension the contracts and agreements of the marketplace.
- Learning the vocabulary of credit and investment.
- Accepting and applying the advice of trusted professionals.
- More personally, encouraging and listening to loved ones talk about their feelings about financial matters.

Finally, let us remember to monitor that all-important self-talk: the tape that plays in our heads all day and sometimes throughout the night. What we tell ourselves about our worth, psychological or material, colors every emotion we feel and every action we take. Thinking to ourselves about our ability or inability to pay bills, our wisdom or naïveté concerning investments, and even our failure to ask for explanations measures how good we are at financial communication. The upside, however, is this: We can get good at it! And learning to get better at communicating about money is crucial for us all—to build our self-respect and to improve our present and future financial well-being.

Communicating about our financial lives, then, involves action and reaction, face-to-face conversations, telephone calls and email messages, letter writing, record-keeping, internal self-talk, and just thinking or talking things over with someone we love.

Sometimes, even after our best efforts, communication can go awry. You have heard it before: "It was just a misunderstanding." But there are specific skills that you can learn to break through barriers and avoid communication meltdown. Combined with your new awareness of your role as a consumer and armed with the knowledge of your Life Values Profile, these specific skills and habits will reduce your vulnerability and enhance your financial competence.

Steps Toward Building Financial Communication Competence

1. Listen effectively and appropriately.

2. Use "I-statements" to express yourself.

3. Keep written statements on-point, concise, free of emotion, and clear.

4. Ask for what you want and need.

5. Become aware of *how* you communicate, not just what and when you communicate.

6. Pinpoint only the central issues and then address them without embellishment.

7. Be aware of your Life Values and respect the Life Values of others.

8. And most important, practice, practice, practice, even though communicating about money at first can make you break out in a sweat.

Let's go over these important steps one by one.

Effective, Appropriate Listening

Rarely can misunderstanding or confusion be blamed on *too little talking*. On the other hand, in most cases of faulty communication, someone failed to *listen* attentively, open-mindedly, or critically—as when listening to that sales pitch. Whether the goal is to get the best deal at the auto mall, make the right job choice, or choose the best vacation this year, your first tendency should be *to listen*:

1. Listen carefully to what is being said and ask for clarification of anything you may not quite understand.

2. Watch for verbal or non-verbal signals that the person is feeling uncomfortable and see if you can help to put him or her at ease.

3. Listen for not just the big ideas but also the small, "oh, never mind" statements that might be important.

4. Listen for cues that something is highly valued and discuss its importance thoroughly, not just for your wallet but for your peace of mind too.

5. Listen for the feelings behind the words when it's personal, the possible hidden agenda when it's commercial and the unattractive but important details when it's complicated.

We wisely choose to listen differently in different situations. When a child wants to discuss an increase in allowance, we want to listen for opportunities to affirm the child and to teach and provide guidance. When a financial planner or loan officer or mortgage broker is talking about our portfolio or a pending investment decision, we want to listen for information, insisting that all our questions be answered and our every concern addressed. Listening to a "money guru" talk on the radio, we are likely to sort his or her advice into two mental piles: what applies to our situation and what does not.

At times we might find ourselves listening to haughty, insensitive, and even demeaning financial talk from someone who wants "to put us in our place," perhaps a bill collector or an inflexible sales clerk bent on being *right*. In those cases, we need to remind ourselves that *we control our own lives*, including our finances. Here's a suggestion that may work in the case of a haughty putdown: The question, *"Am I annoying you?"* can be a quick and effective way to bring misplaced arrogance to a quick halt.

Someone we know once asked that question of a rude and impatient service manager who was reluctant to take back merchandise that had been damaged during the delivery process. The service manager immediately apologized for her behavior and finished the transaction to the complete satisfaction of our friend. Such a retort might work like a charm for you too. Try it!

Learn to Use I-Statements

The concept of taking responsibility for our own statements rather than blaming, threatening, or accusing is not a new concept and is not limited to financial discussions. It would be wise, however, to take a few moments to remind ourselves of the importance of using I-statements and the ground rules for successfully doing so. The most important ground rule is this: *We are responsible for our own manner of talking or writing and for what and how we communicate to others.*

When you express an opinion or feeling about money, begin with "I . . ." and not with you, as in: "*You* always spend more than we agreed upon . . . *You* didn't put the receipt in this drawer . . . *You* charged me too much for this coat." When we reword these statements to begin with "I" instead of "you," it is no longer seen as an attack, but a conversation. It becomes easier both to express ourselves and for the person to whom we are talking to listen: "*I* feel frustrated when one of us goes over budget because I don't want our bank account overdrawn," "*I* worry when I can't find the receipts in the drawer because we need them at tax time," or "*I* am concerned about a discrepancy between the price advertised on the sign and the price on my receipt, because I want to be sure I'm paying the correct amount." What happens with this small change in emphasis is that no one is blamed, and the sales clerk you are dealing with does not feel threatened. You have spoken up for yourself successfully and trampled the feelings of no one in the process.

Let's take a careful look at the three parts of those I-statements:

1. I feel frustrated . . .
   I worry . . .
   I am concerned . . .

   In each case, you say clearly what you are feeling.

2. . . . when one of us goes over budget . . .
   . . . when I can't find the receipts . . .
   . . . about a discrepancy . . .

   You name the specific behavior that caused that feeling, still not blaming anyone for your feelings.

3. . . . because I don't want our back account overdrawn . . .
   . . . because I know we need them at tax time . . .
   . . . because I want to be sure I'm paying the correct amount.

   You identify what can happen as a result of the specific behavior.

I-statements come to mind in other parts of our lives, too. To our benefit, we have all been reminded by personal relationship gurus of the importance of speaking up for ourselves and expressing our feelings in family and personal exchanges. But we are less likely to remember to use I-statements in the marketplace, often causing ourselves and the people with whom we are dealing undue stress. Customer service employees can become intimidated, or embarrassed, or overwhelmed by an accuser and they are likely to respond in kind. Professionals who have important information do not wish to have it demanded of them, and caretakers respond more cheerfully to an upfront request. In short, having the clarity of purpose and courage of will to assert yourself in terms of your own feelings is a key to better communication in all your affairs.

PRACTICE, PRACTICE, PRACTICE

Convert the following accusations into I-statements:

- Your food is terrible! This is the worst meal I've ever eaten!
- You made me wait all afternoon! My appointment was for 1:00, and it is now 2:00.
- You're confusing me with financial jargon I don't understand.

How about:

- I feel frustrated when I have to pay full price for food that was so poorly prepared I couldn't even eat it.
- I feel insulted when I have to wait more than an hour past my appointment time with no explanation or apology from your staff.
- I feel intimidated when you use financial jargon that I'm not familiar with.

Now, think of instances in which—under conditions of high stress, when your heart is hammering and your mouth is dry—you've made similar accusations when I-statements would have served you better. Practicing I-statements in your routine exchanges will help make them a natural response when you are under stress.

Reading and Understanding Financial Documents

Joann and Ted owned three former homes, and all had been covered by homeowners' insurance, but neither Joann nor Ted had ever read the terms of their policies. While Ted was away on a trip out of the country, Joann heard a crash and discovered that the ceiling of their new garage had caved in. A building contractor, who happened to be a neighbor, inspected the damage. He told her the garage ceiling had been improperly constructed and would need to be entirely replaced. Joann called her insurance agent and waited for what she believed would be a quick and reasonable settlement of her claim for damages. She soon learned the costly verdict from an adjuster, who explained, "Your policy doesn't cover faulty construction." Joann placed several frantic—and mutually upsetting—calls to her husband in India until she got her emotions under control, located the insurance policy, and read its terms. There it was: The adjuster had been correct that their policy excluded problems stemming from faulty construction. She felt pretty foolish over her emotional outbursts and her unnecessary lack of consumer savvy!

We may fail to understand messages of financial importance either because they are not written in clearly accessible language, or we simply do not ask the right questions out of intimidation, laziness, or foolish trust. Whatever the cause, we ignore financial terms and conditions in the documents we sign at our peril. Most of us would not own a cell phone or a credit card if having them depended upon reading and understanding our "agreement" with the companies who usually have the edge over the consumers they purport to serve. Worse, we trust sales representatives to explain it to us "in plain English." When we close on a home, making the biggest investment of our lives, we sit mutely as the title officer tells us his or her version of the documents and points at where we should sign. We pay exorbitant bills from medical imaging facilities and treatment clinics without questioning them because the words seem foreign and the phrases convoluted.

Why do we do this to ourselves? Why do we allow it? What is the purpose of a multiple page contract written in 6-point type expressed in sentences that average 35 words in length? Why should a bill be beyond our comprehension? Isn't it supposed to "explain" what *we* owe? Maybe legal and financial documents just evolved that way, but we will never know how clearly they can be re-written if we do not ask for complete and thorough translations of the terms and conditions we routinely accept. And, as a society, we will never achieve real financial competence until we insist on understandable communication each time we are asked for money or for our signature on a binding contract.

Next time you are asked to sign a contract, pay a bill, abide by a directive, or in any way separate yourself from your hard-earned money, stop and read—and then insist on a full and satisfactory explanation (using an I-statement, of course) before you take any further action. Just like learning a new language, understanding contracts and policies does get easier over time. You will soon find that you are understanding more financial jargon, demanding better explanations, and becoming more confident and financially savvy in the process.

Ask For What You Need and Want

The habit of asking for what you want and need goes hand in hand with the patterns and habits we just discussed—insisting on clarity. However, this section covers even more bases: receiving messages, sending messages, and dealing with internal communication. If you were taught to be subordinate to power and authority, you may have difficulty at first dealing with this area. Those who feel they have the right to speak up are more likely to want to take responsibility in communicating about financial matters as well.

You will be able to take control of your finances once you understand that you have both a right and a responsibility to ask for what you want and need. Those who speak up on their own behalf realize four benefits. They

- Feel an immediate sense of relief.
- Stand a good chance of actually getting what they need or want.
- Have an increased sense of self esteem.
- Grow in stature before the person(s) to whom they have made the request.

Here is an experience shared by a new widow who was supporting herself for the first time in her life. She was making it, but just barely, by learning the ropes at the age of 60. Trina had been taught as a child to "be seen but not heard," and speaking up was hard enough, but talking about money was out of the question.

One summer, Trina picked out some new clothes for the season, paid a deposit, and asked the store to hold them because she did not want to finance them on a credit card. As May and June faded into July, she found that she did not have the money to pay off and pick up her clothes, but she was fearful about returning to the store to tell the proprietor. One day she decided that she could no longer bear the discomfort of NOT saying something, so she resolved to tell the store owner the truth—that she could not afford to pay for the clothing.

He was very upset, and repeated over and over, "Why didn't you tell me sooner? Now the clothing must be put on sale because it is so late in the season." Trina apologized and felt terrible for having caused this problem for the proprietor. Though embarrassed and still smarting from the scolding delivered by the upset owner, Trina felt a thousand percent better. She learned a valuable life lesson about her fear to communicate what she had regarded as "bad news." When confronting future financial issues, Trina practiced speaking up sooner, and with that practice, her fears went away entirely.

Practice is important in developing any skill, and it is especially important in developing communication skills. If you are not in the habit of asking for what you need or want in life generally, making requests in the financial realms will not be easy. Like Trina, you must gather your courage, and speak up until you are no longer afraid.

It will get easier with time. As long as you put off asking for what you need or want, the tape recorder in your head will keep playing those needs and wants back to you. Eventually the message might become, "poor me, the victim," or "nasty her, the mean boss," or "stupid guy who cannot figure out what I want." Avoid these messages and instead control your own destiny. Once you have assembled your data and formulated a reasonable case, give yourself permission to:

- Ask for a raise in pay.
- Question a suspicious or incomprehensible charge.
- Request details about credit and investments in lay person's language.

- Ask a finance professional to repeat or to clarify a situation.
- Request more time to make a payment.
- Ask for reimbursement, credit, or a refund.

Point to Ponder

Improving communication skills improves all of our relationships, not just with our family, friends, and colleagues, but with ourselves as well. When we pay attention to the messages we tell ourselves, we can improve the dialog. Try it. Instead of saying "I can't" the next time you are facing a challenge, instead say, "I can do this." To your delight, you will discover that you can!

When we speak up for our own wants and needs, we avoid building silent resentment and unnecessary anger or frustration.

Watch What You Say, but Really Watch How You Say It

We have all had the misfortune of being misunderstood. Sometimes the result is humorous or inconsequential, but at other times the result can be hurt feelings, a stalemate, or even long lasting disharmony. Debra Pankow, North Dakota State University Extension Service family economics specialist, lists six common types of money messages that we might be giving or getting where the intended meaning is lost in language that is counterproductive:

- *Messages that order, direct, or command tell a person their feelings or needs are not important.*

  Examples: "You need to spend less on food" or "You are wasting your money."

- *Warning and threatening messages tell what will happen if something is or isn't done and can make a person feel fearful and submissive.*

  Examples: "If you don't control your charging, I'll cut up the charge cards" or "You will never get that new bike if you keep wasting your allowance."

- *Moralizing or preaching messages that tell what should or ought to be done often result in resistance and defending a position even more strongly.*

  Examples: "You should control the budget better" or "You aren't putting enough money in your savings account."

- *Advising, offering solutions or being told how to solve a problem may make a person feel unable to make wise decisions.*

  Examples: "If I were you, I'd save that extra money" or "You should wait to buy that until the end of the season."

- *Messages that judge, criticize or blame, more than any other, make a person feel inadequate, inferior, or worthless.*

  Examples: "Can't you ever balance the checkbook right?" or "You can't spend your money on that!" or "You bought that useless piece of junk?"

- *Name calling, shaming, or ridiculing can hurt a person's self-image or cause discouragement and anger.*

  Examples: "Okay, Smarty" or "That was a dumb thing to spend your money on."[3]

A good way to avoid the communication pitfalls Pankow describes and to make sure that your message comes through is to put into practice the other skills discussed, especially I-statements. Also be aware that the message is more than just words. It includes your body language, tone of voice, position in relation to the other person, volume, rate of speaking, and even the choice of time at which to open the discussion. If we think through all of the components of our delivery, not just our words, we will greatly reduce the likelihood of being misunderstood.

Stick to the Issues

Financial decisions are much less about how much money you have in the bank than they are about your values, needs, and wants. It is sometimes difficult to identify the real issue at hand when it is surrounded by a fog of seemingly unrelated emotions, observations, and reasons.

You might insist you cannot afford to buy a new car or house or even a pair of slippers, but the real reason is that you may not want to part with the old one. Elderly parents, taken on the circuit to visit assisted living centers, might insist that each one is exorbitantly priced, when the real issue is that they want to stay in their own home. A pre-teen who begs about needing an increased allowance might be feeling peer pressure from others whose socio-economic circumstances are above his or hers. In each case, money is blamed, but the real issue could be something else entirely.

In other cases, finances *are* the issue, but everything else is brought into the discussion. "Florida is too hot, too humid, too far, too crowded," he claims, but the truth is he cannot see how they can afford the trip, and he is reluctant to say so. A job may be "boring, inflexible in terms of hours, managed by a tyrannical boss, the work too difficult," when the real issue is her desire for a pay raise coupled with the fear of asking for it.

Then there are the scenarios in which the conversation is all about money, but the real financial issue never emerges from the foggy communication. Susan insists that the stock her husband Mark wants to buy is too risky; in fact, she wants to share more of the investment authority in her relationship, but does not know how to state her feelings to Mark. Meyer complains about the price of every item his son takes from the shelf in the neighborhood craft store but fails to explain that this store, although convenient, is beyond his limited means. Jeff complains to colleagues about the high-priced, "useless" medical benefits they are getting, but he is really overwhelmed by climbing medical bills not covered by the plan.

Each of these cases can result in confusing, drawn-out arguments in which the real issues never get resolved. When dealing with behavior that appears confusing or out of character, rather than jump to conclusions or react emotionally, look for the motivation and ask, "Why?" Gentle, non-accusatory prodding and keeping the conversation focused on the issue at hand may help cut through the clutter. An effective way to do this is to employ the following final communication guideline.

Stay Aware of Your Life Values Profile

You have completed the profile in Chapter 4, "Your Life Values Profile," so now you have a pretty good idea about how you make financial decisions. You know whether you tend to be motivated more by Personal values (high P score), Social values (high S score), Tangible values (high T score), or Money values (high M score). We hope you also understand how and why your values have evolved to this point. Perhaps your partner or other members of your household have completed the profile and you have shared your results. If so, whenever financial conversations become cloudy or foggy, step back, remind everyone concerned about their Life Values Profile, and then listen before speaking. One partner with a high T (Tangible) score needs to communicate to a partner with a high M (Money) score that the aesthetics of her surroundings are important to her happiness and require a place in the budget. A partner with a high P (Personal) score should help his significant other with a high S (Social) score appreciate his need to invest time—and, yes, money—in his satisfying but *individual* pursuits. The more you use the Life Values Profile, the greater power you will have over your own financial decision making and the more nimble you will be at negotiating fairly to see that everyone's needs are met and everyone's values are respected.

Family Finances

Paradoxically, at home, where our hearts are most engaged and the stakes are highest, we often do our worst listening and communicating. In all discussions of things monetary, we want to choose the right behavior at home so that we can give and take effectively and appropriately to those we care about the most.

When Bill and Jennifer married a few years ago, Jennifer was comfortable turning over the finances to Bill. Four years her senior, he seemed to have more life experience and actually enjoyed talking about mortgages, insurance premiums, and the stock market. Bill shouldered the responsibility but increasingly implored Jennifer to develop a better understanding of their financial picture and perhaps take a more active role in decisions. Jennifer refused, happy to be an artist and raise her family and confident in Bill's financial savvy.

One Saturday morning, Bill realized that weekend breakfast times were good times for bringing up family discussions as the couple lingered over coffee during rare moments of leisure. Gradually, Jennifer began to gain some understanding of the couple's finances but demonstrated little willingness to be a part of their financial decisions. When she and Bill visited an auto dealer to replace their worn out car, Bill asked Jennifer to select a new vehicle. Typically, she had avoided the complexity of all financial decisions, the array of alternatives, and today was no different: She wanted to avoid comparing prices and any other financial consequences involved in making such a large decision. But this time, Bill said quietly that Jennifer had a choice: "It is the car you choose or no car. What will it be?"

As Jennifer tells it, in that moment, she realized that her refusal to engage in financial decisions had been an abdication of her responsibility to Bill, to their partnership, and to their future financial well-being. Today, she actively seeks to understand their finances and joins in offering opinions on purchases and investments. She actively markets her paintings, keeps records, and helps to budget, pay bills, and do financial planning. "It is not only about money," she explains. "It is also about love and respect."

Happy relationships with clear understandings about finances enhance emotional and physical health over the long term, since finances are an important piece in the relationship puzzle. No matter how a family may be defined or characterized, it must come to grips with its financial reality. Increasing individual knowledge about one's Life Values and sharing this knowledge among other family members will strengthen the bonds that unite family members and result in an overall sense of togetherness.

Children's values evolve through their childhood experiences; most of them are learned from and modeled on their parents' values. Parents who fail to share financial rights and responsibilities with children teach them that they are out of the financial loop altogether. Parents who quarrel about money teach their children that financial decisions are troublesome and are to be avoided or used as relationship ammunition. Parents who never talk to their children about saving, borrowing responsibly, and investing wisely teach their children that such behaviors are unimportant, beneath them, or otherwise not a meaningful part of real life. Family life can be a thorny path, and there is no better guide through the briers than open, honest, respectful communication, including communication about money issues, on a daily basis.

Communication, including the all-important I-statements, is the linchpin of financial competence. Once you master this, you can branch out and develop your own support network—family, friends, community resources, and professionals—who will guide you, motivate you, educate you, and cheer you on as you build your financial future.

13

TAPPING INTO THE FINANCIAL MARKETPLACE

N early everything in life is bought, sold, or financed through the capital markets, which makes it possible for us to have homes and community services, own vehicles that we drive on public highways, and enjoy the clothing and the other personal products and services we all use in our daily lives. These goods and services (and public services) are produced by corporations and/or public organizations with corporate and public financing that is taken for granted by most consumers who are unaware of all the transactions that occur each day in the bustling capital markets. By the time the goods and services reach the consumer marketplace, people simply choose to pay cash, write a check, present a debit card, or to finance them once again—this time with credit or charge cards for their personal consumption.

Financial products consist of insurance, stocks, bonds, commodities, mutual funds and many other financial mechanisms—both public and private. Unlike cars and household goods, financial products do not have to be trucked to retail stores or the supermarket, so they can be moved instead at lightning speed electronically by buyers and sellers. Information, contracts, and money are zapped around the globe, and business is conducted in jargon and financial symbols. The men and women who represent us in the financial marketplace hold credentials that resemble alphabet soup, but these credentials reflect the skills, education, knowledge, and experience that help us make informed decisions when we need financial services—insurance products, for example—or become investors in the capital markets.

The keys to fitting into any new environment are (1) learning the vocabulary and (2) getting to know the individuals who reside within the environment. Every change of environment involves a new vocabulary and new networks of people, which at first might seem unapproachable. In fact, you may find some financial professionals intimidating, but others will be welcoming and help you adjust. The first goal, therefore, is learning some financial jargon and how to recognize the professionals who will become most helpful to you. Soon, after you get the hang of things, it is likely that you will feel right at home.

Mission Possible

Josh, a recent graduate of a Master's program in English, was in his new teaching position only a few months when he was recruited to take over the duties of a colleague who had gone on extended sick leave. His assignment was to direct the annual spring musical theater production, something Josh felt ill-prepared to do. While he liked musical theater and taught the classics—including important plays in literature—he had no experience with drama, lighting, scenic sets, costume design, nor any of the myriad other details of a musical production. Worse, Josh couldn't sing or play a musical instrument. Despite his inexperience, his assignment was to guide drama students and to coordinate the work of a choral director and an orchestra conductor—both of whom were 20 years his senior. To Josh, the task seemed formidable and doomed to fail. You may wonder what Josh's situation has to do with the financial world, but it really parallels our own feelings when we must undertake anything we feel unprepared to do.

In Josh's case, he soon learned how talented his new drama students were, and he was able to select leaders and rely on their experience and good judgment. He learned, too, that volunteers regularly helped students design sets and make costumes for the annual production. He also found that both the choral director and orchestra conductor had a wealth of knowledge about musical theater. *In other words, he learned soon enough that he was not alone.*

Despite his initial doubts and anxieties, Josh reached out to the network of skilled and experienced people he found all around him, and they all got down to work. By spring, he and his team had actually pulled it off, and a lively production of *Music Man* was the happy result. Josh realized his success depended on reaching out to others to pull together a team that when combined had all the knowledge and skill that he alone lacked. It had been up to Josh to recognize and learn from those who had the expertise. In the same way, as you reach out to people with financial knowledge and experience, you will become more comfortable with the larger world of finance and use it to your own advantage, maybe even learn to make a "little financial music" on your own.

The Financial Regulatory Environment

Over the past several years, as most everyone knows, interest rates have been at record lows. The good news is that mortgage rates (and homeownership) became affordable for many people. The bad news is that low rates negatively affected the return on savings accounts, certificates of deposit, and money market accounts. Perhaps you were finally able to buy that first house or upgrade to your dream home. On the other hand, if you had invested in CDs or money market funds, you experienced lower returns. Some retirees found it difficult to live on investments that returned interest lower than the rate of inflation. So was it a good season for your finances, and, if not, should you have been able to predict the positive and negative aspects of this financial rate environment?

In fact, too few consumers today follow trends in the general economy. Increasingly, however, we all must develop the will to notice, and the skills to decipher, even subtle movements in the financial markets. We must also become more familiar with the regulatory systems that watch over them. While not perfect, in many respects they are the most sophisticated in the world. Individuals specialize in each facet of the marketplace, and they are available to work with us to help our money grow. Thanks to the U.S. regulatory system, financial professionals must carry valid credentials, work to update them, and maintain unblemished personal records if they intend to retain their licenses and continue to operate in the world of finance.

These individuals prepare our taxes, open and service our savings accounts, help us to prepare financial plans, advise us as we choose and make investments, help us provide for the future financial needs of our dependents, and share educated opinions about trends in the general economy. We need them to act on our behalf when we buy or sell a home, finance consumer goods and services, and help us choose investments to accumulate wealth. We might not fully understand the role each person plays in the financial marketplace, but we need to know how to seek trustworthy, knowledgeable professionals with whom to establish beneficial working relationships. This is essential to help us conduct our financial affairs to our greatest advantage. We need responsive professionals who are familiar with our personal circumstances and who will help us make informed financial decisions.

Sometimes the thought of facing someone who is a financial "authority" can be intimidating. Occasionally our apprehension is justified if the professional is inflexible or insensitive, but first impressions can be deceiving and reflect our own fears, rather than the personality or intent of the person we are encountering. Having the courage to move past our anxieties to make personal connections anyway can be well worth the effort. Here, in her words, is Peggy's story about her meeting with an IRS agent:

> *In my early twenties, as a full-time Master's candidate, I had been living on a shoestring. One day, I received a notice from the IRS that I had failed to correctly report some incidental income from the previous year and owed them "back taxes, penalties, and late fees." The timing could not have been worse. I approached my meeting with the almighty IRS with great anxiety, even though I knew my error had been an innocent mistake. I had no idea how I was going to pay what the IRS said I owed. A tall, intimidating woman nodded a welcome and began detailing the amounts I owed and then asked me how I intended to fix the situation. I fought back tears of fear and frustration as I explained that I had*

no regular income; I was a full-time student; and I had not know-ingly made this mistake. Imagine my surprise when the IRS agent delivered a tissue from her desk to my lap and, in a soothing voice, told me not to worry! The IRS would freeze my account while I was in school and then contact me to make payment arrange-ments when I completed the program. As she ushered me out of the office with good wishes, I thought, "Truly, this was not the visit I expected to have with the IRS!"

EXERCISE

Kick back with pen and paper and list your worst financial fears. Then let your imagination roam through all the prospective solutions that you can think of. Yes, if you want, you can write fantasy solutions like "winning the lottery," but beside each possible solution also add (on a scale of 1–10) the chances of being able to actually pull off that solution. Do this over and over until you have really come up with a few real solutions and then promise yourself to take action to implement at least one of them right away.

If you're in a committed relationship involving shared finances, work at this together. First, independently list your worst financial fears. Comparing notes, settle on a mutually agreeable list. Then, again independently, imagine every conceivable solution to each, rating them for realism of expectation. When you share the lists, your partnership will benefit from the "two heads are better than one" phenomenon. Together, commit to acting on at least one solution. You will be amazed at how good you can become at solving financial problems if you just have the courage to call the IRS, like Peggy did, or call the bill collector, or increase your 401(k) deposit, or open that saving account you have been thinking about. These problems all involve tapping into the financial marketplace—you can do it. In fact, you *must* do it to take control of your own life.

Finding the Right Financial Professionals

So how do you go about meeting financial professionals, and how do you evaluate their character, credentials, and track record so you can get help when you need it?

Begin by seeking referrals, and keep in mind that the value of a referral is based on its source. The more you respect the judgment and integrity of the individual you ask, the more you will respect who *they* turn to for the kind of financial advice or assistance you seek. You can also get referrals to a financial professional from other financial advisors you already trust. For example, your long-time insurance agent might recommend a financial planner or stock broker, or your attorney might know of an excellent tax-preparation professional. Just be sure that the person making the referral has nothing to gain by sending you to the professional referred.

You don't always need an expert to help you find a good resource. Seek out a responsible, approachable coworker, relative, or neighbor who embodies the character traits and success record you admire. Strike up a conversation about annuities or bonds or mortgages—whatever is on your mind. If you get the sense that this person has some valid experience in that area and has enjoyed some success, ask for a referral to his or her accountant, financial advisor, mortgage lender, real estate lawyer, banker, or whoever it is you need to find. A structured way to begin your search is to contact www.cfpboard.net or the National Association of Personal Financial Advisors. Each of these organizations will provide a list of certified financial planners in your area and in the case of NAPFA members, those that are committed to the fee-only model. It is recommended that you interview at least two advisors before you make your selection.

If interpersonal networking such as we have just described is not getting you the referrals you need, call a local referral agency or local professional association. In addition, the Internet offers thousands of resources. (See Chapter 19, "Finding the Help You Need," and the Appendix, "Personal Finance Education Internet Sites," that list online resources at the end of this book.) Your local community college may offer seminars or mini-courses in various aspects of financial education; the instructor could well become your advisor. The Cooperative

Extension System (CES) associated with your local state university or your County Extension office can provide free pamphlets and speakers; one of them might lead you to the professional you seek. And, there are countless periodicals you can buy or read in your public library that will help you gain access to the world of financial advice. Then you can continue to educate yourself in this manner over time.

At this point, you should be developing a list of potential sources. When creating this list, make sure that you are the person who initiates the contact. In other words, be wary of unsolicited offers of help. These may lead you down the road of too-good-to-be-true sales pitches.

Evaluate Credentials and Credibility

As you gather your list of prospective contacts, consider both professional and personal qualities. You are looking for one or more people who not only have just the right expertise, but who also match your temperament—people with whom you feel comfortable discussing your personal affairs. Think along the following lines as you begin your search and meet prospective advisors:

- *How is this person being compensated?*
  Before you even bother about licensing or certification, determine whether you have found an objective, unbiased person who is committed to helping you achieve your goals. If the professional you are considering represents a for-profit business such as an insurance company or broker-dealer, realize that there will probably be some sort of sales pitch—some product or program for sale—and be prepared to separate the sales pitch from the objective advice. Financial professionals have to make a living, and there is certainly nothing wrong with their offering their products to you. Problems arise when you cannot tell the difference between selling and advising. A responsible, trustworthy professional will make that distinction clear *for* you. If the information is not offered, you will want to ask how the advisor is being paid: By commission on the sale of products? By the total volume of assets managed? Strictly by the time spent on your behalf? In other words, are you paying the advisor, is a third party paying the advisor, or is it a combination of both?

- *How objective and unbiased is the advice?*

  Be wary of an "advisor" who insists that there is only one possible point of view on an important issue—their own, but know that advisors should have an investment philosophy and strategy that they recommend for you to follow. In other words, you want to find someone who is knowledgeable, competent and up-to-speed about the current economy and the marketplace. They also need to be open-minded and concerned about you and your goals! The professional should offer information and you should invite their opinions, but anyone who insists his proposal is the only viable solution might be purposely misleading you simply in order to sell you something. There needs to be give-and-take in the conversation. You must feel respected as you seek critical advice. You must also feel comfortable in giving feedback.

- *Is the sales pitch too good to be true?*

  "Bargain loans" are usually no bargain, and investment offers that force you to make up your mind immediately should raise red flags. Companies that specialize in serving those with poor credit or no credit are making their money from some source; will that source be you? Lenders who call you, email you, or knock on your door without an invitation may be predators. Refer back to the chart in Chapter 7, "Who's in Charge of Your Financial Well-Being?" and be alert to possible scams and predatory practices.

As you can see, it is important to use common sense and trust your gut when seeking advice from a financial professional. Take heart, though. Even if you find yourself in a vulnerable position—poor credit rating, needing to buy a house with a low down payment, overwhelmed by debt—there are reliable sources to help you. Even if you *are* vulnerable, there are accessible counselors, and sources of education (and self-education) that can help you evaluate the integrity and reliability of financial companies and their representatives. As you build your network, remember to stay in control. You choose what advice to keep and what advice to disregard. No matter how well-educated or experienced the financial professional is, he or she works for you. You are the boss!

Who Is Licensing or Certifying this Professional?

It is realistic to assume that any financial professional who offers to relieve you of your hard-earned money or transfer it to an investment destination on your behalf should be licensed, certified, registered with a legitimate financial business and supervised by a regulatory authority. Ask to see the individual's license, certification, information about the company, and authorities under which he or she is licensed and/or registered.

If you are meeting in the professional's office, expect to see the license and certification(s) displayed. Go ahead and look at these documents and verify that they are valid and current. Notice what organization awarded it. Ask with whom the professional is registered. If you are unsure what a particular designation means, ask about it, and write it down so you can look it up later. A legitimate financial professional will understand your need "to know" and be happy to explain the details of his or her background and credentials in terms you can understand.

If you go to an estate planner, you can feel more comfortable if that individual holds the AEP (Accredited Estate Planner) designation. Investment advisors or financial consultants who advise you about stocks, bonds and other securities must be registered with the Securities and Exchange Commission (SEC) and licensed by a state securities agency. They hold the designation RIA for Registered Investment Advisor. Now, that does not guarantee their competence, but, without that designation, they are not legally able to advise you.

Stock brokers are licensed by the states in which they buy and sell securities and registered with a company that is a member of the National Association of Securities Dealers (NASD). When they are so registered, they have passed examinations and the scrutiny of the NASD and the company with which they are registered. You can verify your prospective broker's status at the NASD's Central Registry Depository. You can also verify the credentials of an investment advisor or stock broker by calling the NASD at 800-289-9999, or you can call the North American Securities Administrators Association at 202-737-0900.

Life insurance agents receive training from the company or companies whose products they sell, so they might not be knowledgeable about other investment options you may be considering. If they have the CLU designation (Chartered Life Underwriter), they have earned that designation through additional training given by the insurance industry. Some insurance agents are also financial planners and hold multiple designations. To check on an insurance agent's credentials or record, you can call the National Association of Insurance Commissioners at 816-842-3600.

Financial planners work in a broad area of consumer financial services, and their credentials deserve and require your attention. A good financial planner can make a positive difference in your life, so it is worthwhile to seek out the one who is right for you. Credentialing for financial planners is not required by state or federal law. However, you can search for one who demonstrates that he or she has met the standards of well-recognized organizations.

The American College in Bryn Mawr, Pennsylvania, confers many financial credentials, among them the respected Chartered Financial Consultant (ChFC) designation for those who have successfully completed the prescribed coursework. The Certified Financial Planner Board of Standards sets requirements for the Certified Financial Planner (CFP) designation. This credential certifies that the professional has successfully met the board's examination, education, experience, and ethics requirements. A Certified Public Accountant-Personal Financial Specialist (CPA-PFS) is another designation that requires rigorous initial and continuing education, examination, ethical standards, and experience.

Financial planners constitute a huge and growing population of persons from many different financial backgrounds and have widely varying abilities. Perhaps the most common error made by individuals seeking a financial professional is to rely on someone for specialized services that are outside that person's scope of expertise. The next important area to determine is how the financial planner is paid: by commissions from the sale of products, or by fee-for-service.

Some financial planners or advisors represent companies whose products they sell. While they offer valid advice, bear in mind that they are paid by financial companies to represent their products and that their expertise is predominantly with those products. Other financial planners are registered representatives of broker-dealers and hold securities licenses to sell certain securities. A fee-only financial planner, on the other hand, is one who has no such professional affiliation. They may or may not have a broader base of knowledge, but if they do they may also be able to offer you more objective advice. They are beholden to no one but you.

The industries described here and the professionals who work in them are offered as examples in terms of licensing, certification, and registration. Once you determine what sector of the marketplace you need to focus on, take the initiative to learn what the credentialing standards are for people working in that sector. Then follow up on your new information.

Make the Final Cut

When you have identified several financial professionals who offer the kind of advice or support you need, and you have made some initial investigation of each one's qualifications, credentials and suitability, it is time to meet with your top two or three choices in order to make the final selection. Make an appointment or set aside time at the initial meeting for the specific purposes of discussing your needs and exploring the possibility of working together. You are not making a commitment at this point; you are conducting *their* job interviews. Have your questions ready, and do not feel at all uncomfortable about coming in with a written list. The advisor will appreciate your preparation and your respect for his or her time. You might even jot a few notes as they answer. Here are the kinds of things you will want to ask:

- How long have you been doing this type of work? (What did you do before that? What other related experience do you have?)
- With whom are you licensed, certified, registered, affiliated, etc. (as just discussed)?
- How do you usually proceed to help your clients? (or "What is your philosophy related to _____?")
- Can you show me a list of the services you offer?

- What should I expect in terms of timeline, my responsibilities, communication, etc.?
- What will it cost, and how are you paid?
- Will I be working directly with you? (If not, find out with whom you will be working and that person's credentials and experience.)
- Can you show me references from satisfied clients?

After you have interviewed your prospective financial support persons, think about the information you received from each one—on an intellectual level as well as on an emotional level. Your goal is to select a professional who is competent, candid with you, inspires confidence, and can be trusted to represent your best interests. You also want to work with someone who helps you to feel relaxed, comfortable, and valued as a person. These criteria demand a relationship of mutual trust and respect. You will want to feel confident that this person will always act professionally and maintain strict confidentiality. The goal, quite simply, is for you to enter into a professional relationship that will ultimately leave you better off than you are now. Here are some points to consider:

- Was the advisor interested in listening to and understanding my situation?
- How do I feel about the suggestions and advice offered in the initial meeting?
- Will this person be open to my input and the input of other respected professionals?
- Did the advisor make any remarks or reveal any confidential information that should be a red flag to me?
- Will this person be available to me and responsive to my changing needs?
- How did I *feel* during the meeting?

Conducting Business with the Chosen Professional

Once you have identified the financial professional who can help you meet your short-term or long-term goals, you are ready to enter into a comfortable professional relationship that can relieve your stress, improve your financial behavior patterns, and move you along on the road to your secure future. Start off on the right foot.

Discover right from the start what information, records, or other data you will need to bring to the table. Do not delay; gather and organize whatever the advisor is asking of you. In the future, you may be asked to provide some additional information, although most financial resource persons will ask for everything they need up front. Afterwards, most of the flow of information will be from the professional to you.

While your financial professional has distinct responsibilities to you, you are also responsible for your communication. Be clear from the start about the services that will be provided to you, and then hold the advisor to them. An important service that you should request and expect is regular reporting. You have a right to know what is being done in your name and on your behalf. Establish from the start how often and in what way you can expect to be informed of any actions taken or progress made. Then, of course, you have an obligation to attend to the information provided and take any action that might be required on your part.

What if you can't understand the reports? At the first inkling that you will not be able to make sense or good use of the information being provided you, pick up the phone and ask how you can get help. Then train yourself, over time, to get better and better at reading and understanding the financial information you are receiving. You will be surprised at how much more meaningful it will all become after you are comfortable with the format, the symbols and abbreviations, and the "lingo." In fact, as you develop a "history" with the financial resource, a picture will gradually emerge, and you will be able to recognize your own improving financial health. That will be very exciting!

Set up a filing system to store the paperwork or computer files related to this undertaking. If necessary, ask for advice about this too: What needs to be saved, and what can be tossed? How long should various items be saved? What organizational pattern will make the most sense in the long run? (For example, much of your financial data will be needed annually for tax purposes. How can you store it throughout the year in order to reduce the burden on the tax preparer and/or yourself, come January?)

Finally, when you have established a good working relationship with a trained professional in the world of financial markets, you need to attend to the health and well-being of that relationship. Pay attention to any signs that the relationship needs fixing. Do you feel poorly informed? Has the financial professional failed to provide all the services promised? Are you feeling coerced or pressured to make decisions that don't feel right to you? Even worse, is your financial situation declining rather than improving?

In most cases a simple phone call or a short appointment will rectify matters. At a mutually convenient time, simply state the problem as you perceive it. Using the communication skills we discussed in Chapter 12, "Communicating About Money—Count the Ways," talk about what *you* are experiencing rather than making accusations. Take responsibility for your own feelings and, if appropriate, for your own behavior that might have contributed to these feelings. Be open to proffered solutions; you have to be flexible if you're going to change the situation. Even better, consider solutions that *you* might suggest. A healthy, robust relationship with a financial professional—or, more likely, with a growing team of professionals—can be the key to your long-term security.

Committing to Positive Action

It all begins with a personal commitment to financial literacy and positive action. Meredith, 22 years old and single, was just starting her first serious job when she was advised by Pauline, an older coworker, to start educating herself early about her personal finances. Meredith visited the Web site her friend recommended, even though she was not very interested in topics oriented so far into the future. She found that the Web site was full of basic advice even for young consumers, so she stuck with it—reluctantly at first—but Pauline had convinced her that starting early was more important than starting with a lot of money. "Don't wait as I did," Pauline had told her, "Start now to manage money wisely, and you won't be sorry when you get a little older."

Meredith started checking the Web site during lunch breaks for advice about saving and investing, and she followed links to other sites including bulletin boards where she could learn from other people's experiences. Within a short time, she even began posting her own stories on the boards. She bought herself a book on managing her finances, and her confidence grew along with her enthusiasm and net worth as she put into practice the principles and tips she was learning. Something else was happening too: Her spending and saving priorities had shifted. Meredith found that she was more enthusiastic about saving money than about buying the latest fashion or new gadget for her apartment.

Fortunately, Meredith married a partner who also enjoyed watching his funds grow incrementally, and he too appreciated stock market "lows" as good times to buy. Together Meredith and Mark bought and paid off a car, bought a home, and concentrated on paying off their mortgage. They continued to compare notes and post queries on Internet bulletin boards, and they sought the advice of financial professionals as their situation warranted. They didn't get "rich," they recently told us, but they were secure and comfortable when, at age 29, Meredith was able to leave her job and become a stay-at-home mom to care for the couple's first baby—something she had always wanted to do.

Although Mark does not make a six-figure income, the couple is free of the overwhelming debt burden under which many other families struggle. Both Meredith and Mark regularly consult with the financial support network that they have developed over the years and continue to read pertinent books and online financial articles as new circumstances arise. Never in her wildest dreams did Meredith believe that, at the young age of 30, she would "have it all": a like-minded partner, a darling new baby, a home of their own, and the financial security for a promising future.

We need not be passive victims of fate. Like Meredith, we can take note of our financial risks and habits and take practical steps to avoid them or lessen their effect. One important thing we can do is as simple as becoming more active in our own financial affairs and scheduling time to review our progress on the path to fulfilling our material plans and dreams.

Even our best financial intentions can get derailed through the influence of loved ones, friends, and neighbors. Researchers, however, now say that the process of socialization is *life long*, and we can change our old habits and patterns whenever we choose. In fact, our financial savvy really depends on the strength of our choices: reducing competitive impulses to keep up with others, tracking our expenses, committing to save, and taking time to become acquainted with the array of financial services *people* that comprise the greater financial world.

The fact is the financial marketplace is no different from any other social marketplace. Imagine, if you will, your favorite farmer's co-op or flea market or any other collective group of people all selling their products and services to interested shoppers—if you will, a great quilt made up of squares that represent a variety of professions. They are the advisors and professionals who consumers must learn about and link to, in order to obtain its benefits (and avoid its pitfalls as much as possible). To do that, we all need to navigate the maze of financial professionals—advisors, tax-preparers, brokers and agents, realtors, and financial planners that link us to the larger financial world. By doing so, we can create our own support network—a group of not just family and friends, but also professionals who we can turn to for advice and encouragement.

14

BUILDING YOUR ASSETS

You know about how much to put aside each month, but where do you put it? The financial advisors and others in your financial support network will give you specialized guidance to answer this question. To get your conversations going and keep them productive, there are some basics to keep in mind.

Ideally, the bare bones of your financial portfolio should be

1. An emergency fund—a "comfort" fund equivalent to three or more months of expenses kept in a short-term, accessible savings account.

2. Retirement assets.

3. Your investment portfolio.

4. Your home.

The mix depends on your individual goals. Once you define your goals, you have an idea of not only what they are, but how much they will cost. Are you saving for retirement, your children's education, or your own second career? Or is your goal to be financially independent by a certain age—60, or even 45? The structure and timetable of your particular goals will determine the best mix of your financial portfolio. If you are living in retirement, you will usually want your investments to be more heavily weighted in fairly conservative securities. If you are in your prime and planning on early financial idependence, you could be working with a portfolio that is heavy in high earning (and perhaps very high risk) investment products. In other words, there is no generic blueprint about what your financial portfolio should look like. Your plan is *you*; it will have *your* fingerprints all over it—your goals, your hopes, and your aspirations. But it will also be backed by sound, proven financial tools: cash accounts, stocks and bonds, and perhaps investment real estate too.

Money in the Bank—Climbing the Savings and Investment Ladder

If you have been a bank customer for a number of years, you may want to skip this section and go straight to Stocks, Bonds, and Mutual Funds, but if you are one of the millions of Americans who has only a checking account, (or no bank account at all) this section is for you.

No one knows how many people in the United States have no bank accounts. The Federal Deposit Insurance Corporation (FDIC) estimates that people who are "unbanked" represent 10 to 13 percent of all U.S. households. The Federal Reserve estimates that up to 10 million beneficiaries of Social Security have no bank account. In addition, there are uncounted millions of immigrant families who have no checking or savings account. By far the simplest and safest place to save money is in a bank or a credit union, not under the mattress or in a shoebox, even though a few frugal souls have been known to accumulate small fortunes doing just that. The FDIC is an independent agency of the U.S. government that protects you against the loss of your deposits, if an FDIC-insured bank or savings association fails.

Credit Unions function much like commercial banks, but they are nonprofit. Some are available to the public, but generally they are available through an employer or a specific industry, certain location, or university. Credit unions often offer depositors competitive services and more favorable rates and fees. The National Credit Union Administration (NCUA) is the federal agency that charters and supervises federal credit unions and insures savings in federal and most state-chartered credit unions across the country through the National Credit Union Share Insurance Fund (NCUSIF).

Commercial banks and credit unions insure your deposits up to $100,000 and both types of institutions offer a variety of accounts, depending upon how much you plan to set aside and how long you intend to keep your money on hand in an accessible form. One drawback to banking with a credit union is that you will not find branches in several locations as you might find with a commercial bank, but you may not need this particular convenience either.

Basic savings accounts work well if you plan to accumulate money for a short time only. For savings accounts, most banks do not have an initial minimum deposit, but they may charge a monthly fee if your account drops below a certain balance. You would not want to keep much money on hand in a basic savings account, since they generally pay very low interest rates (1–2%, if that much) so they should be considered only as a temporary measure. Basic savings accounts, on the other hand, can be ideal for you when you are just getting started on your savings plan or if you come into a small windfall, such as a gift or insurance payment, and you need time to decide just how and where you will invest your funds.

When choosing a bank or a credit union, choose wisely. First, compare rates and fees. While most banks are fairly competitive, there are some fluctuations. Then look at locations—is there a branch or office convenient to your neighborhood or workplace? Keep in mind that some people consider this convenience a bad thing. If you are concerned that you may be tempted to withdraw money, you may consider a bank in an out-of-the-way location and forgo an ATM convenience card. If you have a high T (Tangible) or M (Money) score and cannot resist a sale, or if you have a high S (Social) score and find it hard or impossible to say "no" to a family member or someone else in need, a less convenient bank might be right for you. That way, the trip to the bank will at least give you time to reconsider your motives for making a withdrawal. Finally, look to your values. There are large, regional and nationwide banks, smaller, community-oriented institutions, and even banks and credit unions that align themselves with social justice or environmental concerns. Your own values might make that institution a good match for you. The bottom line is that not all banks are created equally, so shop around to find the bank best suited to your needs.

A second type of saving vehicle is a **money market account**. These accounts require a higher initial deposit—usually at least $1,000—and you are required to keep a minimum amount in the account to avoid paying monthly maintenance fees. Although these accounts have the look of checking accounts, you are allowed a limited number—usually three—monthly withdrawals. A money market account, therefore, cannot replace your regular checking account. Money market accounts pay a higher interest rate than basic savings accounts, depending of course, upon market conditions. They are ideal for your emergency fund because, like basic savings accounts, they are liquid, so your funds can be easily withdrawn if circumstances warrant.

Certificates of deposit (CDs) are products that pay a fixed interest rate if you keep your money invested for a specific period of time. CDs are a one-time investment that pay interest until the CD matures. Most banks require at least $500 to open a CD, and you can get a CD for a term as short as three months or as long as 10 years. Generally, the longer the term, the higher the interest rate, but check carefully because there can be some variation, especially in markets where short and long-term interest rates do not rise and fall in their usual patterns. Generally speaking, however, a three-month CD rate is comparable to a money market account, and a six-year CD can bear interest at a rate that is three times that amount. Before the stated term expires, you will receive notification from the bank asking if you want to cash out the CD or roll it over into a new CD offered at the current rate. The good thing about these rates is that they are stable. Once you purchase the CD, you are guaranteed to receive the stated rate, no matter what happens in the rate marketplace. These products, however, come at a price in terms of flexibility. You will be charged a penalty, based on several months of interest, if you cash out the CD before the date the certificate will mature.

Stocks, Bonds, and Mutual Funds

Gone are the days when the stock and bond market was the exclusive domain of high rollers. Today, anyone can be a successful investor in this market with a little time and effort. Even though you have a crack financial support team behind you, it is crucial to know how these investments work.

When you purchase **stock** in a particular company, you invest in that company as an owner (shareholder). As a shareholder, you allocate your money for use in the company's operations, and in return for your investment, you are entitled to a share of the profits. Those earnings are either paid back to you in the form of dividends, or the earnings are retained to grow the company's business. As the value of the company grows, so does the value of your shares of stock. On the flip side, as a shareholder, you are also subject to a portion of losses if the company is not profitable. Your loss is usually represented by a decrease in the stock price.

Over time, stocks have proven to outperform virtually all other investments. That doesn't mean that stocks will always beat bonds or real estate in a particular year. But it does mean that over the long-term, stocks, generally speaking, are the investment most likely to grow in value. Since 1961, stocks have returned an average of more than 10 percent per year. The average bank saving account or CD generally returns no more than 2 or 3 percent per year. Even though stocks have historically outperformed other investments, stocks can also deliver significant losses. The rate of return just cited is an average; while some stocks show gain over time, others show losses, some even losing 100% of their value—not only do you not see any growth in your investment, you lose everything you have invested too.

It is worth noting that when a stock goes up or down in value, you only recognize that gain or loss when you sell the shares. These are "paper" gains or losses. Staying in the market over the long-term will mitigate the market's short-term ups and downs. It may be difficult to watch a particular stock go down, but rather than sell in a panic and take the loss, you should first analyze the company, and with advice from your financial professional, try to predict whether or not the trend will turn around.

Avoid the temptation to "play the market" or day trade. This type of strategy attempts to bypass the natural, long-term growth of the stock market, so it can backfire. Also every time you buy or sell a share of stock, you pay a transaction fee, so by repeatedly buying and selling, the transaction fees eat away at your profits. You can probably see that an individual with a high M (Money) score would enjoy stock market trading but might also need to be cautioned not to "play the market."

Another investment option is **bonds**, a relatively steady, safe way to invest. While stocks represent ownership in a business, a bond is a loan to a business (or municipality, government, or utility). Some bonds are exempt from the payment of certain taxes, and all bonds state that you will be paid back by a certain date (maturity date) at a specified rate of interest. Bonds are generally bought and sold on the bond market, which means that even though the term of the bond is for a stated time, you do not have to hold it for that length of time. You can buy and sell bonds with the same speed as you can make stock trades.

Most bonds pay interest semi-annually, and they are redeemed for the face amount when they reach maturity. Since the rate is contractual, bonds are considered safer investments. When you decide to buy bonds, however, you may be tempted to buy ones with the highest yields. But yields can be misleading, so consider the quality of the bond itself and the credit or strength of the company, municipality, or other bond issuer. No yield (promised return on your investment) can make up for the issuer's inability to pay its debt to bondholders if they go out of business or file for bankruptcy. Bond yields are usually expressed two ways: current yield and yield to maturity. Current yield is the annual interest or return on the amount you paid for a bond. Yield to maturity is the total return you receive by holding the bond until the date it matures. It equals the interest you receive from the time you purchase the bond until maturity, plus any gain or loss from whatever price you paid to buy the bond initially. If you purchase a bond with a 6% coupon (interest), its yield to maturity is 6%. If you pay more than its face value, the yield to maturity will be lower than 6%. If you purchased it below its face value, the bond will have a yield to maturity higher than 6%.

One of the ways you can determine the quality of a bond is by researching the credit rating of the issuer. Most bonds are rated by Moody's Investors Service or Standard and Poor's Corporation. Both use a slightly different format of letter grades to represent the overall health of the bond issuer. For example, ratings above Baa/BBB (Moody's/Standard and Poor's) are considered investment grade, which means they generally qualify for commercial bank investment. Ratings below these rankings are more speculative and have a higher risk of default.

Before you buy any stocks or bonds individually, you should thoroughly research the company or other issuer in which you are investing. This can take a great deal of time before deciding to invest and in monitoring their worth over time. These investments should never be bought or sold on whim, impulse, or on a "hot tip" from a friend or family member. If you are leery of investing the time or have little interest in or desire for learning to analyze several companies' investment potential, there are other investments to consider: mutual funds, exchange traded funds, other types of unit investment trusts, and real estate investment trusts to name a few.

Before you invest in any fund or trust, however, be sure you understand the objectives of the investment company offering the fund or trust to investors. Armed with knowledge about the particular goals, objectives, companies, growth potential and other market and legal information, you will still benefit from receiving investment advice from your financial professional(s). Although we go into a little detail in the following sections about certain investments, this is no substitute for the education you will need to become a knowledgeable investor. Take the time to learn everything you can about investing, or join an investment club if you prefer not to go it alone. Investing can be exciting, rewarding and fun, especially when your financial advisor has a knack for helping you become educated.

Many investors choose mutual funds to help them get started, and for good reason. A **mutual fund** is a portfolio of stocks, bonds, or other securities owned by numerous investors. Since mutual funds pool money from many different investors, they have millions of dollars to invest and can build a portfolio of hundreds of individual stocks, bonds, or other investments to achieve diversification. What this means is that the law of averages is in effect—if a particular stock goes down, there are other, better performing stocks that will mitigate that loss. Mutual funds are managed by professional fund managers who make the buying and selling decisions for all investments.

Most mutual funds are built around clear investment objectives. Some focus on only one particular industry such as health care or technology. Other funds are created to meet specific investment objectives such as safety of capital, high income, or growth. There are even funds designed to meet intrinsic social or environmental value objectives. For instance, "green" funds only invest in companies that are environmentally friendly. You can choose a mutual fund, then, that matches your specific values. Research and talk over your options with your financial advisors and carefully read through the prospectus before making an investment. A well-chosen mutual fund is often a smart way for anyone to begin investing, regardless of your Life Values Profile scores.

When you buy into a mutual fund, you buy a number of shares. Much as a stock share represents a percentage ownership in a corporation, a mutual fund share represents a percentage ownership in the entire fund. Many funds require initial investments of only $500. After your initial purchase, once you've become a shareholder, most will accept smaller amounts, allowing you to increase your investment. If you want to sell your shares, the fund is required to buy them back, making mutual funds easy to liquidate.

Some mutual funds charge a fee when you purchase shares. This charge is called a "load." Although loads vary greatly, a 5.75% load fee is not uncommon. That means if you had $1,000 to invest in a mutual fund that had a load of 5.75%, $57.50 would be deducted as a sales charge, leaving you with $942.50 to invest. Many funds do not charge an upfront sales fee. These are known as "no load" funds. Some funds have deferred loads, which means a fee will be deducted from your account if you redeem your shares before a specified period of time.

You may be tempted to think that the fee structure of a fund is tied in to how the fund performs, for example, pay more, get more. Not so. There is no evidence that load or deferred-load funds are better investments than no-load funds. But it is important to look at what the fee structure is, as the same concept applies to mutual funds as to stocks—repeated buying and selling of mutual fund shares can cause you to pay repeated fees (and tax on gains) that can sap your earnings potential.

Retirement Assets

When determining the mix of your financial investment portfolio, pay special attention to your retirement assets. Unlike most other investments, these assets can grow in three potential, and significant, ways:

compound interest, tax savings, and employer match (if your employer is sponsoring the plan). These are designed to replace defined benefit pensions in most companies. The premise behind these accounts is that once your money is deposited, you cannot deduct it until you reach retirement age. Any money you deposit or that your employer deposits on your behalf is not taxed until that time. This allows you to build a nest egg, temptation-free and tax-free.

Whether your plan is employee-sponsored (a 401(k)-type plan) or your own retirement account (one of several types of Individual Retirement Accounts), it will generally be based on stocks, bonds, mutual funds, or CDs. And, thanks to compound interest (which we discussed in Chapter 11, "Committing to a Savings Plan"), if you get an early start, you can significantly build up the assets in your account. Consider these eye-opening calculations:

- $2,000 a year invested starting at age 25 in a tax-deferred account earning 10% average return will become $885,000 at age 65.
- The cost of waiting? Start at 35 with the same investment criteria, and the nest egg would total only $329,000.

That's right, the $20,000 NOT invested in those 10 years cost $556,000.

In addition to compound interest, there are also significant tax savings involved with retirement funds. Because the money is not taxed when you make the deposit, you conceivably have more money to invest. Finally, if your employer offers a retirement plan with matching funds, take it! These matching funds are free money allowing your assets to grow even faster.

Whether or not your retirement plan is employer-sponsored, your savings, plus compound interest where applicable, and tax savings provide compelling reasons to make investing in a retirement account lucrative no matter what your age or Life Values Profile.

Rewards of Real Estate Investing

Whether your only real estate transaction is buying your own home, or if you expand into real estate as part of your investment portfolio, real estate can be a rewarding and potentially fun venture.

Buying a home—and maintaining it well—is one of the surest paths to building your assets. Unless you are an avowed renter, love the carefree lifestyle, have a financial plan, and are streadily accumulating alternative investments that will finance your retirement years, you owe it to yourself and your family to become a homeowner as soon as you possibly can.

Build equity in your home and build wealth. It really is that simple. Homes appreciate over time an average of about 6% a year and provide tax advantages. Home ownership also facilitates increased net worth. Homeowners enjoy, on average, a much higher net wealth per household than those who rent. And if you own your home free of mortgage debt in later life, you will enjoy having the feeling of increased financial security. See Chapter 15, "Choosing Housing Wisely."

POINT TO PONDER

According to a 2003 study by Harvard University's Joint Center for Housing Studies, home ownership builds wealth. At the end of 2001, the median net wealth for homeowners was nearly $172,000, compared to a net worth of $4,810 for renters.

Real estate investments are not limited to home ownership. Purchasing real estate purely as an investment can be an ideal way to complement your investment strategy. While real estate investing does require your time and attention, it can potentially offer you good returns on your investment.

Kevin purchased his first home six years after graduating from college. He purchased a three-level, 80-year-old row house in the Bolton Hill district of Baltimore. He lived on the first floor and rented the other two levels to tenants. The rental income covered most of his mortgage, which freed up his income to invest in more real estate. Today, Kevin owns 12 rental properties, which provide him with a substantial source of income as well as an appreciating asset.

We will talk more in-depth about home ownership and direct real estate investment in the next chapter. If you are interested in investing in real estate, but don't want the hassle of managing properties, consider investing in real estate investment trusts (REITs). REITs allow you to invest in a pool of real estate assets that are managed by professional managers. Conceptually, a REIT is a mutual fund for real estate investments. However, instead of stocks and bonds, a REIT portfolio consists of income-producing properties such as apartment houses, shopping centers, office buildings, warehouses, or a combination of these properties. REITs are sold by brokers and traded on the major stock exchanges every day, making REITS the most liquid form of real estate investment you can find.

Risk and Return

As we have discussed the various types of investments, you may have noticed how some investments have the potential to earn more than others. This is no accident; it involves the relationship between two investment features: risk (how secure the investment is) and return (how much you can potentially earn). In general, the riskier the investment, the higher the potential payoff. Simply put, higher risk investments generally have higher returns because you face a greater chance of losing your investment. For instance, investing your money in a savings account that is insured by the government and that offers a steady rate of interest while keeping the principal intact has very little risk, but the yield is likewise low—typically about 2%. Conversely, investing in speculative stocks provides little to no protection from risk. You could lose every penny you put in, but the investment could yield as much as a 16% return or more.

If you want to increase your rate of return on an investment, you'll have to assume more risk. If you want protection from risk, you'll have to sacrifice some growth. Your investment goal should be to achieve the greatest possible growth for the given level of risk you are willing to take. The worksheet that follows can help you determine your risk tolerance level. Keep in mind that the worksheet is just a guideline to determine your risk profile. Your risk tolerance level is not a one-time thing; it can and will change over time, varying over the course of your life and different life events. For example, a person in his or her 20s can, and should, put their retirement funds on a vehicle heavily weighted in stocks, a riskier investment. But as the same individual ages, they should gradually shift the balance so that, when they are in their 50s and 60s, their retirement funds consist primarily of bonds, a safer investment. Take the following exercise, perhaps as a baseline, if you do not know what your risk tolerance level is. This is an exercise that should also be taken by your partner or anyone else who participates in your financial decision process. It is important that you understand one another's scores on this all-important measure.[1]

EXERCISE

RISK TOLERANCE LEVEL WORKSHEET

<u>Expected return</u>

I expect an above-average return on my investments.

❑ Strongly Agree

❑ Agree

❑ Not Sure

❑ Disagree

❑ Strongly Disagree

<u>Risk tolerance</u>

I can bear an above-average level of risk and can accept occasional years with negative returns.

❑ Strongly Agree

❑ Agree

❑ Not Sure

❑ Disagree

❑ Strongly Disagree

<u>Holding period</u>

I am willing to maintain investment positions ten years or more.

❏ Strongly Agree

❏ Agree

❏ Not Sure

❏ Disagree

❏ Strongly Disagree

<u>Liquidity</u>

I do not need to be able to readily convert my investments into cash because I have adequate liquid net worth to meet near-term expenses.

❏ Strongly Agree

❏ Agree

❏ Not Sure

❏ Disagree

❏ Strongly Disagree

<u>Ease of management</u>

I want to be actively involved in the monitoring and decision-making of my investments.

❏ Strongly Agree

❏ Agree

❏ Not Sure

❏ Disagree

❏ Strongly Disagree

Dependents

There are none or just a few dependents that rely on my income and investment portfolio for support.

❏ Strongly Agree

❏ Agree

❏ Not Sure

❏ Disagree

❏ Strongly Disagree

Income source

My major source of income is adequate, predictable, and steadily growing.

❏ Strongly Agree

❏ Agree

❏ Not Sure

❏ Disagree

❏ Strongly Disagree

Insurance coverage

I have an adequate degree of insurance coverage.

❏ Strongly Agree

❏ Agree

❏ Not Sure

❏ Disagree

❏ Strongly Disagree

<u>Investment experience</u>

I have prior investment experience with stocks, bonds, and international investments.

❑ Strongly Agree

❑ Agree

❑ Not Sure

❑ Disagree

❑ Strongly Disagree

<u>Debt/credit</u>

My debt level and credit history are excellent.

❑ Strongly Agree

❑ Agree

❑ Not Sure

❑ Disagree

❑ Strongly Disagree

Rate your responses:

Strongly Agree = 5

Agree = 4

Not Sure = 3

Disagree = 2

Strongly Disagree = 1

The higher the number, the greater your risk tolerance.

Asset Allocation and Diversification—
The 20% Rule

Before you purchase individual stocks, bonds or even mutual funds, you need to determine your asset allocation strategy based on your ability to manage risk. Asset allocation is the process of selecting different asset classes (stocks, bonds, commodities, real estate) that will enhance the return on your portfolio while minimizing overall risk. Studies have shown that at least 90% of a return on a portfolio is due to asset selection, not individual stock or bond selection. This is important not only because it helps to enhance the return, but it helps investors "stick with the investments" rather than selling at the wrong time. Studies also show that, in practice, a 60% equity and 40% bond portfolio actually performs better overall than more aggressive portfolios because of the simple fact that investors are not as likely to sell out and "give up" due to market down turns.

Minimizing risk does not mean disavowing higher risk investments altogether. It does mean that you create a portfolio with balance—higher risk investments offset by safer investments—and otherwise strive to diversify your portfolio. This is the same principle that makes mutual funds attractive. For example, to diversify your stock investments, invest in several different companies in different markets. Instead of focusing on one company that could go under, spread your money over several companies. That way if one company fails, theoretically, you will have gains from other companies to offset your loss. A good general rule is to have no more than 20% of your investment portfolio in one particular place.

Look at your portfolio from every possible angle and make sure that you are not too heavily weighted in one specific asset class or feature. For instance, geographical diversification involves buying investments based in different world markets. By diversifying globally, you spread out your portfolio over a greater percentage of the world market. You not only gain exposure to potentially higher returns of foreign investment opportunities, you also reduce the overall investment risk of your portfolio as foreign and domestic economies, markets, and currencies rise and fall in different cycles. Also examine industry sectors. For example, health care, telecommunications and energy tend to perform differently in different market conditions. Because there are so many factors that can affect how any single industry sector will perform, it makes sense to diversify your holdings in more than one sector.

To decide if you have fully diversified your portfolio, you may want to bring in members of your financial support team. They can help you sift through the various facets of your portfolio. Remember, much like a diamond, the more faceted your portfolio, the greater the "shine."

Taxes: Taming the Inevitable

One other factor to keep in mind when structuring your portfolio is the impact of taxes. Taxes can derail your financial strategies now, down the road, and for your heirs. Fortunately, there are a variety of approaches that can help you preserve more of your assets for yourself and your family.

- *Tax-deferred investment vehicles.* These investments provide a double benefit. They postpone the tax you pay now, allowing more earnings to compound, tax-deferred. Additionally, since it's likely you'll be in a lower tax bracket when taxes are due, you'll probably have less of a tax bite overall. Retirement assets are among the more common tax-deferred vehicles.
- *Tax-exempt investments.* Theses investments are an especially popular choice for those in higher tax brackets. These investments most frequently include municipal bonds and bond funds. They traditionally yield substantially lower rates than taxable investments such as stocks and mutual funds. However, they tend to be exempt from federal, state, and local taxes. So for those in the highest brackets, they can result in tax savings as high as 39.6%, more than offsetting their lower yield.
- *Estate planning.* A will is one of the single most important documents you can prepare for the protection of your loved ones. It is essential for two reasons. (1) It makes certain that your assets are handled according to you specific wishes. And (2) it allows you to formulate a strategy that preserves from taxes the greatest amount

of your assets for your heirs. There are many strategies and techniques to successful estate planning that, without the help of a professional, can be easily overlooked. Make sure you have a will and one that is drafted by an attorney.

Investment Clubs

Jason fondly remembers playing at his Uncle John's house on weekends when he was a small boy and noticing that people would visit his uncle and give him money. As he got older, he discovered that these people were paying his uncle rent for rooms they rented from him. This sparked Jason's interest in money and investing. As soon as Jason graduated from college he began investing. His investments were modest at first. He wasn't making much money, and he had significant debt from student loans. But Jason was determined to invest at least a small portion of his income. He convinced several of his friends to pool their money and start an investment club. That was 25 years ago. Although the investment club is no longer intact, it helped Jason gain experience as an investor. Today, Jason has an impressive portfolio of stocks, bonds, mutual funds, and real estate holdings.

Investing wisely takes careful research and attention to detail. Sometimes, it can be hard to get motivated to research investments on your own. Investment clubs are a great way to share the effort as well as the rewards of investing. Clubs can be made up of friends, coworkers, or family members. Most clubs have 10 to 15 members and meet monthly to discuss the club's investments. Each member contributes a set amount of money each month. Members may be assigned different tasks such as tracking economic conditions, researching particular investments, or reporting on the club's investment performance. That way, one person doesn't shoulder the burden, and everyone benefits. Investment clubs also have the benefit of being social outlets as well.

Investment clubs have proven to be a successful way to invest money. The National Association of Investors Corporation (NAIC) reports that more than half of its member clubs regularly beat the S&P 500-stock index. That's comparable to a professional portfolio manager's record.

Jason's investment club proved to be an excellent introduction to the world of investing. The club had 16 members at its peak. The members conducted analyses to identify strong companies that had growing sales and profits so they could buy them and hold the stocks for several years. The club picked several winning stocks, along with a few losers, but each member learned a lot in the process. The club eventually disbanded eight years after its inception because many of the members relocated or married and could no longer dedicate time and resources to the club. To this day, Jason has fond memories of the club and credits the experience for helping him build the investment portfolio he has today.

Using the basic savings and investment tools—savings accounts, stocks and bond investments, and real estate—you can build your individual financial portfolio. Once you have the basics in hand, you can then turn to your financial support team to fully flesh out and understand the intricacies of your unique portfolio.

To complete our discussion of building a support system, we have one more relationship that warrants mention in the next chapter, that is the relationship that you have with the place you call "home."

15

CHOOSING
HOUSING WISELY

As you think about your financial support network, consider as well the relationship that shelters you—rain or shine. No other inanimate relationship is so important in life, and little else supports you psychologically and physically like the place you call "home."

No matter your stage of life—whether you are just starting out, raising a family, downsizing for retirement, or considering a reverse mortgage to help with cash flow in later life—your choice of where and how to live is a confluence of many factors. Your budget is an important consideration, but "home" also reflects and impacts your identity, values, career, lifestyle choices, and the needs and desires of those with whom you share your life. Whether or not you are engaged and feel "at home" or live someplace where you simply hang your hat, depends on the costs, comfort, attachments, and other intangible factors of where you live.

Home is something you "provide" for yourself and others. It can bring you needed privacy, or it may be the place you want to spend your leisure time. It is where you feel secure, rest, and rise to meet the pressures of another day. In the best-case scenario, it is your sanctuary. When you see your housing needs in a more holistic way, you will realize that your housing decisions affect every facet of your life:

- Your lifestyle.
- Your livelihood.
- Your physical, emotional, and financial well-being.

- Your safety.
- Your financial security.
- Your intimate and social relationships.
- Your sense of community.

Making Housing Decisions Is Personal

Home ownership is a central aspect of the "get ahead" ideal of the American Dream. This part of the Dream is particularly important because the whole concept of "home" is deeply rooted in our emotions as well as in our heads. Because home is also a personal resource as well as a place to live, a great location, or a secure investment, the best housing decisions engage your heart and head as well as your pocketbook.

Nowhere is using your Life Values Profile more significant than in making housing choices. And when you align your financial behaviors to your Personal Values, you will make housing decisions that can be both financially rewarding and personally satisfying. The more you can distinguish your spending impulses from your values, set realistic goals, and think of your home holistically, the better your housing decisions and your future financial security is likely to be. Return to your Life Values Profile for a moment and review the Personal (P) part of your financial decisions. Then apply them specifically to your housing decisions and choices, past, present, or those you hope for in the future.

EXERCISE

Just as you have been reflectively reading and pondering the ideas in this book, you should now take these important steps to consider how to understand and improve your housing decision-making. After all, it is probably the most expensive item in your budget and financial planning.

1. Reflect on your present home and how it connects you to your lifestyle, relationships, finances, work life, avocations, and ambitions.

---

2. Reflect on a prior housing decision: What factors led to the decision? How did you handle moving details? What emotions were involved?

3. Consider whether a previous move followed or preceded one of life's major upsets.

4. Then evaluate, from the comfortable perspective of hindsight, whether you could have made a better decision under the circumstances.

Being Open About Housing Values

Jack and Cheryl were in love and talking about marriage. Although a wedding date had not been set, the couple decided to go ahead with choosing a home and setting up a shared living arrangement. The marriage never happened, however, and after only a few months, the couple parted ways.

All Cheryl's excitement about gardening and cooking romantic dinners had been sucked through the downdraft vent of Jack's spotless kitchen. Cheryl discovered that Jack was a clean-freak far beyond her own standards of neatness. Jack was disappointed that Cheryl, a fastidious professional woman, was too laid back about housekeeping details for him—even if they could at least partially be done with the aid of domestic help. Shared interests and warm friendship aside, they had failed to include a serious discussion about the meaning of "home" with one another. Cheryl traded daytime perfection for kick-your-shoes-off warmth and comfort at home. Jack shaped his lifestyle around the art and sculpture he collected and the beauty of a professionally decorated home he loved showing off. By not having common lifestyle goals, and—more importantly, being unable to negotiate trade-offs—their relationship did not survive the strain. To make bad matters worse, they had to extract themselves from the financial arrangements they had made to buy the house together in the first place.

Paradoxically, home and hearth, the seat of our strongest and most meaningful relationships, also involve our most important financial decisions, so home can become the arena of our greatest conflicts—a tinderbox waiting for a spark! But it does not have to be that way if you are willing to concede that feelings, money, and housing decisions are best confronted openly. Instead of *assuming* shared values, as Jack and Cheryl did, heart-to-heart talks about your expectations and value differences can help you make needed trade-offs or agree that the differences just may be too great. Either way, the result will be a better joint housing decision and less angst in the long run. (For help in understanding how to make great housing decisions, read *Ten Secrets to Successful Home Buying and Selling: Using Your Housing Psychology to Make Smarter Decisions*, Lois A. Vitt, Ph.D., Prentice-Hall, 2004.)

Financial and other housing difficulties can be minimized and huge roadblocks avoided if couples consider the possibility of dissimilar needs and values and then work through them systematically. It is a good idea to make opportunities for structured discussions away from the hustle of everyday life. Bring as much self-understanding and self-awareness as possible to these sessions. Be aware of what you need and value in your housing situation, taking the time to figure out *why* you need and value the conditions you do.

Share these points, using the Life Values Profile you have both completed, looking together for similarities and differences. Keep the atmosphere positive and try to recognize any challenges that may arise as opportunities for creative problem solving. Above all, in your zest to resolve your differences, do not be overly enthusiastic and make compromises now that will create issues later. Be patient and methodical; get all the cards on the table and work toward mutually beneficial solutions to all problems. Housing decisions, like all important financial decisions, have as much potential for strengthening and reinvigorating a relationship as they do for undermining it. Remind yourself and your partner that housing, more than any other financial decision, is about everything in your lives and is your greatest shared expense.

Move Now or Stay Put for the Long Haul?

Nearly 50 million of us will move this year, heading for college or career, starting married life, trading up or trading down, or finding a retirement home. Reasons vary, but a potential move for any reason can disrupt the equilibrium of all involved. Moving impacts all four of our Life Values: Personal, Social, Tangible, and Money. Even if you have been dreaming of the chance to move for a long time, when the time comes, the move itself can be an expensive process.

All housing decisions fall into four categories: routine, emergency, relationship, and strategic.

1. Routine decisions require little thought: You make your mortgage payments, replace broken windows, and paint the exterior routinely.

2. Emergency decisions must be made as the flood water is rising.

3. Relationship decisions can be the cause or effect of housing decisions and should be treated for what they are: relationship issues.

4. Strategic decisions are those decisions we make in a systematic way. They can be reactive or proactive. It is often a housing choice that can maximize our financial situation as well as our enjoyment of home. Strategic decisions directly involve the "money factors" of your life and require you to follow these six essentials:

- Decide among priorities.
- Assess your financial picture, present and future.
- Adjust your priorities.
- Set goals.
- Turn goals into a specific plan of action.
- Readjust and reset goals and plans as necessary.

To make the best decision, you need to consider the "triggers" that cause you to contemplate moving in the first place. Proceed carefully through each of the four deciding factors. It is important to address what is really at the heart of your housing dissatisfaction. Are you seeking real **Personal** change? If so, changing your environment might make a huge difference, but does that mean moving, remodeling, or perhaps modifying one small part of your environment? Is the underlying motive **Social** in nature, perhaps the inconvenience of a dependent parent across town or the desire to be a part of a community you can share with a number of your friends? Your inner desire for a housing change might be completely **Tangible**, focused on particular features of your home that might or might not be candidates for remodel or renovation. Ultimately, no matter what course of action those three factors (Personal, Social, Tangible) seem to indicate, you will have to conduct a thorough review of the **Money factors** in your life as well.

When deciding whether to move, remodel, redecorate, or find a different solution, a comparative housing cost analysis will help you focus on the financial consequences of the decision you are contemplating. Remember the three money questions from the Life Values discussion:

- *Do I have enough?* This is not a question to be answered only by mental accounting! Put pen to paper and carefully assess your finances, present and future, to find out what your REAL housing budget should be.
- *How long will the source of my/our income last?* Again, do you have sufficient emergency funds set aside? Can you afford this home without sacrificing your other savings—for education and/or for your retirement?
- *Is this home appropriate for my financial reality?* Do I really need a "manor home," or will a townhouse work perfectly well?

To compare the financial consequences of your contemplated actions, you need to establish a baseline, using your current housing situation. Consider the same costs for both your current housing situation and your chosen alternative (and a second alternative, if you have one in mind). In this analysis, it is important to capture all the associated expenses, not just a mortgage or rent payment. Briefly, these are the factors you should consider for current and possible future housing situations:

Housing Costs
- Rental and/or mortgage payments (including second mortgage)
- Association fees/dues
- Property taxes

Utilities
- Gas, oil, electric
- Water and sewer
- Trash pickup
- Phone, cable TV, Internet service

Commuting Costs
- Car payment, repairs, maintenance
- Gasoline
- Registration and fees
- Taxis, tolls, parking fees
- Public transportation

Insurance
- Homeowners/Renters
- Auto
- Other

Income Taxes
- Federal, State, Local

Other Costs
- Furnishings, maintenance and repairs
- Other debt payments or expenses unique to your situation
- Moving costs

Are you now contemplating a move? You will be more comfortable with your housing decision and sleep better if you make the decision process a conscious one. Try not to skip these important questions and then justify your housing decisions later. You can start by setting your housing priorities. Once you recognize the trigger(s) that are causing your housing discomfort, work patiently through all four deciding factors, paying particular attention to the Money factors. Then you should know whether you will be most successful moving, remodeling, redecorating, or looking for another alternative.

Rent or Buy?

You have decided it is time to move—your current housing situation no longer serves your needs. Now you face the big decisions: Continue to rent or take the plunge into home ownership? Or, give up your own home and return to renting? Which makes the best sense financially?

If you have never been a homeowner, home ownership should definitely be your goal, either short-term or long-term. The American Dream aside, investment in real estate makes sense for everyone at some point. But timing is crucial. Buying a house just because it seems like a good idea or because analysts predict that the market is ripe could be a mistake if the time is not right for you. Accurately and objectively, take stock of your financial situation. Using the analysis just detailed in conjunction with your overall savings plan, determine how much "home" you can afford and meet with a mortgage lender to get a sense of the mortgage you can comfortably handle.

Do not spring for exotic mortgages unless you have a sound plan for meeting all the future terms and obligations. In fact, we would advise that unless you are a wise and confident homebuyer with assets to spare, anything but a long-term, fixed-rate mortgage that you know you can afford, makes no sense for you. Housing can also include many unforeseen expenses: damage needing repairs, rising utility costs, and life changes that require longer commutes or other cost issues. But remember too, that housing decisions are more than financial, so you are only halfway there.

The next step is to look at your personal situation. If there is any instability in your life—if you are contemplating a career change, going through a relationship shift, or you are experiencing angst or friction in any area of your life, *now might not be the right time to commit to a new home.*

New housing does not repair relationships; more often than not, it causes even more upheaval, and many housing decisions are better when there is stability in your personal affairs. There is one exception, of course, a move that will help you avoid instability in a living situation.

If you are contemplating a second home or an investment property, however, you need a housing plan. While investment income, or a second home for pleasure now and retirement later makes a lot of sense for many people, such decisions should not be made lightly or in haste unless you have plenty of extra cash to rely on in case of a sudden change in your personal circumstances or a market downturn.

Sometimes renting can be your best option. This is the story that Carolyn and her husband shared with us:

> *My husband and I were both self-employed and living in New York City. Following September 11th, the revenues from our respective businesses dried up almost entirely. We needed money, and since our best source of cash was tied up in our home, we decided we had to sell our co-op, use the funds for living expenses, and rent a house until things got better. We banked the profit from the sale and saved about $1500 a month in expenses by renting. After three years, as our work picked up, we were able to use some of the remaining proceeds from the sale as a down payment to buy a home in a wonderful, moderately-priced area of Brooklyn, which we got to know as a result of renting there.*

If, like Carolyn and her husband, your analysis strongly suggests that for financial reasons you should rent for the time being, set that goal and, despite your misgivings, make your plans anyway. Even if you must leave a home you love, the sacrifice usually proves to be worthwhile.

Although this type of move will require budgeting, saving, and maintaining good credit, the rewards of planning for home ownership later—when the timing is better—can be considerable. It is important that you accumulate some savings while you are renting, even if only a small amount. Begin watching the housing market as well. Make decisions about the living arrangement you want in the short and long-term and also in retirement, and set these as goals to work toward. Modify your housing plans realistically through the years and live up to them. Anchor your retirement planning with the home of your dreams and save regularly to make them come true.

Buyers and Sellers Beware

Buying a home, (or selling a home for that matter,) can be a tricky, emotional, time-consuming, and expensive process—sometimes with good reason. There are far too many opportunities for making financial and other mistakes during the home buying or selling process to even begin to cover them adequately here. If you are a homebuyer, especially a first-time buyer, we strongly suggest is that you take a homebuyer course, stay alert through every aspect of your decision making, and read, read, read before you sign your contract to buy and again before you go to closing. Educate yourself even though you may feel you have all the answers. Here is a brief personal account that indicates what might happen at the last minute. It is from Josh:

> Although both my wife and I considered ourselves pretty sophisticated buyers—I wrote about financial topics and she is an attorney—we got taken by our mortgage broker. They changed the deal on the day of the closing, claiming we had "misinterpreted" our original contract. Could we have walked? Sure. Would it have cost us the house of our dreams? Probably. Bottom line: We have been paying about $6000 more a year in mortgage payments than originally planned. That old-cliché, "if it seems too good to be true, it is," surely applied in our case.

Is the idea of "seller beware" in connection with selling a home new to you? It is to us. Recently, however, the following happened to someone we know:

Linda and her husband sold a home under a "clean contract" with no contingencies or identifiable uncertainties of any kind. The sale was to an affable couple, and they celebrated with hugs all around at the closing. The outstanding loan balance that was paid off at settlement, however, *was for a different property.* That's right. The mortgage company and the title company actually paid off the mortgage secured by an investment property the sellers also owned, not the property that was being sold. The mistake was discovered by the sellers two weeks later, when the next payment on the investment property *also was applied to the wrong property.* They immediately notified both the mortgage company and the title company. Neither company owned up to their mistake, however, despite many months and much correspondence.

The companies did pay off the correct mortgage nearly six weeks after closing, but the funds due the seller from these mistakes disappeared down a black hole. Nearly $3000 was at stake, and repeated requests that the monthly payment (and the proceeds due at closing) be properly paid to the sellers went totally unheeded by the mortgage lender and the title company. Nothing has been resolved to date.

The crucial lesson of this experience is that if you are selling your home, be certain that you know the exact amount you should be paid at closing. Hire your own attorney to represent you and know the details of the transaction before you accept, and cash, the check that pays you the proceeds of your housing sale. You could be being short-changed and never know it. Especially count the days of interest your lender is charging between the date of closing and the date the mortgage loan proceeds are actually applied.

Refinancing Your Home

If you are a homeowner, love your mortgage! It is a unique investment tool that helps you leverage a number of major financial transactions to improve your quality of life. You can buy many consumer goods—not just homes—on credit, but none of them will pay you back quite like your mortgage. That's why it is important to manage your home equity as you build your financial security. You may elect to put it in a drawer and forget about it until you own your home outright, or you can maximize its financial potential, which may mean refinancing.

According to Dr. Gary Eldred, real estate authority and educator, more than 10 million homeowners who should have refinanced in recent years did not take advantage of the opportunity. He suggests three reasons for this mistake:

- They did not understand the refinancing choices available to them.
- They received bad advice from so-called "loan experts."
- They did not know how to shop for property financing.[1]

There are good, tangible reasons to refinance your home, taking on a new mortgage in exactly the same way as you took on the first:

- A lower interest rate can reduce your monthly payments.
- A shorter-term loan lets you build home equity quickly.
- Converting from adjustable-rate to fixed-rate allows for payment-size certainty.

- A different adjustable rate than the original rate might offer you better features.
- A cash-out refinancing can provide funds needed for home improvement or repairs or to jumpstart savings accounts for emergency or retirement.
- Equity recovered from a refinancing might allow you to buy a second home or rental property.

Of course, not all homeowners refinance for sound purposes. Using cashed-out equity to fund a lavish vacation or pay off credit card debts that will just re-occur is not a wise use of home equity.

It is important to understand your refinancing choices, and they are numerous. One option is to contact the lender from whom you obtained your current mortgage and find out what terms are available for refinancing. Then check out your lender's competition to obtain the same information. And don't forget that book stores, libraries, magazine racks, and the Internet offer hundreds of excellent resources with "can-do" details to help you decide if, when, and how to refinance. Look for advice aimed at consumers and provided by objective, independent sources. Make sure you get good advice from the local experts, too: Turn to your support network for advice on finding reputable lenders.

When you are ready to go to those lenders, think of yourself as an interviewer. Have your questions ready, ask the same questions of each lender, and then ask for references. As you later compare the details from all the interviews, make sure you are comfortable in your (P) Personal Life Value decision areas (autonomy and control, feeling secure, personal and social identity, and "trusting your gut") when you make the decision to refinance. Keep in mind that refinancing is exactly the same process as applying for an original mortgage, so you need to have an accurate picture of your financial status: income, expenses, assets, liabilities, balances, and terms. This is serious business; do not be tempted to impulse shop.

Financing a Remodel, Rebuild, or New Construction

Another housing option you may be considering is to enter into a construction project. You may decide that you are unhappy with certain aspects of your current home but that a move isn't the right answer, or you may decide to start from scratch and build a new home. If you do decide to pick up a hammer, consider this: A home construction project can be your worst nightmare or a creative, exciting experience. Even if it proceeds smoothly, such a project can generate stressful interactions. So be ready to practice your communication skills when you enter a remodel or building project. You will need to work hard to keep a cool head with lenders, contractors, and even your loved ones at home. Home construction projects do not solve relationship problems, but they can create them. If there is a partner, you must be able to communicate preferences without emotional turmoil.

Here are a few tips to get you started:

- Do not go overboard. Remember that your home is your best investment. Keep it that way.
- Do not make your home, through this project, the biggest or best in a low-end neighborhood.
- Do not remodel or rebuild in an area in which homes are decreasing in value.
- Avoid under-budgeting. Research thoroughly and add 15–20% as a margin of error.
- Assume the project will take 15% more time than originally anticipated.
- Take the long view, envisioning future remodels/renovations, and consider doing the whole job at one time, a more cost-effective way to proceed.
- Do not cut corners in terms of permits, zoning ordinances, licenses and insurance.

Whether you are building from scratch or making major changes to an existing home, you have an opportunity to paint your domicile on a blank canvas. The results will be pleasant only if you (and your partner if you have one) work well together on such projects, know what you want, and know what to expect during the building process. Take time to reach all of those milestones before you begin. Then be prepared to control the building process. Do not underestimate the impact of the right (or wrong!) builder, sub-contractors, mortgage loan, and location. As knowledgeable and skilled as you might be, consider stepping aside and turning over the reins to objective, detached professionals.

But there are some things you should not cede control of. All financial details must be openly discussed and documented, including those with your builder, sub-contractors, real estate and mortgage experts, and any others involved. Stay involved in keeping the costs under control: Know the price of every added detail and be alert to less-expensive alternatives as decisions need to be made. Research theses options yourself; don't rely on your builder. Also if costs start creeping up, be prepared to compromise and make trade-offs that you can live with. Above all, be available. Plan to spend time at the site, making decisions, answering questions, and making requests as the project unfolds.

Inevitably, satisfaction or dissatisfaction with a home building project comes down to the contractor's performance and compatibility with the owners. Interview contractors who come highly recommended and choose one with whom you can communicate successfully and often. Before you sign on the bottom line, consider the following:

- **Make sure** your contractor is licensed and that you check references.
- **Bids** should be true cost estimates, especially if you plan to do some of the work yourself. A square footage or price-per-foot estimate will not do.
- **Estimates** should contain a breakdown of the cost of labor and materials and a profit calculation.
- **Phases** of the project should unfold without surprise, in agreement with the signed contract and plans. Still, you should be allowed to request changes along the way, provided you are willing to pay the additional costs.
- **Contracts** should be specific about what is and is not included. Such contracts can be difficult to understand. That is why you must hire a reputable, trustworthy contractor.
- **Inspections** by you at critical points should be planned for and written into the contract.
- **Models** on which homes are based can present special challenges. Insist on a clause guaranteeing that your house meets the model's quality standards, specification of the model and standards to be used during each phase, and a satisfactory extended warranty.

Proceed with due diligence and determination—with your eyes wide open.

Investing in Real Estate

If you have your primary housing needs squared away, you may decide to venture into real estate as an investment. Or maybe you're thinking of buying a second home for vacation or for your future retirement, or maybe even renting out the home you now own because you must relocate. Becoming an owner of rental homes has made millionaires of many who chose to take this investment path, but it has brought others to ruin. Owning and keeping a primary residence running smoothly and in good shape requires good "business" sense. Owning a second home requires all that plus timing, financial savvy, patience, maintenance and management skills, and an eye for spotting value. Any type of real estate ownership should come after you have stabilized both your employment and your personal relationships.

There are many good scenarios for investing in a second home:

- You can vacation in your own dwelling, in a special area, while the home appreciates in value.
- You can purchase your retirement home early, in a well-chosen place, and rent it out until retirement.
- You can invest with potential for a good return on your invested capital.
- You can enjoy a family vacation residence now that you plan to retire later in life.
- You can invest systematically in a series of rental homes as opportunities arise.

Second-home ownership can be complex, so you want to learn your way around before committing your capital. There are many ways to hold title to property, including partnerships, timeshares, condo ownership, or ownership in fee simple. No matter what your reason for owning the second home, keep in mind that "location, location, location" still applies. If you are thinking of investing near a tourist attraction or vacation spot, understand that the quality and performance of that attraction will directly impact the value of your home.

Using real estate as an investment strategy involves some special considerations. What is your risk tolerance based on the facts of your age, income, and savings as well as on the realities of market timing, interest rates, credit availability, and inflation? When considering the potential value of an investment, it is important to remember that buyers generally overestimate the earning potential of the investment. Even analysts and other market experts tend to be overly optimistic about general trends, so keep your cool to avoid getting caught up in the excitement. Remain practical and objective.

With these caveats in mind, though, owning a second home can be a good investment option provided you have enough cash flow and property management skills and you experience good price appreciation. Your return might come in the form of cash flow, price appreciation, or both. The tricks are to maximize your rental income, minimize your out-of-pocket expenses, and meet the needs of reliable tenants. Such an endeavor can help you gain financial independence while being your own boss. You can set your own goals, make your own decisions, and work at your own pace. The experience, when shared with a partner, can even enrich your relationship.

Finally, here is a quick—but certainly not comprehensive—checklist to get you started:

- Make an extensive search, using many sources, before committing to a house.
- Engage a buyer broker and start studying "comps" in interesting neighborhoods.
- Crunch the numbers, just as for a first house, to define your spending limits.
- Estimate value from an informed position, knowing tax assessments, lot size, zoning, subdivision and association requirements, easements, etc.
- Plan for covering your financing costs and maintenance expenses by verifying the market rental; set up a cash reserve to cover those costs in case of an emergency.
- Plan to cover costs during vacancies.
- Use your camera and a notebook at every house you visit.
- Be realistic and objective about major repairs that might be called for.
- Consider yard size and landscaping needs in your figures.

- Evaluate the neighborhood and its likely impact on the home's future value and rent revenue potential.
- Keep your emotions under control. Don't fall in love too quickly.

Using "The System" to Your Best Advantage

You have considered a variety of housing possibilities as significant parts of your total personal financial management plan. Now you deserve the really good news: There is a system in place to help with all of this, and it's a good system, albeit complex, but it will make your life easier—*if* you learn to use it well. This system, which is really an alliance of financial and government institutions, big and small business, and nonprofit organizations, educates you, sets interest rates, reduces red tape, and can save you taxes. The system can intimidate, but an understanding of it can help you prevent costly housing mistakes and reap financial benefits.

First of all, as with all aspects of personal finance, educate yourself. It is never too early or too late to take advantage of the huge store of books on real estate and personal finance. Visit your library or favorite bookstore and select a few titles that will teach you the nuts and bolts of buying all types of dwellings. Choose from books for "dummies," first-time buyers, the upwardly mobile, pre-retirees and retirees, and housing investors. Learn how to avoid mistakes, protect your nest egg, buy, renovate, build, finance, and sell.

Remember that almost anything available in print is rivaled in the offerings of the Internet. That source also offers interactive Web sites that allow you to browse available homes, calculate a mortgage, or find lenders. Find out how real estate professionals work, how they are paid, and the difference between agents and brokers. Enroll in local real estate education classes to develop at least a passing familiarity with the world of home buying and selling.

When you are ready to buy your next home, chances are very good that you will need to borrow money. In that case, you will pay interest, the fee charged for using someone else's money. The "system" sets the interest rates. Today's adjustable rates make payments more affordable in the early stages of homeownership. Use books and Web sites to sort out the difference between fixed-term, adjustable, and variable-rate mortgages. Before you commit to a mortgage, you will want to understand the interest rate and mortgage term as well as the intervals of your loan. There is much to learn about mortgages, and the "system" is prepared to help you learn it.

The "system" does more than set interest rates; it reduces red tape and saves you taxes. The processes of buying, selling, and borrowing have been substantially streamlined over time. Credit reports and credit scores can now be obtained in seconds. Mortgage loan applications can be made via the Internet or telephone. With disclosure laws, professional ethics enforced within the real estate world, and stiff competition among mortgage lenders, every step is now made as easy and smooth as possible.

Once you own a home, you benefit from the "system's" offer of tax advantages, including the deductibility of your real estate taxes and mortgage interest and your ability to avoid tax on any exempted gain on your home when you sell it. The tax benefits and consequences of owning residential property should become a knowledge priority in your life.

We have provided a broad overview on the most substantial investment you will make in your lifetime. No matter where you find yourself along the spectrum of housing decisions—Buy or rent? Move or stay? Refinance or hold? Build or remodel?—every housing decision is complex, important, and multi-faceted. You can make the right decision, no matter what your individual circumstances, if you take a holistic approach and look at your home not just in a financial light, but as an expression of your Life Values. By creating a relationship with your home and considering it part of your support network, you will make housing choices that are enriching in ways too numerous to count, including finances, of course.

You have the tools that you need to work toward your financial goals—to spend wisely in order to save for what matters most to you. You have reached out and developed a support network to help in this building process, and you have not underestimated your need to be educated about what you are undertaking. You are on your way to success.

Sometimes, however, life throws us a curve ball. Or even two or three. We are now ready to embark on the final step and discover how to plan for the unexpected. What do we do when, while reaching for our *New American Dream*, we find adversity and loss instead?

Part IV

COPING WELL WITH CHANGE AND LOSS

16

PLANNING FOR LIFE
TRANSITIONS

Maintaining the status quo, at times, is comforting. When we get into a routine, we lull ourselves into "knowing" that when we go to sleep at night, we will wake up the next morning and do whatever it is that we do. Being in the same groove, however, can also give us a sense of false confidence. Developing financial awareness, savvy consumer behaviors, and a plan for routine saving and investing, on the other hand, feeds our confidence in numerous beneficial ways. As we practice these behaviors—develop a positive attitude, become more engaged in our own financial affairs, and reach out to others for information and assistance—we find that we are in a "new groove." We are building financial competence and are growing more assured that we can handle whatever life happens to throw our way because life is about more than the status quo.

Face it, life is really about change. And that's okay because change is part of the human condition—who we are and what we are all about. Without transition periods, our confidence groove would become a stagnating rut. Change, whether through traditional transitions—getting married, having a baby, sending our children to college—or transitions due to natural disasters and adversity, can represent a healthy period of growth, *if* we are prepared to fully appreciate and embrace it. Take the case of Bob.

Five years ago, Bob's wife left him. She moved out, taking their twin eight-year-old sons with her. She believed that Bob's job kept him away from home too much, and she felt alienated and isolated as a result.

Before Bob knew what hit him, she filed for divorce and petitioned the court for alimony and child support. The emotional turmoil alone was difficult, but Bob was also in dire financial straits. He had been out of the loop in managing the family finances since he typically signed over his paycheck and relied on his wife to handle all of their financial affairs. Suddenly, on top of a house that was too large for one person (not to mention too crowded with memories), his living expenses, legal bills, alimony, and child support obligations piled up, and Bob was emotionally and financially adrift. Uncharacteristically, Bob began to spend evenings at the local bar and longed for the status quo, wishing he could go back to the way things were, to what had always been so comfortable for him.

Bob managed to confront his demons over time, but he tackled his finances within only a few months. He stopped crying in his beer, sold the family home, settled with his wife, took his share of the proceeds, and purchased a small townhouse. He engaged a fee-based financial planner and an accountant to work out a plan that allowed him to live within his means and save for his goal of providing help for his sons' college tuition. He admits now that his marriage had not been happy, and he is glad things worked out the way they did. In fact, he is looking forward to his next life transition. After his sons go off to school, and he no longer has to pay child support, he says he is going to sell his townhouse and move to Nassau, Bahamas, to run a charter fishing boat. He sees this as a realistic goal toward which he is diligently working rather than the far-off dream it was in his youth. The difference between this transition and the last is that this time his eyes are wide open. This time he has control over his finances and (he says with new confidence), his life as well.

Part IV is all about planning for, and coping with, change. As we embark on the final step in this process of building financial competence, we will learn how to manage periods of transition, handle income interruptions and potential loss, and overcome adversity (in coming chapters). As you have gone through the earlier steps, you may already have transitions in your mind. If you look at the goals that you defined earlier, some of them may involve making a transition, changing your lifestyle and your former ways of thinking.

There are many lessons we can take from Bob's story. One is the understanding that many of us *react* to life transitions instead of *planning* for them. When we are in reaction mode, the stress component that is already a factor in transitions is heightened. The financial impact of even those transitions that we expect to happen can take us by surprise. And then there are, of course, the transitions—like divorce—that we might not expect. Either way, if we are not aware or in control of our finances, we are adding an extra stress layer that can overwhelm us, causing us to lose sight of the tremendous growth opportunity that transitions almost always bring.

A number of years ago, psychologists were inviting people to take tests that could measure their points and severity of stress. Stress points were ranked in importance and then accumulated so test-takers could assess their impact, with major life issues chalking up more points than lesser, more common events. The same is true of managing your finances. When you are under stress, it can be difficult to think straight and formulate an effective financial strategy. You can easily lose the awareness, commitment, and control needed to stay on top of your finances. That is why it is important to have a financial plan in place long before significant events occur. With a plan, you can almost ensure that you will not be thrown off guard.

EXERCISE

RECOGNIZING AND TAMING LIFE'S TRANSITIONS

The following chart outlines some major life transitions. First, go through the list and check off the ones that you have gone through in the past. Take a moment to reflect on how the transition affected you. Think about these transitions not just in terms of their emotional impact, but also how they affected your finances. Were you prepared, or not? Think about how this level of preparedness made the transition easier or more difficult. Now, go through the list again and check off any transitions that have a likelihood or possibility of occurring. Finally, compare this with your defined goals. Do they match up, or do you need to revise your goals?

Table 16–1 Major Life Transitions

Life Transition	Did you go through this?	Likelihood of going through this in the future
Landing a new job		
Going to college		
Getting married		
Getting divorced		
Death of a partner		
Voluntary job change		
Getting laid off or fired		
Having children		
Sending children to college		
Death of a child		
Caring for aging parents		
Death of a parent		
Retirement		

I Do, Until Divorce Does Us Part

Managing your finances is trickier when another person is involved. You must anticipate your partner's Money Values, which may be different from your own. Before you consider tying the knot, come to an understanding with your future partner about your values and goals: where they are the same and where they differ. Marriage is a big transition no matter what stage of life you are in or whether either or both of you were married before. You might already have to deal with the emotional turmoil of merging homesteads and lifestyles and saying goodbye to old habits and possessions while adjusting to new ones. One way to smooth the transition is to work out your financial plan beforehand so that you can start your new life together without this potentially divisive factor hanging over your relationship.

We talked about the importance of sharing goals and discussing values in earlier chapters and situations. Another important consideration when coming into a new marriage is how your finances will be managed. Once you step over the threshold of a new life together, do not abdicate your financial involvement. As Bob's story illustrates, staying in the dark about your family finances can backfire. No matter who manages the checkbook, whether it is one or both of you, you should share control and meet regularly to discuss any issues or to review how well you are working toward your goals.

The mega-rich of the world are not the only ones considering prenuptial agreements. While this may seem contrary to love, commitment, togetherness, and sharing goals, it really is not. In fact, as family counselors know, it is better to discuss the sticky details of money and finances before you marry than to deal with them for the first time in a divorce settlement, especially if one or both of you is entering the marriage with high financial stakes. For everyone who is thinking of marriage, a prenuptial agreement is an excuse for opening up the frank, honest, and thorough discussion about money you should have as you plan your life together.

Consider a prenuptial agreement when either or both of you:

- Earn a high salary and have significant assets to protect.
- Own a business.
- Have agreed to pay for the professional education of your soon-to-be life partner and want to be sure that you will benefit from the income he or she will receive in the future.
- Want to ensure that your children inherit all or part of your assets and property after your death.
- Are paying child support for children from a previous marriage. If your marriage fails, you want to be sure that the assets to make those payments are not used.

If you decide that a prenuptial agreement is for you, do not attempt to create it by yourself. Each person should have a lawyer who has experience in family and contract law. And do not sign it under duress or if you are not 100% satisfied with the terms. If you are feeling any angst as you put pen to paper, trust your instincts and go back to the drawing board—you and your future life partner have more talking to do.

Financially related issues are the number one reason for divorce in this country. But as difficult as money issues are within a marriage, they pale in comparison to the complexity and animosity that comes into play when a couple is divorcing. You will be dealing with complex emotional issues, but, as Bob discovered, getting a handle on the financial aspects of your marriage is the kindest thing you can do for yourself and the other loved ones in your life—even the person you might be leaving. This is particularly important if you have deferred financial decisions to work through. While you tend to your broken heart, keep your wits about you and take the following steps as you prepare for divorce:

- Consult with an attorney. It's wise to seek legal counsel about the laws and your rights within your state *before* you start divorce proceedings.
- Estimate your worth (yours individually, your partner's, and your joint assets). List your assets and liabilities and gather documentation to support your claims.
- Check your credit report and determine if you need to take steps to build or repair your credit history. (See Chapter 7, "Who's in Charge of Your Financial Well-Being?") Remember, you will be living independently for at least a period of time.
- Assess your living expenses. Can you afford to live on your own? Analyze your income and expenses as best you can using the savings plan outlined in Chapter 8, "Becoming a Savvy Consumer."
- Review your insurance. Do you have health insurance through your employer, or are you covered by your partner's company health plan? If your partner works for a big company, you may be able to continue the health coverage for 18 months under COBRA, but you must pay the premium. If need be, investigate other, independent, ways to obtain this all-important insurance.

Marriage and divorce are both transitions that are often guided only by our emotions. Take note that these contracts of life do not stop there.

Whether you are embarking on a new life together or are dissolving a relationship, as you transition to the next stage, stay grounded in the financial basics.

Your Children's College Education

Education costs are rising faster than inflation rates. In some cases, colleges and universities, although well-endowed, continue to raise the costs of tuition because, like the businesses they aspire to be, they *can*. This part of the changing societal landscape is burdening young adults with college loans so high they will take years to repay after college. Parents of college-bound children too are in a quandary about the alarming rate of tuition cost hikes in the U.S. As we have noted before, saving and learning to invest are crucial to your future well-being. But today it seems that people must save for everything: emergencies, homes they own, pension substitutes (401(k)-type plans), increasing costs of health care, helping older parents, retirement, and of course, college tuition costs. But like other "markets," colleges and universities can continue to raise tuition rates because consumers, both parents and students alike, continue to pay—no, *compete* to pay—them. In many cases, this is using poor financial and emotion-based judgment.

Unless you have planned for, and can *afford* these high tuition costs, our advice is to look for in-state schools, smaller colleges, and junior colleges as alternatives to higher-cost name colleges and universities. Never, under any circumstances, forego your own emergency savings or retirement savings altogether to send your child to college. Do some serious financial planning for your child's education; yes. Help your child become educated at a lesser-rated school; yes. Seek out sources of scholarships, student loans, and grants; yes. Do all you can to be of help, but nearly bankrupting yourself in the process is an unacceptable outcome. This is not depriving your child; it is modeling prudent and sensible behavior. In the long run, it will help him or her learn to be independent, self-sufficient, and lighten future debt burdens as well. Someday, they will thank you.

If you have children that you *plan* to educate, it is never too early to start putting tuition money aside. Encourage your children to save their own money too. When time is on your side, say you have 10 years or more, engage a financial planner who is an expert in tuition planning. While most experts suggest that you invest the bulk of your college savings in stocks, since stocks have historically outperformed other investments when investing for the long-term, do not undertake this type of investing without doing your homework.

If you feel comfortable about investing, you can create your own stock portfolio or choose investment funds that are heavy in growth and value stocks. Look for funds run by a reputable company and try to contribute at regular intervals—even if you can only manage $50 a month. When your child is five years away from entering college, you may want to start moving part of your college savings into volatility-proof investments such as CDs or U.S. treasury bonds.

You have other options as well. *State-Sponsored College Savings 529 Plans* are becoming increasingly popular. States that offer these plans permit their residents to deduct contributions from state taxes. When withdrawn to pay for higher education, gains are taxed at the child's rate, which can be significantly lower than your own. (In addition, some states levy no state taxes on gains.) Keep in mind that the plan's investment strategy is decided by plan administrators, not by you. Investments may not be aggressive enough for risk-tolerant investors who think they can earn more than enough on their own to balance the tax advantage. Also bear in mind that, like other state and federally-sponsored programs, the terms of these plans can be changed to meet changed conditions in the general economy.

Education IRAs. These types of IRAs allow your money to grow tax-free and be withdrawn to pay for higher education. However, your maximum annual contribution is limited and may be further restricted if you are also utilizing other tax-free plans such as the state-sponsored 529s. Due to changes in the tax laws, money from all IRAs can now be withdrawn without penalty when used to pay for higher education. Regardless of the type of IRA you choose, the federal government imposes annual contribution limits. Check with your bank or other financial institution to learn what age-appropriate current limits are each year. After 2008, the contribution limit will raise in increments of $500 depending upon the level of inflation. Again, we advise that you carefully weigh using IRA accounts to meet education costs, depending, of course, on your overall retirement savings strategy.

Prepaid Tuition Plans. These plans allow you to pay current tuition rates for an education far in the future. However, full tuition is only covered if your child decides to go to an in-state college. Also prepaid plans replace financial aid, so they may not be a good deal for a child who would qualify for substantial aid. If, down the road, your child develops a different agenda for his or her college years, perhaps deciding to attend a private college—or none at all—you can cash out the plan.

As with all transitions, when planning to help your children with all or part of their tuition expenses, it is important to note that you have many choices. The choice that you ultimately make should depend on your overall financial position. For example, should you invest in an IRA, or is that your vehicle of choice for your retirement plan? Likewise, should you invest in a mutual fund, or would it make more sense from a tax strategy standpoint to be able to shelter some of your current income? Involve your financial support network, if need be, to sort through these and any other questions you may have.

Caring for Aging Parents

People over 85 are the fastest-growing segment of the population, and they are living longer today than ever before. With longevity rates on the rise, increasing numbers of adults are finding that family roles might suddenly become reversed. Caregiving is a common result of the sudden illness of an older parent, and in extreme cases, adult children must assume "parenting roles" to their own older parents.

If you are one of the growing numbers of adult children faced with this dilemma, whether or not your parents live with you, you will go through an adjustment period as everyone gets used to new roles and responsibilities in this changed family structure. Even your teenage children may have to take on increased responsibilities, and you might be doubly stretched and living out the problems of the "sandwich generation" with its dual demands of raising young children and caring for elderly parents. If so, you may find that college, care expenses, and retirement savings can cause problems if you are unprepared. While you may not be able to prepare in advance for the emotional adjustment of caring for aging parents, there are several steps you can take to prepare financially:

Get Information

Find out as much as you can about your parents' financial situation. What are their sources of income, their assets, and their debts? As they age, do they plan to live with you or in a retirement community? Do they have enough income to do what they want and need to do? Learn where they keep important documents like wills, insurance policies, pension and social security records, and tax returns. Make sure each parent knows where to find these records in an emergency and ask for copies to keep in your own records.

Draft Key Documents

Are you prepared to take action if your parents become incapacitated? Often, a debilitating illness or accident can happen without warning. Coping with a catastrophic illness is difficult enough, but being forced to make life-or-death decisions or even routine decisions for a parent when you do not know his or her wishes can be daunting. Do not wait for a crisis. Choose a quiet time now, and have a candid conversation with your parents to determine their wishes. If they do not have a will and advance directives drawn up, then—with their permission and their participation—visit a lawyer.

Together, prepare a living will, a durable power of attorney, and a health care proxy. A living will outlines a person's wishes regarding the use of feeding tubes, intravenous fluids, mechanical ventilation, and other procedures that might be used to prolong life in the event of a terminal illness or accident. A durable power of attorney allows your parents to delegate someone to make legal, financial, and medical decisions on their behalf. A health care proxy is similar to a living will, but this document outlines a parent's wishes regarding care (not just end-of-life issues) and grants a designated person the power to make health care decisions for the incapacitated parent. This document also gives the proxy authority to choose or dismiss doctors and to consent to surgery.

Determine Housing Options

If your parents are not sure where they want to live, you can research different housing options in keeping with their wishes and finances. Their options include independent living communities, assisted living facilities, nursing homes, and continuous care retirement communities. Independent living communities offer healthy seniors basic services such as housekeeping, meal preparation, and on-site health clinics. Assisted living facilities provide a bit more care. These facilities provide round-the-clock assistance for residents who cannot manage completely on their own. They provide residents with a variety of daily social activities and with help from paying bills to bathing or dressing. These facilities generally have a nurse on duty during the day. Nursing homes provide the highest level of care with a nurse on duty 24-hours-a-day and doctors and clergy on call. They are very expensive and usually require having financing in place for long-term care. Continuing care retirement communities offer a range of living options under one roof including independent living, assisted living, and a nursing home. Residents may move into the independent living section initially and later move into the assisted living or nursing home sections as they require more care and assistance.

In addition to helping your parents manage their finances and other practical concerns, do not forget to adjust for the impact this may have on your own financial well-being. You will be incurring extra expenses if your parents live with you or if you help cover their health care or living expenses. You may also incur travel expenses and lose time away from work (and pay) if your parents live far away. While it is a lot of work, caring for your elderly parents can be emotionally enriching, as long as you are financially and emotionally prepared.

Retirement

Ah, retirement! This is the subject that got society started on the path toward financial education and the crucial need for everyone to smarten up about personal finances. Why?

- We are all living longer, and we have to support ourselves as we age.
- Our parents' generation is living longer, and they might need our help to make it during their later years.
- The average Social Security income is about $11,000 per year, and that is not enough to live on.
- It takes *time* and *willpower* to accumulate savings and investments.
- To save anything at all, one's living expenses *must be lower* than their income.
- Costs of living expenses, including transportation, education, and health care are soaring.

So, what do we do about all of this?

Thanks to public campaigns, public service messages, and community programs, most people are getting the message that their future well-being is in their own hands. High schools having savvy administrators are introducing financial topics into the curriculum, and some college graduates are beginning to think about retiring as soon as they start working. Boomers are all over the place: Some are taking retirement needs seriously and are making big changes in their lives; others deny the facts of aging and ignore later life entirely until it is nearly upon them. The rest, according to a 2006 Harris Poll, are stressed out about money—75% are worried about rising prices, 60% have concerns about money for emergencies, and 38% worry about not having money for basic necessities. Whatever group you belong to, or if you are somewhere in between, your retirement promises to be what you plan for and what you make of it. There is no longer any set formula for how to approach later life realities.

The concept of retirement from working life can be a pleasure to anticipate, both financially and emotionally, if you are prepared. When you retire—this does not mean you will be *unoccupied*—you will be trading current income from employment for a mix of income from other sources, most of it of your own making: Social Security (with its much-publicized uncertainty), perhaps pension income, part-time earnings, and your savings and investments. There is no magic source of income unless you are expecting a big inheritance or other windfall, so careful planning now will help ensure that you have the comforts in retirement that will bring you peace of mind. Some of us will stay busy with volunteering, take up a hobby, or start a second career, and others might be planning not to retire at all.

If you or someone you know has a never-to-retire goal—to keep working as long as possible at a profession you love—the fact is that a sudden illness or other unforeseen event or condition might change your plans involuntarily, and you must be prepared for that. The bottom line is that everyone, like the public messaging, employers, communities, financial educators, and the markets have been indicating, must now get smart about what to do as they approach their later years. Here are some things to consider:

If you have not yet thought about your future security, kick-start your thinking by taking a cue from the animal kingdom's "fight or flight" mentality and scare yourself into action: Do something *now* to assure your survival, or you might end up homeless, hungry, sick, or all three.

1. Take a course on basic money management from the Internet, your employer, your faith-based organization, your community, or your local college or other learning center.

2. If you are living above your means, take immediate steps to start lowering your living costs and your expectations. Remember that happiness does not depend upon your bank account, but it does depend upon your peace of mind.

3. Get involved in local politics and learn what your representatives are doing to help you keep your job and your benefits, improve the certainty of health care and Social Security, and afford housing, transportation, and other necessities of basic living. Stop allowing politicians to deliberately divert your attention from your personal money and financial issues by leading you into partisan fights over moral issues.

4. When thinking about how much to save, there are some important considerations to keep in mind. Estimate your retirement

income level realistically. Rules of thumb, such as 70% to 80% of your pre-retirement income, may or may not work for you, depending on what you "see" for your future. Be realistic! When projecting this forward, remember that inflation can impact your retirement budget and so can periods of low interest earnings. For projections, assume inflation rates in the 3% to 4% range. Get help doing this from the many Internet sites that offer retirement savings calculators and consult an advisor.

5. When will you retire? 20 years from now, in five years, tomorrow? If you are close to it or are already retired, how long must the money last? Now think about your retirement investments. Is the bulk of your money positioned for long-term growth (equity funds, stocks, real estate) or short-term stability and income (bonds and U.S. Treasuries)? The mix you have in these instruments is something you must decide for yourself, but there is plenty of help available as you face these decisions: your 401(k) provider, financial planners, advisors, financial educators, and the Internet, to name a few.

There are several tools to help you calculate your retirement needs. There are retirement planning worksheets and several online retirement planning calculators. Use either of these tools to calculate an estimate of how much you'll need for retirement. Once you calculate your estimate, don't be so frightened by that number that you run and hide. This is exactly the time you need to start thinking about paring down the expenses in your retirement planning, plan to supplement your retirement income with part-time work, or take any number of actions that are open to you when you *plan* for your future instead of letting it just happen to you.

In an earlier chapter, we discussed the various vehicles available to save for retirement. We want to end this chapter on this positive note: Your contributions to plans such as a 401(k) lower your taxable income dollar for dollar, so you immediately cut your income tax bill. Plus, the investments grow tax-deferred: There is more money in your account to compound over the years because you do not pay taxes on the growth and income until you make withdrawals in retirement. As another incentive, your employer might pay you to save by matching your contributions. *Take full advantage of this opportunity and always deposit the maximum you can into this valuable savings vehicle.*

Here are more ways to get involved in your forthcoming retirement NOW whatever your age or life stage:

- Lobby your boss to increase employer matching funds and to offer financial education programs for employees.
- Be informed about any proposed changes to the laws that give you retirement benefits or funding that can impact the quality of your later life.
- Be aware of political or market changes that will hurt your retirement income. Do not be fooled by political or financial interests that want to divert your attention away from your future financial well-being.
- Stay on point with your representatives and get smart about *money politics.*

Finally, all of your life transitions can end up being a pleasure for you to experience: a new job that you highly value, your career advancement or change, your child's looming independence, and even your own aging. Adjust your thinking, if you can, that "life is predictable with blips along the way" to "life is a series of transitions with periods of stability in between." Then you can approach your financial strategy the same way—as an organic, ever-evolving process. You will minimize the stress that can accompany transitions and come to see these changes for what they are: exciting opportunities for personal growth and vibrant new experiences!

17

PREPARING FOR DISASTERS

All who have been in the direct path of a natural disaster have felt its effects both in their souls and in their livelihood. Other disasters can also strike without warning and be just as devastating. Divorce, a sudden casualty or death in the family, collapse of a business, an official finding of liability, can sweep away investments, dry up savings, and even drain your cash on hand. Despite our best planning, the fruits of anyone's life's work can disappear in the wake of a financial tsunami—whether caused by nature, the general economy, an accident, attack from out of the blue, or by personal circumstances.

While it is true that some disasters—an earthquake, flood or hurricane—cannot be avoided, there are actions we can take to sidestep or mitigate most others. The first, crucial step is refusing to settle into these two mental extremes:

1. *Victimhood.* The state of living in constant fear of some unforeseeable crisis.

2. *Ostrichthink.* The act of avoiding unpleasantness by believing it is unlikely that a disaster could happen to you, (or that if it did, there wouldn't be anything you could do about it anyway).

By being proactive instead of reactive, you can *prepare* for possible financial trauma. If some unforeseen event should happen, you can experience it more like a close call or a bump in the road than an all-engulfing tidal wave.

Only a short time ago, the thought of being harmed or losing one's home as the result of a terrorist attack on U.S. soil was unheard of. In the aftermath of September 11, 2001, however, whether openly talked about or not, the possibility of harm and loss has crossed the minds of many Americans. Natural disasters too may be on the rise. If you do not know anyone personally who has been caught up in a financial disaster, think of the TV images of people whose homes were flooded, or blown away, or reduced to rubble by a tornado, or burned down, or covered in a mudslide or an earthquake. These events happen to thousands of Americans every year, and the numbers of events that result in people's total or partial loss of home are *increasing* every year.

In May 2004, the Institute for Business & Home Safety (IBHS) and the Tampa Museum of Science & Industry launched a partnership to create the country's first interactive learning center for understanding and surviving natural disasters. The National Center for Disaster Safety is now only one of many cities, towns, and organizations that provide the public with information about preparing for and surviving the many types of disasters that can threaten the safety of our homes and loved ones.[1]

But natural disasters account for only one type of financial trauma, and there are others to learn about and prepare for as well.

POINT TO PONDER

Relax and carefully consider each of the following events in turn. Take your time and really think about what may happen if any of these were to occur in your life. Recall whether you or someone you know has already experienced one or more of these life crises. Try to imagine how they felt or consciously remember the details of your own experience—even though it may be painful:

- Unemployment, especially long-term unemployment.
- A natural disaster that leaves you heartbroken and homeless.
- An illness, accident, or health crisis—yours or a loved one's—that carries a price tag far beyond your health care coverage.

- Financial setbacks caused by divorce.
- A death in the family, particularly the death of the principal wage earner.
- The theft of something extremely valuable to you.
- A huge loss in your investment portfolio caused by a market decline or a villainous funds manager.
- The onset of frailty or inability to work as an older adult when you need the income to survive.

Even if faced with situations such as these, which are all too commonly a part of life, there are steps you can take to protect yourself and your loved ones. But it is important to take action *before* disaster strikes—incorporating simple behaviors and habits as part of your daily activities. Here are some of them:

- Do not engage either in *victimhood* or *ostrichthink*. Be aware of trends in the general economy, policy shifts at work, threats by a partner to leave your marriage, unsafe conditions in your home, or other situations in your personal environment that need your attention and action.
- Insure reasonably against losses and check your insurance policies annually to see whether changed circumstances might call for a change in your level of coverage.
- Get and stay organized. Keep your records and important papers in secure places and make sure that someone else knows where they are in the event of an emergency.
- Be disciplined. Just as those who live in flood zones routinely check weather reports and lay in sand bags when the skies turn gray, we can forestall disasters or, at least, take steps to lessen the damage before they strike. The floodwaters may rise, but we can be protected from heavy damage.

Develop Your Financial Awareness

It is certainly true that the more you have your head in the sand, the less able you are to look around. The reality is this: Instead of *ostrichthink*, you need to stay aware, be able to look down several roads at a time, and react quickly if necessary. The information that you need is out there—in newspapers, journals, and on the Internet. You can check on trends during conversations with friends, colleagues, and those in your support network. In other words, you need to read the writing on the wall about anything that may have an impact on your finances or livelihood. We discussed in an earlier chapter the importance of communicating with your partner and other loved ones about finances, but you also need to expand that communication habit into other aspects of your life. You must learn to stay up with the times so that you can nip potential problems in the bud. Unfortunately, only those individuals who score high in the M (Money) category on the Life Values Profile are likely to have a lot of interest in preparing for possible financial disasters. Yet all of us, no matter what our Life Values scores, need to become more aware of our financial affairs as they relate to our social and natural environment and to trends in the general economy.

Your Career or Employment

These days, the most critical area that you can protect is your income. If you are an employee, be aware to the best of your ability of your employer's general philosophy, operating style, and financial situation. Your employer's business is your business too. Whether your job or career is banking, manufacturing, high-tech, food service, or something else, make it your business to understand the industry you work in as well as the particulars of your specific employer. In other words, treat your employer as a company you would buy stock in because, as an employee, you are already an investor. You are investing your time, skill, education, diligence and trust for your earnings. Think of your paycheck as the *return* on your investment.

Remember that your Life Values color your perception of "work." If you as an employee have a high P (Personal Values) score, you might focus on a job that offers personal fulfillment above everything else. But take care not to become so caught up in your employer's mission and vision that you ignore the company's financial health. If you have a high S (Social Values) score, you might focus on the relationships the job offers, possibly even putting greater emphasis on the needs of coworkers than on your own employment outlook. A high T (Tangible Values) score should alert you to the possibility of complacency as long as your current paycheck meets your needs. What about next year's paychecks? Whatever your Life Values score, you need to be attuned to your employer's current status in the marketplace and be positioned to make a move if necessary.

If you work for a publicly traded company, read the company's annual report. Also scan the Internet, the business pages of your local paper, and the *Wall Street Journal* for news and articles about your company or industry. Are similar companies merging or going out of business? If so, yours could be next.

If you are self-employed, are you aware of trends in the marketplace? If you are only dreaming of having your own business, why not test the feasibility of such a career change now? You can enroll in a course to produce your own business plan, and have it ready when the time may be ripe. Watch for industry trends, review national debates on new laws, regulations, and funding initiatives and also read reports on new research related to your own career or industry specialty. No matter what your work consists of today, follow the debates on outsourcing and new recruitment. Both have and will continue to have a tremendous impact on U.S. business formation and the workforce. Keep your eyes on what is going on so that you can take action, rather than risk becoming frozen like a deer caught in the headlights of a layoff.

You are not protecting your job, but your *income*. The subtle, but crucial, distinction involves being aware not only of trends in your company and/or your industry, but where you fit into the picture as well. Be on high alert about your employment situation: your skills, knowledge, untapped abilities, and do not forget to factor in your desires for fulfilling and challenging work. What could make you a more productive employee or further your career? Are you doing everything you can to meet your personal career goals and maximize your earnings potential? Keep in mind that this is not your parents' job market where a job was for life. Today's markets are more fickle, no matter what industry you work in, so do not get too comfortable. Instead, be nimble in assessing possibilities—all of them.

- Keep your resume updated. Do not wait until you think you might need it. Have it ready, like your umbrella.
- Keep your skills current to stay competitive. Take advantage of or ask for mentoring relationships, professional development, or on-the-job training opportunities. Consider taking night courses at your local community college or university.
- Remind yourself how valuable you are. Provide your boss with periodic updates, in writing, on projects you have successfully initiated or completed and ways that you have saved the company money. Keep your updates handy, in case you decide to jump ship and start your own new company.
- Establish solid habits of attendance, teamwork, initiative—and remember to stay positive. These are the hallmarks that will get you noticed, that a future employer will seek, or that will give you the confidence to "go it on your own someday."

Even if you are content and secure in your job, understand the job market; know which industries are hiring and what the upcoming "hot" jobs are. Be flexible and ready to move on if and when the time ever comes.

Increasing Costs

There are other markets you should be aware of as well. As consumers and citizens, we are all a part of what is going on in the world around us. We no longer have the leisure to leave the economic forecast of our state or nation to others. In our global village, the financial twists and turns of China and India are as relevant to us as local indicators such as inflation rates or increases or slumps in American housing statistics. Although you may not be buying or selling a home right now, you will want to be attentive to housing market conditions.

Whether you own millions of shares of stock or no shares at all, the rise and fall of the stock market will affect your daily living. And even if you avoid or limit your driving due to rising gas prices, you are still affected;

you might not be traveling that much, but the goods you consume—everything from bananas to automobiles—are traveling to get from the producer to your local market or dealer, and the increase in shipping costs is reflected in higher prices. What all these examples illustrate is that the web of marketplaces, both here and abroad, touches all our lives. Keep in mind the valuable lessons learned from the "oldest old" in Chapter 1, "The Right Stuff," which is that two of the reasons individuals achieve their life goals is their willingness to reach out to others in the community and their determination to remain engaged in any affairs impacting them.

Health Care

Financial disaster can result from a health crisis, either your own or a member of your family. National health care spending is climbing by more than 7% a year. In 2004, according to U.S. Census data, nearly 46 million people of all ages were uninsured, an increase of six million over the year 2000.[2] Even if you have health insurance, health costs can still eat away at your savings. And if you are the principal income provider in your household, an illness or injury can have a double impact by decreasing earnings and increasing health care expenses. So take care of yourself, eat your veggies, and look both ways before crossing the street. Also keep track of your medical appointments including routine screenings for such things as cholesterol, blood pressure, and colon and prostate cancers. Be aware of your own health, and use the same awareness to protect your family, particularly the senior generation.

If you are an adult son or daughter, be in close touch with the reality of your parents' lives. Pay attention to your parents' health trends. Engage them in conversation about their insurance, their desired care in an emergency, and the housing they want as they age. Speak candidly and compassionately about inevitable health problems experienced by nearly all older adults and try to determine how you can best help them. Are they comfortable asking for aid, or do they want to avoid "being a burden" until it is too late to make their own wishes known? When the time is right, they might even like to discuss their funeral and burial plans with you. At this critical stage, don't balk or let any emotional baggage or sentiment get in the way. You may not want to face losing your parents, but you don't do either them or yourself any good by making the transition more difficult than it has to be.

In addition to talking directly to your parents (or other elders whom you may be responsible for), pay attention to what they may not be telling you outright. Regular visits or phone calls will let you gauge their spirits—depression is a common illness among the elderly. Also gauge the effects of any medication they may be taking. Talk to them about what has been prescribed and do some research yourself, looking for potential drug interactions. Keep a list of their medications, both prescription and over-the-counter. Don't be shy—tell them what you are doing as you take periodic inventories of their medicine cabinets. (They may forget to mention a particular drug or not think to tell you that they have been taking aspirin along with prescription pain killers, for instance.) Listen for slurring speech, vagueness, or forgetfulness; these all may be signs that a potential health issue is in the making. In taking these proactive steps, you are in effect guaranteeing your parents that all-important support network cultivated naturally by those who live the longest, healthiest lives.

At home, on the job, and in the global and domestic marketplaces, taking the time to become informed now can help forestall the trauma and expense of a financial disaster later. A little knowledge and awareness can go a long way.

Be Adequately Insured

Insurance companies are profitable businesses, and sometimes it hurts to give them your money. Indeed, when looking for costs to cut, the temptation might arise to cancel insurance. After all, if you do not file any claims, might it be worth the gamble? Absolutely not. Today everyone needs insurance because financial setbacks can so easily snowball into financial catastrophes. But make sure you become educated as to what type and level of coverage you really need. Be wary of insurance agents who encourage you to invest in more insurance than you need or in the wrong type of insurance for your situation. The basic categories of coverage include:

- *Auto.* Do not even think about getting behind the wheel if you are uninsured (or worse, if you do not hold a valid driver's license). If you do, you will drive straight down the road to financial ruin. Autos are insured according to their replacement costs as well as liability, should you be the cause of an accident. Rates are determined, in part, by your age and experience, the number of accidents you may have had, and the car itself. In fact, you might be able to get a break on your premiums for installing certain safety features and theft protection devices.
- *Health/Medical.* Few of us can afford to avail ourselves of the wonders of modern medicine unless an insurance company is helping us pick up the tab. Your employer probably offers a group plan and might even pay part of the premium. If so, take advantage of this benefit since it is most likely your most affordable source of insurance. But think, too, of specific areas that might or might not be covered under your group plan and seek adequate coverage for dental, prescription drugs, and vision care, including any pre-tax medical savings plans that may be sponsored by your employer. If you are self-employed or you work for a small company that does not offer health insurance, consider joining a trade association that offers to find insurance for you or seek out an independently sponsored plan.
- *Homeowners/Renters.* Imagine the cost of replacing everything you own. Even if you own little (perhaps a high P score?), chances are you do not have the cash to replace what you have in the event of loss. Conversely, if you have disposable income, chances are you also own a collection of valuable items that bring you satisfaction (a high T score?). In either case, it would be costly to replace the contents of your home unless they are insured. If you own or are planning to purchase a home, your lender will see to it that your home itself is insured, but make sure the contents of the home are covered as well. If you are a renter, think about the contents of your dwelling. They might be all you have. A renter's policy would be appropriate for you.

Most homeowner policies guard against hurricanes, fire, and other types of natural disasters, but times are changing in the wake of huge and more frequent storms and other natural disasters, *and insurance terms are changing as well.* Check carefully to see exactly what damages your policy covers, and if you have questions, be sure you ask them and get straight answers from your agent. Also consider the risks inherent in where you live and insure accordingly—you might need specialized protection against earthquakes or flooding. In addition to having adequate insurance, it is vital to keep your insurance up-to-date. Keep an eye out for renewal notices and take that opportunity to review the terms of your coverage. As property costs and values appreciate, make sure that you are not underinsured.

■ *Life Insurance.* Don't leave home without it if the future of your loved ones depends upon your income. Think rationally and communicate with your partner about your need to "insure your paycheck" in the event of your untimely death. There are many types of life insurance, and this is a big and critically important subject. Life insurance comes in many different forms, and it is important for you to understand that it is a big and complex subject, but one that is crucial during much of your life. At other times, when you have sufficient assets to assure the financial future for your dependents, insurance is not so important. If you are single with no dependents, no debts, and the means to provide for your own internment in the event of your death, you do not need life insurance.

This section is intended to alert you to your need to be insured, not to teach you about insurance. What we ask you to do, however, is to become proactive and knowledgeable about every kind of insurance you already carry or think you might need. Find a book, a course, an article, a knowledgeable friend, pay an insurance consultant, or do anything you have to in order to learn about the insurance you already have or are planning to obtain. You may be surprised by what your insurance actually covers.

Once you decide that you need an insurance policy, shop carefully and resist the urge to simply go with the lowest premiums. Consider the extent and type of coverage you need, thinking carefully about how well it will serve your purposes. Another consideration is customer service. If the time comes when you need your insurance company, you must be able to reach them easily. That is when you want a company and an agent who will be responsive, reliable, and fair. Insurance is a key part of the support network you are establishing as you become financially competent and prepared; reviewing your insurance and making adjustments is a big part of being actively engaged in your own affairs.

Be Organized

There is comfort to be found in being organized. Much like the security you feel when the smoke and carbon monoxide detectors are functioning, an organized filing system can provide the same level of assurance. By setting aside one place to keep all of your important papers and contact numbers, you will always know where to find anything you might need, without wasting critical time searching. Titles and deeds, insurance policies, wills, contact information for family members, medical information, and banking records should be kept in a fireproof, waterproof container, with copies stored in another location, such as a bank safe-deposit box.

Also set up a file cabinet, keeping copies of tax returns and receipts. While the recommended length of time to keep tax returns is from three to seven years, we recommend that you keep them indefinitely. There is a wealth of information in these returns, such as work and salary history, home addresses, investment data, bank and mortgage information, all concisely organized by year. Considering the information they contain, they take up very little space, and if you ever need personal background information, for whatever purpose, it will be right at your fingertips. Also keep in your files warranties and appliance instruction manuals and tickler files to remind you of upcoming insurance renewals, vehicle registration expirations, anything that may require your attention that you are likely to overlook. Becoming organized is part of being proactive, having a positive attitude about the things in life that you value.

Our friend, Nancy, keeps a backpack hidden in her home, ready to grab and go at a moment's notice. In it, she has a copy of all of her important documents and more: cash, traveler's checks, credit cards, birth and marriage records, health care ID, deeds, coded bank account and insurance policy numbers, and everything else she thinks she might need in the event of an evacuation or other emergency that would require her to leave her home.

We talked in a previous chapter about setting up an emergency fund. This fund should be earmarked to help you face catastrophes such as major illness, loss of employment, a lawsuit, natural disaster, sudden death, or an unanticipated need to travel or relocate. However, you may not be able to readily access this account in an extreme emergency. Take a cue from our friend, Nancy, and be as prepared as you can be. Think about having to stay in a hotel in the unfortunate event of a housefire or flood. In other words, take charge of all the corners of your life, including preparation for that emergency we hope you will never have to experience. Think of those who lived to be 100+. Their lives were not disaster-free; they simply prepared themselves to face the disasters.

Develop Financial Discipline

Above all, being prepared to face a potential crisis involves discipline. Discipline of any kind is difficult, especially when it involves resisting the dominant American culture of buying now and paying later!

Financial discipline involves delaying gratification. It also involves setting goals and making a step-by-step, manageable plan to reach them. All of this takes time and effort. The reality, though, is that your investment of time and effort will actually get you what you want. Developing the sense of discipline required to follow through on the preparedness plan outlined in Part IV, "Coping Well with Change and Loss"—indeed in all four parts of building financial competence, can prove to be valuable in every facet of your life. You will never regret developing self-discipline, and you might just enjoy a much longer and productive life!

> *Point to Ponder:*
>
> Living can be a pretty risky business. Nearly everyone faces hard financial decisions, and most of us will face true financial hardship at some time in our lives. You may never be in that position because of great good luck or, more likely, because you are prepared. If you are prepared, you might not have to look calamity in

the eye helplessly because you can position yourself now to take cataclysmic events in stride and avoid falling off the cliff.

There are no sure things. Some of us will face actual adversity, situations that come from nowhere and blindside us. In the next chapter, we take a close look at particular financial traumas that can bring a person to the brink of disaster, and we'll help you learn how to recover from them.

18

RECOVERING FROM ADVERSITY

L ife is not always "fair." We can live prudently, devise a savings plan, and diligently build assets. We might be well on our way to reaching cherished goals and even have planned strategies to avoid serious mishap. Despite our best efforts, trouble can happen anyway, and on occasion, it will hold us firmly in its painful grip.

Our difficulties can be gradual—a job loss or long-term health problem—and result in a slow erosion of assets. Or we can be hit by a sudden financial calamity. Our retirement savings can disappear in the blink of an eye through the actions of an unscrupulous money manager or the changed pension policies hammered out in a corporate boardroom and ratified by a federal bankruptcy court to "save the company."

What about *you*?

Who is looking out for your interests? How can you be expected to recover from crises like these? Landing on your feet after a fall takes gratitude for what you have left, the courage to share with helpful people and avoid hurtful ones, stick-to-itiveness, and the resolve to rebuild no matter how long it may take. Using Dave Ramsey as an example for ordinary people to follow may at first seem light-headed of us, but there are several hundreds of others who have "made it" and then lost it all and never recovered from financial adversity. But Dave Ramsey did, and now he makes a living by teaching others how to avoid or beat debt.

Ramsey, who has established Financial Peace University and reaches 2 million listeners weekly with his syndicated radio show, knows exactly what financial peace means in his own life— mainly because he lived with financial anxiety for several years. By age 26 Ramsey had established a $4 million real estate portfolio; by age 30 he had lost it all. He has since rebuilt his financial life and authored best-selling books of financial advice based on his own dreadful experience. He has also returned to real estate investing, but he never goes into personal debt to buy property. His radio program features an interesting adjunct: He employs "partner advisers" at the local level who welcome listeners in their community and help them understand the forces behind their financial distress and how to set things right. Today Dave Ramsey's message is not about extravagance or irresponsible spending, but about commitment and accountability. He advises listeners to eat beans and rice today, if that is what they can afford, exhorting them to, "Live like no one else, so later you can live like no one else."

No, we do not think that many people will enjoy a $4 million real estate portfolio at age 26, but Ramsey's story proves two things: first, there is no adversity too large to recover from; second, no situation lasts forever. The difference is in our attitude, our refusal to cave inward, and our ability to cope well with loss. Dave Ramsey did not roll over. He did not give up, nor did giving up (or giving in) ever occur to him. He faced bankruptcy with guts and resolve. Hearing others talk about similarly crushing debt experiences and wanting to be of help, he learned radio hosting through on-the-job training, and the rest is history. Each week he honestly acknowledges his mistakes and his strengths to the world, building a new empire while spreading the good news about realistic money management.

It's Not Just the Money

Job loss, health emergencies, divorce, the death of a significant wage-earner, and being the victim of a natural disaster are all significant setbacks that drain our finances. Although these situations impact our basic financial management, they are also emotion-laden, often heart-wrenching events.

When we lose a job, we lose not only an income stream, but we can also temporarily lose our sense of self-esteem. We can endure feelings of failure at being unable to provide for our family or not being "good enough." It does not matter whether we lose our job to outsourcing, downsizing, or some other corporate policy that also affects our coworkers. We take the loss of our own job personally—that's just the way it is. The nagging question, "What could I have done better?" can plague us until enough time passes, and we are able to see the situation through clear eyes and with strong resolve.

A friend, Peter, lost his job as Marketing Director of an up-and-coming investment firm, just when he was feeling on top of the world. He had built a prize-winning sales network, enjoyed an expense account, led trips to exotic places for high sales performers, and was beginning to accumulate his own savings and investments. He owned his home, his family life was thriving, and he recently surprised his wife with the belated "engagement" ring they decided to forgo in leaner times. Out of the blue, Peter was dumped by his autocratic boss after a dispute about an impromptu meeting scheduled when Peter could not be present.

Peter had enrolled in an evening course and had used up all his allowable absences from class. One more absence and he would automatically fail the course, but this excuse did not sit well with his boss. Peter was called the morning after the meeting, and he was fired—just like that. Peter's self-image, his status as "provider" for his family, his social networks, and his reputation in the industry seemed just as shattered as his financial livelihood, and it took several months for him to recover from the shame of having been fired. At first, he stayed home and slept or watched TV to pass the time, and he refused to face his feelings or look for work. It was only after he consulted a psychologist and worked through his feelings of unworthiness that he was able to concentrate on his financial situation and regain his sense of self-esteem and inner resolve. Peter had a very high S (Social) score on his Life Values Profile, so it was natural that losing his ability to provide for others caused him great pain. That social focus, however, turned out to be his redemption a little later. With the help of friends who had watched the debacle and knew how talented Peter was, he started his own business that soon was able to compete successfully with his former company.

Feeling unworthy, as Peter did, caused him to feel separated from others—his friends, former coworkers, his social contacts, and others within his industry. Until he found the help he needed to work out his inner disconnectedness, Peter was unable to get on with his work life. The reason, if you think about it, makes perfect sense. Feeling disconnected inside causes us to disconnect from people—from life itself. We have no choice in this untenable situation but to do exactly what seems the most difficult of all to do: reach out for help and keep reaching out to others until we are able to reconstruct our shattered sense of self.

Victims of embezzlement also suffer feelings of loss and emotional pain—shame, guilt, and fury over their stupidity in an investment choice or misplaced trust. They know they have played by the rules, sacrificed to build up their assets, and in all likelihood they took pride in watching them grow. Don and Linda are a case in point.

Don and Linda, in their seventies, were retired and living in Florida on Social Security and lifetime savings that were securely invested in bonds and CDs. But these investments were returning a paltry sum by comparison to the stock returns in the 1990s. Charlie, a financial advisor and "close personal friend," lived nearby, and when they spent evenings together, the subject always turned to those fabulous stock returns. Charlie did not ask them to invest; he did not have to. His glowing accounts of investment successes soon had Don and Linda asking Charlie if he would manage their savings. Charlie assured them their funds would be safe with him, but months later both Charlie and Don and Linda's managed account had disappeared. They soon discovered that many of Charlie's "close personal friends" had suffered the same fate.

Don and Linda, who both had Personal Values scores fairly balanced between M (Money) and S (Social), immediately listed and sold their Florida retirement home and set about "starting over." They found an area where they could affordably settle and re-entered the workforce as real estate agents. Fortunately, they chose both a growing location and a hot real estate market, which helped their financial recovery. They doubt that "retirement" as they knew it in their former life will ever again be an option for them. But get this—they say they are *glad* it all happened. They report feeling more youthful, more engaged, and more purposeful these days and have plans to sell the investment properties they initially bought for a song and move closer to their children when they do.

In the aftermath of adversity, we often hear that life has *improved*. The combination of facing financial loss and emotional upheaval can be overwhelming, but once faced squarely, we can be re-energized to live our lives differently—and better. If we can learn anything from Dave Ramsey's story, it is this: No matter how devastating your loss, this period of time is a mere blip in your lifetime, and you will get over it. The lesson we can take away from Don and Linda's experience is that it is never too late to start over. The moment you are in may seem like a lifetime, but you have a lifetime of moments, some good, some just OK, some even great. You just need to get through this one.

Dave Ramsey said, "Broke is normal. Why be normal?"

You too will survive.

Dealing with Tough Times

Remember when you were little and you learned to ride a bike? You didn't think that you could do it, and sure enough, that first time going solo, you wiped out—big time. If you are now faced with adversity as an adult, envision your childhood self falling off that bike. To that child, falling may have been devastating. You might have felt like a failure, especially when you saw the other kids zipping around on their bikes. You might have believed you would never get past that moment, sitting on the curb with a bloody knee, crying. But you did and went on to ride with the best. Granted, as an adult, your adversity is significantly more severe, but it is still really just about getting past that disappointment and temporary feeling of failure. Getting a grip on both the financial setback and the emotional fallout is crucial; it is also a time to practice resourcefulness and resilience—*even if we don't feel like it*. We must get up off the curb and wipe our eyes. To succeed during tough times requires patience, focused attention on the issue, and a willingness to make gradual progress. And, just as your moment is a mix of financial and emotional issues, it will take a mix of financial and emotional strategies to see you through. These strategies can be sorted into four categories: taking control of the situation, turning the adversity around, back-pocket strategies, and maintaining a healthy frame of mind.

Taking Control of the Situation

STAY CALM

The first reaction that most people have when faced with a crisis is to panic. Although these feelings are human nature, it is important instead to remain calm. Impatience, scattered energy, and anger do little more than impede our progress in overcoming adversity. If you are feeling unstrung, it is virtually impossible to make smart decisions. To make matters worse, when you stress about a situation, that stress spills over into other parts of your life. Stress can affect your health and your family relationships, and you may begin to feel that you are losing control of your whole life. Staying calm during tough times may be difficult, but it is one of the most important things you can do for yourself and your family.

ACKNOWLEDGE YOUR FEELINGS

There is a variety of emotions that go along with difficult situations—feelings of devastation, anxiety, fear, panic, or anger. These feeling are not always pleasant, and they may run counter to the image that we like to project. However disagreeable these emotions may be, psychologists agree that these feelings are normal reactions to tragic events. To get past them, it is important to acknowledge them and communicate them to friends, family members or a counselor. If you cannot bring yourself to admit your innermost feelings to others just yet, start by admitting them to yourself.

Write in a journal; putting your thoughts and feelings onto paper can help you sort through your emotions. Don't worry, no one will read it, and when the crisis is past, you are free to include, as part of your personal celebration, a ripping up of your former angst. If writing isn't your thing, then lock yourself in the bathroom and have a conversation with the bathroom mirror. Or talk it over with your dog, cat, or goldfish. Silly as it may sound, the key is to get your emotions out in the open. Saying them or writing them down will make them real, and once they are out there, you can deal with them and move on.

OBJECTIVELY ASSESS YOUR SITUATION

How bad is it, really? Once you have calmed down and faced the reality of the crisis, it is time to take stock. Objectively assess your situation and research all of your remaining resources. When you identify your resources, you may realize that your situation is not as bleak as you thought. If you are the victim of a natural disaster, you may have insurance to cover all—or nearly all—of your claims. Review your policies, gather all relevant paperwork, and file claims promptly. Determine how much coverage you have and the out-of-pocket expenses you will likely incur. Calculate transition costs, such as temporary living quarters. Review your spending plan to identify areas where you can save money and adjust for any decreases in income. Identify others who can help you stay objective and involve your financial support network fully in looking for ways to adjust, and readjust, your plan. Use your emergency fund, but use it wisely. Go through this same process no matter what type of adversity you may be facing.

If you believe you have "lost everything," take heart. Your most important resource is the inner strength that will seem to emerge from nowhere, and the people, even strangers, who will appear just when you most need their support.

Turning the Adversity Around

MAINTAIN CONTACT WITH YOUR CREDITORS

Try to make the minimum required payment on your bills, but if that is not possible, get in touch with your creditors. Don't procrastinate. Before you skip a payment, let your creditors know about the difficulty you are experiencing. These may be uncomfortable calls to make, but they are essential. Explain the situation and ask to work out acceptable alternative payments. If you fall behind on paying your bills, keep your creditors informed about your progress and contact the three major credit bureaus to enter an explanatory statement into your credit record.

SEPARATE MONEY AND EMOTION

As you pick up the financial pieces, do not let anxiety, fear, or anger cloud your perspective. As you work through both sides of the situation, realize there is an appropriate time for each side. Take the time to grieve your losses and properly heal, but when it comes to dealing with the financial issues, be concise, thorough, and professional. Treat it as a job or special project.

BE CREATIVE ABOUT RAISING FUNDS

You might have a second marketable skill that may help you to get another full or part-time job. Consider any hobbies you may have; there may be a way you can use what you love to get through this crisis. For example, if you are a skilled knitter, consider teaching a class or selling custom-knitted fashions. Be open and creative as you review all of your assets and your skills to determine if any might be used to produce additional income.

LOOK AT HOME EQUITY

If your home has risen in value, you may have a resource to tap into. But use this resource cautiously. Taking out equity on your home may increase your monthly mortgage payments. The biggest drawback of a home equity loan is the fact that your home is on the line, and you could lose it if you default on your payments.

LEARN HOW OTHERS RECOVERED FROM A MAJOR SETBACK

David was a sales representative for a major food and beverage company. When he lost his job, he thought he'd be unemployed for just a few months. But he has been out of work for over 11 months with no strong job prospects in sight. While the situation could have been bleak, David took control quickly. As soon as he got his layoff notice, David revised his expense plan so the family could live on his wife's salary as a computer technician and the unemployment checks he would receive. These amounts totaled just 50% of their former income and when the unemployment checks stopped, David took a part-time job to allow him time to keep looking for a better full-time job. The $250 a month the family used to spend eating out is now $50, and the grocery bill has been trimmed from $750 to just $400. It helps that the couple had very little debt and that they own both their cars—a 12-year-old Camry and an 8-year-old Accord. These are not happy coincidences, by the way. They are the result of smart financial planning long before disaster struck.

Back-Pocket Strategies

Bankruptcy. This is one of the strategies that you should resort to only if you have exhausted all other resources. In other words, keep it in your back pocket and consider it very cautiously. A bankruptcy filing will stay on your credit report for ten years and make it difficult to obtain future credit. Ten years is a long time. Although you may have long since resolved your crisis, a bankruptcy will continue to appear on future credit reports to your detriment, and you will be required to explain the circumstances many times to prospective creditors or lenders. On the other hand, when bankruptcy is the only or best strategy you have to start over, recognize there is "life" after bankruptcy. And you will recover your pride, dignity, credit rating, and upbeat attitude about your repaired finances in time.

Seek financial help from family. If this is something you are considering, keep in mind that your relative will expect to be repaid, no matter how generous and willing to help he or she may be. Be sure that the person can afford to make a loan without any kind of hardship. Some family members may feel obligated to help even though they really don't have the money available. Remember, money doesn't always mix well with family and friends, so if you do agree to accept a loan, treat it as seriously and professionally as a bank loan. Put the entire agreement in writing including all of the repayment information and the loan-interest rate, which should be competitive. Insist that both parties sign the document and retain copies.

Do not tap your retirement funds. It can be tempting to use your retirement funds in times of financial crisis, but the taxes and penalties may be severe. Learn whether you qualify for a "hardship distribution." Then, use your retirement funds for absolute dire emergencies and carefully check the penalties you will incur and the permissions you will need. Not only can you lose money to taxes and penalties, but you will also lose the tax-deferred returns—and compound interest—you could have earned. And that's not small change: A $10,000 withdrawal now from your IRA or 401(k) means $109,000 less for your retirement, assuming the money would grow at an average 8% annual rate for 30 years. Also if you drain the account, especially in your later, pre-retirement years, it will be difficult to rebuild, leaving you with a potentially larger crisis later on when you may be less able to recover.

Maintaining a Healthy Frame of Mind

Reach out. Find out about local support groups led by trained and experienced professionals. These can be especially helpful for people with limited personal support systems. Consult the community board at your local library, YM/WCA, or church. In addition, seek professional help if you or a family member has had a prolonged reaction to your stress, such as depression, and it is disrupting your daily life.

Live well. Avoid alcohol and drugs, eat regular, well-balanced meals, and get plenty of exercise. You will be less helpful to yourself and others if you let your health slide. At this particular time, especially, you need to remain sharp and focused, and you simply cannot do that if your body is not at its peak performance level.

Get plenty of rest. Try to get a full 7 to 8 hours of uninterrupted sleep. If you experience ongoing difficulties with sleep, you may be able to find some relief through relaxation techniques, yoga, or meditation. Avoid caffeine, including coffee, tea, cola, and chocolate (yes, chocolate!) for several hours before bedtime. If you still can't sleep, consult a physician. But be wary of prescription sleep aids; they can be addictive and may mask the underlying causes of your insomnia.

Don't dwell in adversity. Keep busy and continue to enjoy your life during this crisis. Even during the bad times, make sure you take time for your family and yourself: Rent a favorite movie, read a motivating book, have coffee with friends. Find something that you enjoy that doesn't cost a lot of money. Yes, this period of adversity is serious business, but that doesn't mean you can't enjoy the feel of sunshine on your face or the laughter of a child.

Avoid the blame game. Do not blame yourself or others. At this point, that will solve nothing and will just be counterproductive. Learn from your mistakes and move on, focusing instead on resolving the crisis.

Pace yourself. While well-meaning friends or family may try to help by giving you advice and telling you what you *should* do, understand that everyone handles trauma and stress differently and give yourself permission to go at your own pace.

POINT TO PONDER

They say that we are tested by adversity, that overcoming obstacles is a way to prove our character, mettle, and inner fortitude. Or, in more casual parlance, what doesn't kill us makes us stronger.

As we wrap up this section about coping well with loss, the message we want to leave you with is that actively sidestepping adversity through careful planning is a necessary component of developing financial competence. But it is more than just gaining the knowledge on how to avoid risk and potential danger. Coping with loss is about gaining the understanding that if adversity strikes you, you can work through it. It is about gaining the peace of mind and confidence to rebound and to be successful once again.

You now understand the four traits you need to achieve financial competence: have a positive attitude; be engaged and active in your financial affairs; reach out to others for advice, education, financial resources, and financial help; and learn to cope well with loss when you must.

As you put them into practice, you will find that they get easier and easier. And the reward for your hard work? The ability to realize your dreams.

Congratulations!

19

FINDING THE HELP YOU NEED

You are on a journey to financial competence, but this is one trip you do not have to take alone. On the contrary, reaching your destination will *depend* on your ability to obtain the help and information you need on the road to financial security and independence. You will find that strengthened communication habits can pay big dividends as you feel more comfortable asking for guidance—both from people you already know and from others you have yet to meet. If you do not yet feel entirely comfortable communicating about money, remember to practice, practice, practice until you do!

If you have finished reading this book, congratulations on taking this step to renew your personal vision and plan for a more secure future. You have the basic knowledge you need to get smart about money and to create a bright financial future. As you go forward, you are bound to have questions and find that you need additional information or advice on particular topics. To help you, there are numerous organizations, Web sites, periodicals, and magazines that provide a wealth of information. Many of the organizations listed in this section offer free or low-cost classes and seminars to help you learn about financial matters.

It has been said that the Universe sends us just what is needed as we reach out to others, and this saying seems especially true when it comes to developing any social support network, including a financial network. You might begin to recognize financial talent among family members and close friends when you start being more open about the financial areas of your life. You may also find new support just by meeting people who work for various financial companies—banks, mortgage companies, credit unions—and by attending seminars or taking advantage of other financial education opportunities.

Financial professionals also stand ready to help you plan and navigate your financial journey. Some will surface as you become more interested in personal finances (under the Universe-providing-whatever-you-need concept), and you will have to recruit others. As with any profession, there are saints and charlatans, those who genuinely want to help you succeed, and those who are all too happy to take advantage of your naïveté and inexperience. *Ask for and check references* and learn to trust your instincts about your financial advisors and the source of the financial information you receive. Ask many questions and do not stop asking questions until you feel comfortable that you understand the answers. Always be wary of any professional who wants to handle all your needs and thinks you should rely totally on his or her wisdom and experience alone. Check the performance of your investments frequently and change advisors if you do not feel welcome or comfortable along the way.

Although the world of financial services may at first seem alien and difficult to navigate, with the tools you have learned and a little courage, you can easily gain the savvy to get in there and mix it up with the array of financial services companies and *people* who make up the greater financial world.

Knowledge Is Power—Get Educated and Stay Aware!

Here is a partial list of personal finance organizations that have consumer information and learning Web sites where you can find answers to pressing questions and problems. If you cannot find an answer to your particular inquiry, check the financial education resources in your community and take a course. Stay active politically and complain loudly to your community representatives if you believe you have been treated unfairly. Unfair practices persist because we are too timid to talk about money and finances—*we think we are the ones who have made the problem.* And being too timid, or staying in the dark where finances are concerned, just keeps us vulnerable to unfair practices and policies. It can be a vicious circle.

To overcome your vulnerabilities, stay upbeat, connected, active, and courageous. And get and stay financially educated. Learning is a lifelong process, and financial learning means staying on top of current events in your workplace, neighborhood, community, and the general economy. Check out the following organizations, but know that there are many more organizations that have personal finance educational Internet sites and are ready to be of help to you. We have listed them in a directory in the Appendix.

Good luck and Godspeed on your journey to financial fitness.

Resources

AARP

http://www.aarp.org/

AARP is a private, nonprofit membership organization for mature Americans that promotes financial education through its extensive programs and activities. AARP offers information on the latest consumer issues. It focuses on how to avoid scams and how best to manage money. Its "Money and Work" section on the AARP Web site features tips and additional resources on a variety of consumer topics.

AMERICAN BANKERS ASSOCIATION (ABA)

http://www.aba.com/

Click "Consumer Connection" to find advice on banking and personal finance from the ABA Education Foundation. The Web site features learning modules on the financial basics, identity theft, predatory lending, scams and other security risks, personal calculators for financial decision making, information tip sheets on using ATMs and finding banks, and links to other sites related to personal finance. Remember to compare banks for interest rates and fees before you decide to choose a bank to work with. If you feel uncomfortable dealing with one bank, do not hesitate to choose another.

AMERICAN SAVINGS EDUCATION COUNCIL (ASEC)

http://www.asec.org/

ASEC is a coalition of private and public-sector institutions working to raise public awareness about what is needed to ensure long-term personal financial independence. ASEC, through its program "Choose to Save" makes its Ballpark Estimate calculator available online and offers a series of learning modules about saving. You can also find a clearinghouse of information under "Resources" on many topics that lead to the people and organizations associated with financial education, including saving initiatives—particularly about retirement. Selected materials are available in hard copy as well as online.

ASSOCIATION FOR FINANCIAL COUNSELING AND PLANNING EDUCATION (AFCPE)

http://www.afcpe.org/

AFCPE is a nonprofit, professional organization of financial educators, researchers, and financial counselors and planners with a common goal of improving the quality of life of families and individuals. This site is not suitable for finding consumer information, but the AFCPE certifies financial professionals, educators, and housing counselors. Ask your financial advisors to tell you what specialized certifications they received and what organization(s) stand behind them. The AFCPE might be one of them.

CONSUMER ACTION (CA)

http://www.consumer-action.org/

CA, a nonprofit, membership-based organization, serves consumers nationwide by advancing consumer rights. CA refers consumers to complaint-handling agencies through its free hotline. CA publishes educational materials on credit banking, insurance, utilities, and HMOs in Chinese, English, Korean, Tagalog, Russian, Vietnamese, and other languages, and it provides outreach and technical assistance to a national network of 4,500 community-based and government agencies.

CA's National Consumer Resource Center (NCRC) distributes free multilingual educational publications that can be browsed online and printed out by community agencies to help them educate and inform their customers about current consumer issues.

CORPORATION FOR ENTERPRISE DEVELOPMENT (CFED)

http://www.cfed.org/

CFED's mission is to foster widely shared and sustainable economic well-being. CFED's IDA (Individual Development Account) Learning Network is an online connection to IDA practitioners and policymakers as well as a clearinghouse of IDA programs, policy, and research information. Resources available include a quarterly newsletter, IDA handbooks, introductory information on IDAs, news articles, access to the IDA list server and list server archives, the latest IDA research, updates of state and federal IDA activity and a searchable archive of IDA programs.

DEBT COUNSELORS OF AMERICA

http://www.getoutofdebt.org/

Debt Counselors of America is a nonprofit organization that helps consumers overcome problem debt by providing educational information, programs, services, and support. Debt Counselors of America features downloadable self-help publications on credit and debt management. The Web site also includes a chat room, the "Get Out of Debt" radio show and articles from "Breaking Debt News."

DEPARTMENT OF HOUSING AND URBAN DEVELOPMENT (HUD)

www.hud.gov

HUD is the federal agency responsible for national policy and programs that address America's housing needs, improve and develop the nation's communities, and enforce fair housing laws. In the Consumer Information section of its Web site, HUD has consumer tip sheets to avoid fraud, information on home buyers' and borrowers' rights, and many resources for potential home buyers, including information on shopping for a mortgage, working with a realtor, and calculating an affordable mortgage.

FANNIE MAE FOUNDATION

www.fanniemaefoundation.org

The Fannie Mae Foundation creates affordable home ownership and housing opportunities through innovative partnerships and initiatives that build healthy, vibrant communities across the United States. The Foundation provides free, multilingual information on credit, borrowing basics, home ownership and getting a mortgage loan.

FEDERAL DEPOSIT INSURANCE CORPORATION (FDIC)

http://www.fdic.gov/

Congress created the FDIC in 1933 to restore public confidence in the nation's banking system. The FDIC insures deposits at the nation's more than 10,000 banks and savings associations, and it promotes the safety and soundness of these institutions by identifying, monitoring, and addressing risks to which they are exposed. The FDIC publishes information on consumer rights via its online quarterly newsletter, pamphlets, and handbooks. The FDIC maintains a consumer hotline number, 800-934-FDIC, for inquiries.

FEDERAL RESERVE SYSTEM

http://www.federalreserve.gov/

The Federal Reserve System, founded by Congress in 1913, is the central bank of the United States. It was founded to provide the nation with a safer, more flexible and more stable monetary and financial system. The Federal Reserve Board provides a clearinghouse of consumer publications on banking, finance, protection, home ownership and mortgages, interest rates, and loans and credit. The clearinghouse contains publications that can be ordered, online brochures and teaching materials in different formats.

FEDERAL TRADE COMMISSION (FTC)

http://www.ftc.gov/

The FTC enforces a variety of federal antitrust and consumer protection laws. In addition to carrying out its statutory enforcement responsibilities, the FTC advances the policies underlying Congressional mandates through cost-effective non-enforcement activities, such as consumer education. As part of its consumer education campaign, the FTC maintains an extensive clearinghouse of consumer fact sheets in English and Spanish and lists of rules and acts that protect consumers on a variety of topics, including credit, privacy, and investments.

FREDDIE MAC

www.freddiemac.com

Freddie Mac is a stockholder-owned corporation chartered by Congress in 1970 to create a continuous flow of funds to mortgage lenders in support of home ownership and rental housing. Freddie Mac provides information and tools on credit and home ownership.

INSURANCE EDUCATION FOUNDATION

http://www.ief.org

The Insurance Education Foundation's mission is to improve public understanding of the role of insurance in society through the education of teachers and students. The Insurance Education Foundation provides access to insurance-related teaching materials aimed at high school students. The foundation lists descriptions of insurance-related education materials by type of insurance and supplies links for obtaining more information.

JUMP$TART COALITION FOR PERSONAL FINANCIAL LITERACY

http://www.jumpstartcoalition.org/

Jump$tart seeks to improve the financial management skills of young adults by evaluating the financial literacy of young adults; developing, disseminating, and encouraging the use of guidelines for grades kindergarten through 12; and promoting the teaching of personal finance. Jump$tart maintains a database of curricula and other teaching materials, as well as one on national training programs for educators. Contents may be searched by a variety of methods including grade level, media type, and descriptor. The coalition also produces a quarterly newsletter for educators that contains personal finance education tools and concepts, sample lesson plans and upcoming events and activities.

NATIONAL CENTER FOR FINANCIAL EDUCATION (NCFE)

http://www.ncfe.org/

NCFE develops and makes available financial education curricula and other materials to schools and consumers nationwide. NCFE has over 150 resources listed in the Money-Book Store Catalog that include programs and materials for parents, younger children, students and teachers. NCFE also produces a quarterly newsletter.

NATIONAL COMMUNITY REINVESTMENT COALITION (NCRC)

http://www.ncrc.org/

NCRC was formed by national, regional, and local organizations to develop and harness the collective energies of community reinvestment organizations across the country to increase the flow of private capital into traditionally underserved communities. NCRC sponsors a variety of technical-assistance workshops and trainings throughout the year to build the capacity of community-based organizations, neighborhood groups, and other community reinvestment advocates. The Web site features links to member organizations and other related sites.

NATIONAL CONSUMER LAW CENTER (NCLC)

http://www.nclc.org/

NCLC is a nonprofit corporation founded at Boston College School of Law. NCLC acts as a consumer law resource center for legal answers, policy analysis, technical assistance, and legal support, particularly on issues involving consumer fraud, debt collection, consumer-finance law, and sustainable home ownership programs. NCLC provides free consumer information on topics such as credit, scams, fraud, foreclosure prevention, and reverse mortgages and sponsors conferences, trainings, and other events on consumer issues. NCLC's "Surviving Debt" can be ordered from the Web site for a fee.

NATIONAL CONSUMERS LEAGUE (NCL)

www.natlconsumersleague.org

The NCL uses research and education to advocate for consumers. NCL sponsors national conferences and legislative briefings that address consumer issues and develops training materials, low-cost brochures and publications on subjects such as consumer credit. NCL also operates the National Fraud Information Center, a toll-free hotline at 800-876-7060, which offers help and support to victims of telemarketing and Internet fraud.

NATIONAL COUNCIL ON ECONOMIC EDUCATION (NCEE)

http://www.nationalcouncil.org/

NCEE is a nonprofit partnership of leaders in education, business, and labor devoted to helping youth function in a changing global economy. NCEE publishes and distributes books, teacher strategies, and resources for teaching economic principles to grades kindergarten through 12th grade.

NATIONAL CREDIT UNION ADMINISTRATION (NCUA)

www.ncua.gov

NCUA is an independent federal agency that supervises and insures federal credit unions and insures state-chartered credit unions. It is entirely funded by credit unions and receives no tax dollars. A monthly newsletter, *NCUA News* (available by print or online), covers news of credit unions around the country and spotlights topics of interest to credit union members.

NATIONAL ENDOWMENT FOR FINANCIAL EDUCATION (NEFE)

http://www.nefe.org/

Established as the parent organization of the College for Financial Planning, NEFE provides financial-planning education to the general public and creates personal financial education projects and programs with leading national organizations. NEFE also created the High School Financial Planning Program (HSFPP) to increase the financial literacy of teenagers. NEFE maintains a clearinghouse of financial education curriculum, publications, and resources. The clearinghouse can be accessed at the NEFE Web site.

NATIONAL FOUNDATION FOR CREDIT COUNSELING (NFCC)

http://www.nfcc.org/

NFCC is a network of 1,450 nonprofit agencies that provide money-management education; confidential budget, credit, and debt counseling; and debt repayment plans for both individuals and families. The Web site has a debt test for individuals and facts about bankruptcy. Brochures about budgeting, credit, and solving debt problems are also available from the NFCC offices.

THE OFFICE OF THE COMPTROLLER OF THE CURRENCY

www.occ.treas.gov

The Office of the Comptroller of the Currency (OCC) was established in 1863 as a bureau of the Department of the Treasury. The OCC charters, regulates, and supervises national banks to ensure a safe, sound, and competitive banking system that supports the citizens, communities, and economy of the United States. The OCC also serves as an outreach resource for banks and their community development partners and provides technical assistance to organizers of community development financial institutions. The OCC Web site includes materials for consumer education and for professionals working in the fair housing and fair lending fields. A quarterly newsletter is available in print and online.

OFFICE OF THRIFT SUPERVISION (OTS)

www.ots.treas.gov

OTS was established as a bureau of the U.S. Treasury in 1989. OTS's mission is to ensure the safety and soundness of thrift institutions and to support their role as home-mortgage lenders and providers of other community credit and financial services. OTS's Web site offers research and policy write-ups on a variety of community lending topics.

ONE ECONOMY CORPORATION

www.thebeehive.org

One Economy is a national nonprofit organization created to be a cat-alyst for innovation and change. Its mission is to maximize the poten-tial of technology to help low-income people build assets and raise their standard of living. One Economy sponsors an Internet-based por-tal of information and tools to help low-income people build assets called The Beehive. It can be accessed from www.one-economy.com or from www.thebeehive.org.

SECURITIES AND EXCHANGE COMMISSION (SEC)

http://www.sec.gov/investor/

The SEC's Office of Investor Education and Assistance provides a vari-ety of services to address the problems and questions you may face as an investor. It cannot tell you what investments to make, but you will find great information about how to choose a financial professional, invest wisely, and avoid fraud. You can check the credentials of your broker, file a complaint, find investment calculators, and other infor-mation that will help you become an informed investor.

U.S. FINANCIAL LITERACY AND EDUCATION COMMISSION

www.mymoney.gov

The U.S. Financial Literacy and Education Commission promotes access through its Web site to financial education tools that can help Americans make wiser choices in all areas of personal financial man-agement, with a special emphasis on saving, credit management, home ownership and retirement planning. The Financial Literacy and Education Commission was established under Title V, the Financial Literacy and Education Improvement Act, which was part of the Fair and Accurate Credit Transactions Act of 2003, to improve financial lit-eracy and education of persons in the United States.

USDA COOPERATIVE STATE RESEARCH, EDUCATION, AND EXTENSION SERVICE (CSREES)

www.csrees.usda.gov

CSREES cooperates with many institutions, or partners, in providing personal financial education courses and Internet sites for consumers. The most prominent among CSREES many partners are the more than 100 colleges and universities that comprise the nation's Land-Grant University System. A land-grant college or university is an institution that has been designated by its state legislature or Congress to receive unique federal support.

WISER

www.wiser.heinz.org

The Women's Institute for a Secure Retirement works to provide low and moderate income women (aged 18 to 65) with basic financial information aimed at helping them take financial control over their lives and to increase awareness of the structural barriers that prevent women's adequate participation in the nation's retirement systems. Although women have entered the labor force in record numbers, their access to retirement benefits has not followed at the same level. As the only project to focus exclusively on the specific inequities that disadvantage women, WISER seeks to improve the opportunities for women to secure retirement income.

APPENDIX

PERSONAL FINANCE EDUCATION INTERNET SITES

The following listing of educational Internet sites was originally compiled for the Institute for Socio Financial Studies (ISFS) study, *Personal Finance and the Rush to Competence: Financial Literacy Education in the U.S.*, funded by the Fannie Mae Foundation. The listing was updated and expanded by the ISFS for the AARP study, *Goodbye to Complacency: Financial Literacy Education in the U.S. 2000–2005*. Because Web sites are constantly changing, some of the URLs that are listed below may also have changed.

4-H Cooperative Curriculum—www.n4hccs.org

101 Financial Lessons—www.101financiallessons.com

A

AAFCS American Association of Family and Consumer Sciences—www.aafcs.org/

AARP—www.aarp.org/money

AARP Investment Program—www.aarp.scudder.com

ABA Education Foundation—www.aba.com/consumer+connection

ABC News Business—www.abcnews.go.com/Business/

About.Money—www.about.com/money/

AFSA Education Foundation—www.afsaef.org

A.G.Edwards—www.agedwards.com/public/content/fcgi/bma/frontpage.fcgi

AICPA—www.360financialliteracy.org

Alliance for Investor Education—www.investoreducation.org

American Association of Individual Investors—www.aaii.com

American Bankers Association Education Foundation—www.aba.com/Consumer+Connection/default.htm

American Bankruptcy Institute—www.abiworld.org/Template.cfm?section=Consumer_Education_Center

American Center for Credit Education—www.cwcid.com

American Century—www.americancentury.com

American Express Financial Services—www.americanexpress.com

American Savings Education Council—www.asec.org

Ameritrade—www.ameritrade.com

AOL Personal Finance—pf.channel.aol.com

Australian Securities & Investments Commission—www.asic.gov.au

Australian Stock Exchange—www.asx.com.au

B

Bank High School—www.bankhs.com

Bank Junior—www.bankjr.com

Banking on Kids—www.bankingonkids.com

Banking on Our Future—www.bankingonourfuture.org

Bank of America—www.bankofamerica.com/financialtools/index.cfm

Bank Rate, Inc.—www.bankrate.com

Barron's (Wall Street Journal Interactive version)—www.barrons.com

Biz World—www.bizworld.org

Bloomberg—www.bloomberg.com

Bonds Online—www.bondsonline.com

Brill's Mutual Funds Interactive—www.fundsinteractive.com

Broadwaybank—www.broadwaybank.com

Bubblebank—www.bubblebank.com/

Bull and Bear Securities, Inc.—www.bullbear.com

Bureau of Engraving and Printing, The New Color of Money—www.moneyfactory.com

Business Week—www.businessweek.com

C

Calvert Group—www.calvertgroup.com

Canadian Bankers Association—www.yourmoney.cba.ca/eng/index.cfm

Canadian Savings Bonds—www.kidscansave.gc.ca/loaded_homepage.html

Canslim.net—www.canslim.net

Capitalist Chicks—www.capitalistchicks.com

CardRatings—www.cardratings.com

CBM Credit Education Foundation—www.cbmfoundation.org/educational_materials.html

CBS Marketwatch—www.cbsmarketwatch.com

Certified Financial Planner Board of Standards—www.cfp.board.org

Charles Schwab & Co.—www.schwab.com

Chase Financial Education Library—www.chase.com

Chicago Board of Trade—www.cbot.com

Chicago Board Options Exchange—www.cboe.com

Chicago Mercantile Exchange—www.cme.com

ChoiceNerd—www.choicenerd.com

CIGNA—www.cigna.com

Citigroup Financial Education Program—
financialeducation.citigroup.com/citigroup/financialeducation

Clearstation—www.clearstation.com

CNN Financial Network—www.cnnfn.com

CNN Money—money.cnn.com

College for Financial Planning—www.fp.edu

College Savings Bank—www.collegesavings.com

Columbia Funds—www.columbiafunds.com

Columbia Funds—www.younginvestor.com

Consumer Credit Education Corporation—www.ccecorp.org

Consumer Debit Resource—www.consumerdebit.com

Consumer Education for Teens—www.atg.wa.gov/teenconsumer

Consumer Federation of America—www.consumerfed.org

Consumer Information Center—www.pueblo.gsa.gov

Consumer Jungle—www.consumerjungle.org/

Consumers Union—www.consumersunion.org

Co-op America—www.coopamerica.com

Credit Report—www.annualcreditreport.com

Credit Union National Association—www.creditunion.coop/

Credit Union National Association Youth Initiatives—
www.cuna.org/initiatives/youth/index.html

CyberInvest.com—www.cyberinvest.com/cybinv/broker-infospace.html

D

Darwin—www.darwin.ameritrade.com

Datek online—www.datek.com

Decision Point—www.decisionpoint.com

Depository Receipt Services—www.bankofny.com/adr

Dog & Pony Shows, LLC—dogandponyshow.server101.com/program.htm

Dorsey, Wright, & Associates—www.dorseywright.com

Do Something Financial Education—www.dosomething.org

Dow Jones & Co.—www.university.smartmoney.com

Drip Investor—www.dripinvestor.com

Dupree Funds—www.dupree-funds.com

E

EdWise—www.edwise.org

Eleve Group—www.elevegroup.com

Emerging Markets Companies—www.engmkts.com

Empire Financial Group—www.empirenow.com

Equis International—www.equis.com

Ernst & Young—www.moneyopolis.com/new/home.asp

Escape from Knab: the Adventure—www.escapefromknab.com

Etrade securities—www.etrade.com

F

Fairmark Tax Guide for Investors—www.fairmark.com

Fannie Mae Foundation—www.fanniemaefoundation.org

Federal Citizen Information Center—www.pueblo.gsa.gov

Federal Deposit Insurance Corporation—www.fdic.gov

Federal Reserve Bank of Atlanta—www.frbatlanta.org

Federal Reserve Bank of Boston—www.bos.frb.org

Federal Reserve Bank of Dallas: A Beginner's Guide to Securing Your Financial Future—www.dallasfed.org/ca/wealth

Federal Reserve Bank of New York—www.ny.fed.org

Federal Reserve Board—www.federalreserve.gov/consumers.htm

Federal Reserve Education—www.federalreserveeducation.org

Federal Trade Commission—www.ftc.gov

Financial Peace for the Next Generation—www.daveramsey.com/hope/youth

Financial Planning Magazine Online Edition—www.fponline.com

Firstrade.com-First Flushing Securities—www.pathfinder.com/fortune

Forbes—www.forbes.com

Foundation for Financial Literacy—www.ffltx.org/index.cfm

Foundation for Investor Education—www.foundationforinvestoreducation.org

Franklin-Templeton Funds—www.franklin-templeton.com

Freddie Mac—www.freddiemac.com/creditsmart

FTC Facts for Young Consumers—www.ftc.gov/bcp/online/pubs/young/redycrdt.pdf

Fundalarm—www.fundalarm.com

Futures Industry Association—www.fiafii.org

Futures Trading Group—www.futurestraining.com

G

Gabelli Mutual Funds—www.gabelli.com

Galaxy Funds—www.galaxyfunds.com

General Electric—www.ge.com

Genworth Center for Financial Learning—
www.centerforfinanciallearning.com

Girl Scout Council of Greater New York Investing Pays Off (IPO)
Program—www.gscgny.org/HTML/girls/ProgramsIPO.htm

Girl Scouts—www.girlscouts.org

Girls, Inc.—www.girlsinc.org/gc/page.php?id=2

Globe Information Services—www.globeandmail.ca

Good Money—www.goodmoney.com

Got Moola—www.gotmoola.com

Green Jungle—www.greenjungle.com

Greenmoney online guide—www.greenmoney.com

I

IBC Financial Data, Inc.—www.ibedata.com

ICI Mutual Fund Connection—www.ici.org

Infusing Personal Finance into Language Arts and Math—
www.economicstexas.org/LessonPlans.htm

InCharge Institute, Credit Compass—www.creditcompass.com

ING Direct—www.orangekids.com/po_intro003.html

Innovative Teaching—www.surfaquarium.com/newsletter/bank.htm

Institute for Financial Literacy—www.financiallit.org

Institute of Consumer Financial Education—
www.financial-education-icfe.org

Insurance Education Foundation—www.ief.org/edu/edudefault.asp

Insurance Information Institute—www.iii.org

Insure.com—www.insure.com

Internal Revenue Service—www.irs.ustreas.gov

Internet Closed End Fund Investor—www.closed-end-funds.com

Invesco—www.invesco.com

Investing in Bonds.com—www.investinbonds.com

Investing in KIDS Corp.—www.investinginkids.org

Investment FAQ—www.invest-faq.com

Investment Research Institute—www.options-iri.com

Investopedia—www.investopedia.com

Investor Guide—www.investorguide.com

Investor Home—www.investorhome.com

Investor Protection Trust—www.investorprotection.com

Investors Alley—www.investorsalley.com

Investors Business Daily Web Edition—www.investors.com

Investorwords—www.investorama.com

IPO Intelligence Online—www.ipo-fund.com

Irajunction.com—www.irajunction.com

It All Adds Up—www.italladdsup.org

J

JH Darbie & Co—www.jhdarbie.com

Junior Achievement Worldwide—www.ja.org

K

KidsFinance—www.kidsfinance.com

Kiplinger Online—www.kiplinger.com

Knowledge Adventure—www.knowledgeadventure.com

L

Lavamind—www.lavamind.com/index.htm

League of American Investors—www.investorsleague.com

Learn to Save, a Site for Children & Their Parents—
www.learntosave.com

Levitt & Levitt Trutrade—www.trutrade.com

Liberal Financial—www.younginvestor.com

Life and Health Insurance Foundation for Education—
www.life-line.org

Loomis Sayles Funds—www.loomissayles.com

M

Making Allowances—www.makingallowances.com

Market Watch—www.marketwatch.com

Maryland Public Television-Sense & Dollars—
senseanddollars.thinkport.org

Mastering Your Personal Finances—www.yourpersonalfinances.com

Midamerica Commodity Exchange—www.midam.com

Monetta Funds—www.monetta.com

Moneylife, Inc.—www.moneylife.com

Money Math: Lessons for Life—www.publicdebt.treas.gov/mar/
marmoneymath.htm

MoneyMinded.com—www.moneyminded.com

MoneyPaper—www.moneypaper.com

Money Savvy Generation—www.msgen.com/prod/assembled/
home.html

Money Skill—www.moneyskill.org

Moonjar—www.moonjar.com

Morningstar—www.morningstar.com

Mosaic Funds—www.mosaicfunds.com

Motley Fool—www.fool.com

Mr. Stock Online Trading—www.mrstock.com

MSN Moneycentral Investor—www.moneycentral.msn.com

Mutual Fund Investor's Center—www.mfea.com

Mydiscountbroker.com—www.mydiscountbroker.com

N

Nareit Online—www.nareit.com

NASD Regulations, Inc.—www.nasdr.com

NASDAQ—www.nasdaq.com

National Association of Investors Corp. (NAIC)—
www.better-investing.org

National Center for Financial Education—www.ncfe.org

National Consumers League—www.nclnet.org

National Council on Economic Education—www.ncee.net;

National Endowment for Financial Education—www.nefe.org

National Discount Brokers—www.ndb.com

National Foundation for Credit Counseling—www.debtadvice.org

National Fraud Information Center—www.fraud.com

National Youth Involvement Board—www.nyib.org

Native Financial Education Coalition—www.nfec.info

New York Board of Trade—www.cbot.com

NFA Futures—www.nfa.futures.org

Northwestern Mutual & NCEE—www.themint.org

North America Military Financial Education Center—militaryfinance.umuc.edu

North American Securities Administration Association—www.nasaa.org

O

Options Industry Council—www.888options.com

P

ParentWare—www.parentware.org

Payden & Rygel funds—www.payden.com

PBS News Hour—www.pbs.org/newshour/on2/budget.html

Philadelphia Stock Exchange—www.plx.com

Pitmaster—www.thepitmaster.com

Premier Educational Services—www.goodcreditnews.com/homepage.html

Prosperity4Kids, Inc.—www.prosperity4kids.com

PRS Online—www.countrydata.com

Q

Quicken.com—www.quicken.com

R

Regal Discount—www.eregal.com

Ric Edelman—www.ricedelman.com

S

S&P Personal Wealth—www.personalwealth.com

Salomon Smith Barney—www.smithbarney.com/yin/home.htm

Seaport Securities Corporation—www.sea-port.com

Securities & Exchange Commission for Students & Teachers—www.sec.gov/investor/students.shtml

Sherry Bruce State Discount—www.state-discount.com

Smart Money—www.smartmoney.com

Social Investment Forum—www.socialinvest.org

Social Security Administration—www.ssa.gov/schools.htm

Society for Financial Education and Professional Development—www.societyforfinancialeducation.org

Sovereign Bank—www.kidsbank.com

Springboard Non-Profit Consumer Credit Management—www.ncfe.org

State Bank of the Lakes—www.thisisyourbank.com/future/index.html

State Farm—www.statefarm.com

StreetSage—www.streetsage.com

Stock Market Game—www.smgww.org

Stockwinners.com—www.stockwinners.com

Strong Funds—www.strongfunds.com

Strong Kids—www.strongkids.com

Student Credit—www.studentcredit.com

T

Tamarack Funds—www.jbfunds.com

TeachMeFinance.com—www.teachmefinance.com

Teen Analyst—www.teenanalyst.com

Tesco—www.tescofinance.com

The Gay Financial Network—www.gfn.com

The Money Camp for Kids—www.themoneycamp.com

The Stock Market Game TM—www.smgww.org

The Street.com—www.thestreet.com

Thinking About Dropping Out of School—www.dol.gov/asp/fibre/dropout.htm

Thrivent Financial for Lutherans—www.thrivent.com/planning/index.html

Top 10 Dot Coms (Scams)—www.ftc.gov/bcp/conline/edcams/dotcon/text.htm

Tradehard.com—www.tradehard.com

Trade-well Discount Investing—www.tradewell.com

Trading Direct—www.tradingdirect.com

True Life Interactive—truelifeinteractive.com

Tucker Anthony—www.tucker-anthony.com

U

University of California-Cooperative Extension—www.moneytalks.ucr.edu

University of Minnesota-Extension Service—www.extension.umn.edu/topics.html?topic=3

University of Missouri Center for Entrepreneurship & Economic Education—www.umsl.edu/~econed

USA Funds Life Skills—www.usafunds.org/financial_aid/debt_management/usa_funds_life_skills

US Mint—www.usmint.gov/kids

US Securities and Exchange commission—www.sec.gov

US Treasury—www.ustreas.gov/kids

V

Valueline Investment Research & Asset Management—www.valueline.com

Vanguard—www.vanguard.com

VISA's Practical Money Skills for Life—www.practicalmoneyskills.com/english/index.php

W

Wachovia Bank—www.wachovia.com

Wall Street Journal Classroom Edition—www.wsjclassroomedition.com/index.html

Washington State Attorney General's Office—www.atg.wa.gov/teenconsumer

Waterhouse Securities—www.waterhouse.com

Wayne Hummer Funds—www.whummer.com

WEBS—www.websontheweb.com

Wells Fargo's Hands on Banking—www.handsonbanking.org

Wise Pockets—www.umsl.edu/~wpockets

Women's Institute for Financial Education—www.wife.org

Worldly Investor—www.worldlyinvestor.com

WorldWideLearn—www.worldwidelearn.com

Y

Young Americans Center for Financial Education—www.yacenter.org

Young Biz—www.youngbiz.com

Young Money—www.youngmoney.com

Z

Zillions—Consumer Reports 4 Kids—www.zillions.org

ENDNOTES

Preface

[1] Elizabeth Warren was recently interviewed on a PBS Frontline Special.

[2] This analogy is borrowed from Shapiro, David. *Retirement Countdown*. Upper Saddle River, NJ: Financial Times Prentice Hall, 2004.

Chapter 1

[1] As widely reported, Federal Reserve Chairman, Alan Greenspan, warned Congress on February 25, 2004, to move quickly to fix the nation's swollen budget deficit by making "significant structural adjustments" to Social Security and Medicare. See: http://money.cnn.com/2004/02/25/news/economy/greenspan/.

[2] Originally published in *Lawyers Weekly USA*, a Dolan Media publication, "IRS to perform more audits as part of emphasis on compliance," appeared in the *St. Louis Daily Record* on January 4, 2006. See also *National Profile and Enforcement Trends over Time*, TRAC/IRS at http://trac.syr.edu/tracirs/newfindings/v09/.

[3] See www.isfs.org (Institute for Socio-Financial Studies) to download the text of *Personal Finance and the Rush to Competence: Financial Literacy Education in the United States* and *Goodbye to Complacency: Financial Literacy Education in the U.S. 2000–2005*. These and other studies involved the evaluation of over 150 financial literacy education programs, including focus group and individual interviews with participants in financial education studies across the nation.

[4] The study was conducted by the Institute for Socio-Financial Studies at the Mid-Atlantic Regional Maintenance Center (MARMAC), United States Navy, Norfolk, VA.

[5] Boothby, Rita McAllister. *The Golden Rules of Parenting*. VA: Capital Books. 2002.

[6] *Guida degli Stati Uniti per L'Immigrante Italiano* was the Italian name of this book.

Chapter 4

[1] Personal values are the standards or principles people use for evaluating the actual or potential consequences of their action and inaction. They are used as guidelines for discerning priorities, for making tradeoffs, for forming preferences among available choices, and for taking action or deciding not to act. Discussions about values and how values function at personal levels have occurred over centuries. They can be found in all fields of the social sciences, in law, the physical sciences, education, philosophy, and religion. (See: Feather, Norman T. 1999. *Values, Achievement, and Justice: Studies in the Psychology of Deservingness*. New York: Kluwer Academic/Plenum Publishers, 1999 and Milton Rokeach. *The Nature of Human Values*. New York: The Free Press, 1973.)

Chapter 5

[1] Billie Jean King interview in the April 29, 1991, issue of *Sports Illustrated*, p. 72.

[2] Ibid, p. 113.

[3] Vitt, Lois A. et al. *Personal Finance and the Rush to Competence: Financial Literacy Education in the US, 2000*. Washington, DC: Fannie Mae Foundation. pp. 31–35.

[4] Pfeffer, Jeffrey and Robert I. Sutton. 1999. *The Knowing-Doing Gap: How Smart Companies Turn Knowledge into Action*. Harvard Business School Press: Cambridge, MA.

[5] Vitt, Lois A., Gwen Reichbach, Jamie L. Kent, and Jurg Siegenthaler. 2005. *Goodbye to Complacency: Financial Literacy Education in the U.S. 2000–2005.* Washington, DC: AARP.

Chapter 6

[1] Vitt, Lois A. and Noel A. Schweig. "Ten Money Myths: Help Your Clients Avoid These Financial Mistakes." *Perspectives on Retirement and Life Planning,* March 2000.

[2] Gonzalez, Ruben, "Failing Your Way to Success," www.thelugeman.com.

[3] Sappenfield, Mark, "How Olympians handle the jitters of big moment," *The Christian Science Monitor,* February 13, 2006, p. 1.

Chapter 7

[1] See references to Tang, T. (1992, 1993, 1995) and colleagues (Tang and Gilbert, 1995; Tang et al, 1997) concerning the Money Ethic Scale (MES) in Adrian Furnham and Michael Argyle, *The Psychology of Money,* 2000. London: Routledge, pp. 42–43.

Chapter 8

[1] The NCPA's Consumer-Driven Health Care Web site is a one-stop-shop for information on consumer-driven and consumer-centric health information for consumers, researchers, policy-makers and the media. It features a large collection of health care policy experts who believe health care competition and quality go hand in hand. The Web site is an initiative of the National Center for Policy Analysis' Rapid Response in health care—the purpose of which is to promote consumerism in health care and correct misinformation while promoting sensible solutions to America's health care problems.

[2] Consumer Driven Healthcare, Volume 2, No.4 (April 2003) Atlanta, GA: National Health Information, LLC.

Chapter 9

[1] Board of Governors of the Federal Reserve System. "The Profitability of Credit Card Operations of Depository Institutions," An Annual Report submitted to the Congress pursuant to Section 8 of the Fair Credit and Charge Card Disclosure Act of 1988. (June 2005) Washington, DC: Federal Reserve.

[2] Federal Reserve Statistical Release G19, *Consumer Credit,* July 10, 2006. See http//www.federalreserve.gov/release/g19/current.

Chapter 10

[1] Brokamp, Elizabeth. "50 Simple Tips for Big Savings," *The Motley Fool,* August 26, 2006.

[2] www.crimesofpersuasion.com.

Chapter 11

[1] Boston Center for Adult Education, Summer 2005 catalog.

[2] Organization for Economic Cooperation and Development (OEDC) Economic Outlook, December 2006 No. 78, Vol. 2005; 2. from Annex Table 23 "Household saving rates."

[3] As indicated in Table 11 "Life expectancy by age, race and sex," from the National Vital Statistics Reports, Nov. 2004.

[4] . . . More than half of workers saving for retirement report total savings and investments (not including the value of their primary residence or any defined benefit plans) of less than $50,000 (52%). However, the large majority of workers who have not put money aside for retirement have little in savings at all: Three-quarters of these workers say their assets total less than $10,000 (75%)," from: EBRI Issue Brief No. 292, "Will More of Us Be Working Forever? The 2006 Retirement Confidence Survey," April 2006.

[5] This quote appears online at http://www.ruleof72.net/rule-of-72-einstein.asp and also in a lesson on compound interest taught on The

Motley Fool Web site (www.motleyfool.com), but variations of it can be found in other writings about compound interest as well.

Chapter 12

[1] The "2006 Retirement Confidence Survey." Mathew Greenwald & Associates, Employee Benefit Retirement Institute (EBRI) and the American Savings Education Council (ASEC), Washington, DC. www.asec.org.

[2] See Lois A. Vitt, *10 Secrets to Successful Home Buying and Selling: Using Your Housing Psychology to Make Smarter Decisions*, published by Prentice Hall in 2004. The research cited about hoped-for activities in retirement was reported by Mathew Greenwald & Associates in its 2003 "Retirement Confidence Survey," for the Employee Benefit Research Institute (EBRI) and American Savings Education Council (ASEC).

[3] Pankow, Debra. Communicating about Money and Money Issues, North Dakota State University Extension Center, #FS-592, April, 2003.

Chapter 14

[1] The Risk Tolerance Level Worksheet was adapted from a variety of similar self assessments that appear on the Internet to help consumers become better investors. In recent research, John Grable, Michael Roszkowski, So-Hyun Joo, Barbara O'Neill, and Ruth Lytton ("How Well Do Individuals Assess Their Own Risk Tolerance? An Empirical Investigation," *Consumer Interests Annual*, Volume 52, 2006) found that individuals taking such a self assessment do a reasonably good job of understanding their own risk tolerance.

Chapter 15

[1] Eldred, Gary W. *106 Mortgage Secrets all Homebuyers Must Learn – But Lenders Don't Tell.* Hoboken, NJ: John Wiley & Sons, Inc., 2003.

Chapter 17

[1] See the list of organizations with Internet addresses and other resources listed in Chapter 19, "Finding th Help You Need," and also in the Appendix, "Personal Finance Education Internet Sites."

[2] The Commonwealth Fund. Gaps in Health Insurance: An All-American Problem. www.cmwf.org/publications/ publications_show.htm?doc_id=367876.

INDEX

SAVING FOR RETIREMENT WITHOUT LIVING LIKE A PAUPER OR WINNING THE LOTTERY

Gail MarksJarvis

The perfect book for anyone who's concerned about saving for retirement, from baby boomers to "Generation Y." Most books on retirement investing are either too complex, too superficial, or too gimmicky to help you. Instead of starting with some lofty financial planning theory, the author walks individuals through the beginning of the process with IRAs and 401(k)s, leaving no basic questions unanswered. Gail MarksJarvis is one of the nation's leading personal finance columnists. Her syndicated columns currently reach millions of readers in many of the nation's leading daily newspapers, including the *Chicago Tribune*. She was named Best Financial Columnist by the Medill School of Journalism at Northwestern University.

ISBN 0132271907 ▪ ISBN-13 9780132271905 ▪ © 2007
272 pp ▪ $17.99 USA ▪ $21.99 CAN

YOUR CREDIT SCORE
How to Fix, Improve, and Protect the 3-Digit Number that Shapes Your Financial Future, Second Edition

Liz Pulliam Weston

In the past five years, a simple three-digit number has become critical to your financial life: your credit score. It not only dictates whether you get credit: it can dictate how much you'll pay for it. What's more, it's being used by insurers, employers, and others who can determine your financial future. A bad score can cost you tens of thousands of dollars in higher interest costs, bigger insurance premiums, and missed employment opportunities. Now, MSNBC/*L.A. Times* personal finance journalist Liz Pulliam Weston rips away the mystery surrounding credit scoring and tells you exactly what you need to do to build, rebuild, and maintain your good credit in the second edition of *Your Credit Score*. In this updated edition, you'll learn how many credit cards you should have; whether carrying a balance helps or hurts you; when you should or shouldn't close a credit account. Weston explains how to bounce back from bad credit and bankruptcy and tells you exactly how credit counseling, debt negotiation and other credit "solutions" can affect your score. Above all, this book offers an action plan for discovering and improving your credit score and reaping the benefits.

ISBN 0132254581 ▪ ISBN-13 9780132254588 ▪ © 2007
224 pp ▪ $18.99 USA ▪ $ 23.99 CAN